Marketing the Populist Politician

Marketing the Populist Politician

The Demotic Democrat

Robert Busby
Lecturer in Politics
Liverpool Hope University, UK

First published 2009 by
PALGRAVE MACMILLAN

Palgrave Macmillan in the UK is an imprint of Macmillan Publishers Limited, registered in England, company number 785998, of Houndmills, Basingstoke, Hampshire RG21 6XS.

Palgrave Macmillan in the US is a division of St Martin's Press LLC, 175 Fifth Avenue, New York, NY 10010.

Palgrave Macmillan is the global academic imprint of the above companies and has companies and representatives throughout the world.

Palgrave® and Macmillan® are registered trademarks in the United States, the United Kingdom, Europe and other countries.

ISBN-13: 978-0-230-52227-5 hardback
ISBN-10: 0-230-52227-0 hardback

This book is printed on paper suitable for recycling and made from fully managed and sustained forest sources. Logging, pulping and manufacturing processes are expected to conform to the environmental regulations of the country of origin.

A catalogue record for this book is available from the British Library.

Library of Congress Cataloging-in-Publication Data

Busby, Robert.
    Marketing the populist politician : the demotic democrat / Robert Busby.
        p. cm.
    Includes bibliographical references and index.
    ISBN 978-0-230-52227-5 (alk. paper)
    1. Marketing – Political aspects – Great Britain. 2. Marketing – Political aspects – United States. 3. Communication in politics – Great Britain. 4. Communication in politics – United States. I. Title.

JA85.2.G7B87 2009
324.7'30941—dc22   2009013178

10 9 8 7 6 5 4 3 2 1
18 17 16 15 14 13 12 11 10 09

Printed and bound in Great Britain by
CPI Antony Rowe, Chippenham and Eastbourne

To Mia

Contents

Acknowledgements

I would like to thank my wife Louise for her support through the writing of this project. Mia and Anna assisted in their own special way.

Alex Waddan, Michael Holmes and Bill Jones provided valuable support through the final stages of writing and gave up valuable time to assist. Thanks too to colleagues and friends at Liverpool Hope who have endeavoured to assist across time in bringing this work together.

Introduction

In the contemporary era the political identity and character of a political leader is pivotal in dictating the success and failure of government and opposition. In both the United Kingdom and United States attention upon political leaders has become saturated, with issues above and beyond their political and ideological objectives becoming subject for discussion and debate. Indeed across a broad and diverse array of media productions significant attention is now directed at politicians as much for who they are and how they socially and morally conduct themselves as for their policies or executive or legislative skills. This has been fuelled by changes in media coverage across time, the evolution of celebrity culture and its interplay with politics, alongside a willingness by the political elite to use their personal backgrounds and circumstances as political tools to be utilised to compete for power.

In the realm of political marketing and in the selling of the modern politician to the electorate, leadership has had a significant role to play in shaping popular interpretations of modern politics. Across a broad swathe of theory on political marketing, leadership is only one component part amidst a broader array of policies and ideas advanced to a demanding voting public. However, the increasing prominence of leaders who are cast as both political leaders and as individuals suggests that, at the least, the voter is likely to take instruction and guidance from the social attributes of a political leader as much as from an in-depth study of their policy issues or from long-term retrospective considerations. This in part helps to explain why short-term poll fluctuations are common irrespective of whether policy announcements have been made and why leaders, such as the leader of the Conservative party in Britain David Cameron, could manufacture changes in poll statistics even though new explicit policy directions were not spelled out for some time after his successful party leadership election in 2005.

This text evaluates the relationship between wealth, social class and leadership and how it is interpreted by the electorate. It argues that in the modern political era candidates and leaders, across a spectrum of political dispositions, have attempted to portray themselves as representing an imaginary and largely artificial class niche. They have used this portrayal so as to give themselves social and emotional ties with both mass and niche voting blocks. This has taken place across several decades with leaders generally trying to suppress the features that elevated them to high levels of power and potential leadership, such as elite education and economic well-being, in favour of stories of hardship and struggles against adversity. There have been pronounced changes across time in this area of political presentation. There has been a transformation from a period in 1960s America, where the American voter witnessed Camelot and the election of the 'best and the brightest', to a political culture which now seeks to elect candidates who, although they are largely from the same stock of society, seek to accentuate issues of hardship and ordinariness rather than issues of elitism or exceptionalism. The paradox here is clear. In order to get to positions of political power leaders need to avail themselves of the facilities offered by elite positions and status. Thereafter, in order to address the needs of the mass public the appearance of elitism is marginalised in favour of a manufactured position grounded upon market considerations. This has been a challenge for both presidents and prime ministers and for leaders of governments and opposition parties. The marriage of elite and ordinary is prevalent on both sides of the Atlantic through the interaction and communication between political parties and, as a consequence the exchange of political advisors and information, the approach to the political marketing of the elite nature of political candidates has become similar in both countries.

This work evaluates how political leaders have addressed the problem of class portrayal since the 1960s in the United States and United Kingdom and have used social and emotional issues to form meaningful bonds with the electorate. It does this by looking at a select number of political leaders and addressing how they manufactured changes in their public image and rhetoric, or accentuated points of weakness, in order to be more palatable and marketable to the electorate. In doing this it provides information on the comparative strategies used in both countries, allows an appreciation of which strategies worked and which did not and, through a chronological evaluation, charts how and why an evolution in this approach to political leadership and marketing has taken place.

The selected political leaders in this text are those who tried to market themselves as ordinary when, in large part, they emerged from traditional political backgrounds, that is they were wealthy and had lifestyles which were not typical of the general populace. Even in cases where the political leaders, such as John Major and Richard Nixon, were from relatively ordinary backgrounds they endeavoured to market their childhood experiences as points through which they could advance images of their past as political assets. The intent and purpose of this work therefore is to give a general profile of how the political marketing of individual character, especially that related to elitism and wealth in politics, has evolved on both sides of the Atlantic through selected case studies. Naturally in a study of this type many political figures who might have been appropriate for consideration have to be left out of discussion. Individuals such as Prime Minister Harold Wilson and Presidents Ford and Carter all have attributes and aspects of the marketing of their identity which would have made for meaningful case studies. However, in order to allow an appropriate combination of both breadth and depth, concentration has been directed at political leaders who give meaning and in some cases, such as John F. Kennedy, provide contrasts in the issue of political marketing and wealth. There are also omissions in the chronological evolution, but the candidates and political leaders who are discussed provide adequate coverage of the nature of, and problems posed by, the issue of marketing wealthy individual politicians to an electorate which perceives itself as detached from, and doubtful of its associations with elite society.

Political marketing with respect to political identity and socio-economic standing has long-standing roots. In the nineteenth century in the United States several presidents made play of their humble origins in the prelude to political office. The pursuit and acquisition of the presidential office was advanced as one based on individual merit rather than elite standing or personal wealth. Although these marketing roots are important, this text takes as its foundation the politics of the 1950s and 1960s and the emergence of mass communication to inform voters of candidate attributes. This analysis of leadership and wealth initially looks at the leadership strategies employed by Kennedy and contrasts the presentation of his leadership and his emotional connection with the voter with the strategies employed by Richard Nixon. Across the period in question political presentation changed, albeit slowly, with a greater consideration of the visual image and an enhanced appreciation of voter expectations about how the identity of the political candidate could be marketed so as to satisfy perceived voter demand. Much has been made of the 1960 election contest, and the communications strategies adopted by Kennedy and Nixon. In part these were about conveying political platforms but, in addition to this, efforts were made to accentuate some of the trials the candidates had endured in their personal lives. Kennedy was forced to address queries about the impact of his religion upon his political responsibility, and played tactfully to the elite standing of his family background and military experience. By contrast Nixon was largely unable to market his genuinely regular background, and while internally holding some resentment against the 'eastern liberal elite', was unable to transform this into a tangible and meaningful political criticism of Kennedy. He was unable to demonstrate that elite social standing was detrimental to the marketability of a political candidate. In this context, as a snapshot, elitism and the elite social position of candidates appeared to be of little consequence in the electoral process. This is in stark contrast to the contemporary era, where perceptions of elitism are consistently and actively suppressed, for fear that associations with elite standing and the wealth that accompanies it may have a corrosive impact on the relationship between the elector and the elected.

There have been significant changes with candidate portrayal and its association with wealth and social class in both the United States and United Kingdom. Not all candidates are suited or comfortable with a manufactured or re-branding of their character, and some have proven to be uncomfortable with the utilisation of their private lives as facets for political advancement. This has presented marketing issues related to family, with concerns about exploitation and matters of privacy coming to the fore. However, even given the reservations it is clear that the evolution of modern politics demands a combination of the selling of the personal and the political, with consideration about the message that is delivered to the public, and its salience, being important in shaping the political fortunes of both political parties and their leaders.

In advance of changes in communications and the exposure of the private lives and private wealth of political figures there appeared to be an acceptance on the part of both those who were elected and those who elected them that there was a social and class gap between the two groups. However, it is evident that by the 1970s there was a slow and gradual change in how the political establishment was viewed and, accordingly, its key players were forced to address and accommodate changing societal views about the personal profiles of those subject to election. Wealth appeared to be an issue which shaped perceptions of how political figures might understand the electorate, and conversely how the electorate perceived the character and political identity of politicians. For example, a slow but purposeful modification by Margaret Thatcher of her image and background was implemented so as to present her as a female political leader in keeping with the experiences of both men and especially women, in the 1970s. This incorporated discussion of her past, her homelife, and her experiences as a woman and mother. These had emotional salience and played to stereotypical images of a woman working to conquer a predominantly male environment. Social and class issues were managed so as to portray Thatcher as a political figure who was legitimate and authentic as a voice for ordinary Britons. It involved an effort to market a modified class position and to downplay any accusations of elitism. A 'them and us' environment was to be avoided, and a classless one accentuated. This was not only directed at contemporaneous political campaigning and marketing, but towards shaping Thatcher's permanent political legacy.

This is in keeping with a broader remit within political marketing where the image of social inclusiveness and ordinariness is continued into the period following the occupation of the political office. In the memoirs of virtually all politicians who have left office, and those discussed in this text who have produced memoirs, suggestions are made that they were of a lower social standing than they actually were, or that they, on the grounds of character, could associate easily with members of all social classes. In 2008, Barack Obama continued this trend with discussion of his humble roots and financial difficulties prior to his legal and political career. This further enhances the general concept of a reworking of class interpretations and emotional connections with the voter and social positioning as a central component in the marketing of a political identity.

In both British and American politics there has been a marked and rapid evolution in image manipulation and political marketing directed at conveying manufactured political identities. Through the 1980s on both sides of the Atlantic the preferred political image, and the one that has remained into the contemporary era, has been one where the elected politicians have been portrayed as ordinary and unexceptional in their origins, yet exceptional and gifted in their leadership. This is borne out through the analysis of a number of political figures addressed in this work. John Major presented himself as the son of circus performers and the product of a working-class background. President Clinton cast himself as the product of a problematic and disrupted childhood and as a politician who could empathise with the problems of recession hit America. He conveyed issues to the electorate that gave a profile of him as a person as well as a political leader. Only a limited political knowledge was needed in order to form a bond with the candidate, and this played heavily upon weaknesses in the 1992 re-election campaign of President Bush. Blair followed suit in the United Kingdom by casting the Conservative party as out of touch with ordinary people and elitist in its membership and leanings. He engaged personally in a series of populist oriented actions designed to make him and his entourage appear at one with the interests and emotions of 1990s Britain. This was achieved by using focus groups, spin-doctors and effective media presentation. Blair's elite background, which had helped to elevate him to assume the leadership of the Labour party in the first place, was downplayed, while his family activities, social meetings and interests were accentuated to give a him universal appeal. Efforts were made by the Conservative party to follow this lead, but the legacy endured by the party and its leadership from its prior time in government during the 1980s and early 1990s, alongside prevailing stereotypes concerning its elite interests, ensured that it was hard to convince voters that the leadership had undergone a personality change or that the party represented and understood the needs of the ordinary person.

By 2000 the benchmark in the political marketing of class and social origins was clear in British and American politics. Candidates and leaders could no longer afford to be perceived as elite or products of wealthy backgrounds, nor could they be perceived to be out of touch with the daily concerns of the electorate. Conspicuous wealth and the lifestyle that it offered was thought to be a potential barrier to gaining affinity with the voter. The political response was balanced and considered, reflecting extensive research into what voters wanted, and what candidates could realistically offer in presenting themselves at one with the populace. Underpinning the need of the political elite to understand the electorate was the use of poll statistics, market research into the nature of the voter as a consumer, media investigation into the role of character in political life, and the treatment of the political candidate as a 'celebrity', as well as a political figure. Often issues were raised for discussion that were not part and parcel of political debate, with political leaders and opposition challengers appearing on daytime chat shows, discussing lifestyle habits and family issues designed to make them appear at one with the nation. This was important in shaping David Cameron's challenge for the Conservative leadership in 2005, and in the re-branding of Gordon Brown following Blair's decision to relinquish his leadership position during 2007. Both played down their pasts, accentuated trying personal issues, particularly involving health care, and fought to hold to a social, emotional and political position which would endear them to the British public.

The development of a manufactured political identity has followed a relatively predictable path in the contemporary era. Both Gore and Bush, alongside the other candidates in the 2000 presidential primaries, sought to cast themselves as ordinary and regular Americans. This continued into 2004, when Bush and Kerry cast themselves as sharing the interests, feelings and emotions possessed by ordinary Americans. All of the major candidates in 2004 read from the same hymn sheet, identifying areas of hardship, impoverishment and trying circumstances which aligned them with the American people. Personal childhood hardship and family health concerns were favourite areas for political reinvention and exploitation. This was achieved through strategic and selective presentation, no candidate overtly criticising any other on account of their wealth or social background, and all candidates casting themselves as being from similar backgrounds or in one form or another as not having been affected by wealth in an untoward manner. The result was a competitive endeavour to highlight personal characteristics, past troubles, social habits and the ordinary attributes of each candidate.

The presentation of leadership identities, both political and personal, as major components in modern marketing is evidently a component of modern politics that now occupies a prominent role in political communication. An emergent feature is that political leaders may be judged for who they are and the lifestyle choices they make, rather than for the policies they advocate. The concentration on the selling of political identities, rooted in the presentation of ordinariness, gives the opportunity for the voter to determine political outcomes having considered issues that have little political meaning. Yet, social and emotional presentations, conveyed with authenticity and legitimacy, allow voters an additional component through which to make a political choice. In an era where concentration in the centre-ground of politics is commonplace and policy differentiation between political parties in terms of policy may be difficult, this may give additional indicators which enhance the information available to the voter. Evidently wealth and trappings of elite society are factors that appear to alienate the voter. Because the social origins of most notable political figures are still from esteemed and wealthy sections of society, it has become the norm to reinvent the pasts of candidates and convey selected aspects which will resonate with the voter. While class, wealth and social standing are presented as being issues which no longer create a divide between electors and the elected, part of the reason for this is that it has been marketed so as to be an issue which no longer matters. That the political strategists and politicians themselves give the issue considerable time and attention suggests that it is an issue which does matter and is an important component in the modern search for popularity and power.

1
Leadership and Ordinariness

The evolution of political marketing in the modern era has been rapid, with significant study of its practice, significant investments in its refinement, and marked improvements in its implementation taking place over the last 20 years. A large proportion of the marketing changes have taken place against a mixed background of political successes and failures, and these have informed its evolution. It is clear that changes in the demands of the electorate and understandings of what might be desired from a political candidate have had a meaningful role to play in determining the type of leadership candidate required in western democratic societies.

There are limitations in the type of candidate that can be marketed to an electorate. For each political party involved there are limitations in the ideological disposition of the candidate that can be chosen on account of their political allegiances, voting record and their chosen mandate, particularly relating to issues considered important by the party elite and political membership. For example, candidates must choose domestic and foreign policy positions in keeping with the general ideological thrust offered by the party which has elected them as leader. While ideological or platform reform can take place with respect to overall party disposition, sometimes rapidly, often it is slow to change and is subject to internal debate and dissent about abandonment of tradition or deviation away from party roots. The challenges faced by Bill Clinton and Tony Blair in creating the New Democrats and New Labour are testament to this with respect to party modernisation and change.

Although traditional party frameworks create a number of marketing constraints one area that can be addressed with much more freedom is that of the character and the socio-demographic profile of the candidate.

In theory candidates will be drawn almost exclusively from elite social positions where individuals have the connections and wealth to access political institutions and have the social networks necessary to pervade party structures. Indeed, historically that has been the case in both the United Kingdom and, to a large part, in the United States. Yet in the contemporary era there has been a pronounced effort to distance candidates from their social and economic roots and to cast them as something other than their real selves. To be seen to be of the elite is to be seen to create a political liability and an impediment to elected office. This has had pronounced consequences for political marketing as this outcome gives candidates a challenge in accentuating the parts of their social and economic background that can honestly and legitimately be marketed to the mass, but it also adds an additional component. Parts of the candidate's background will be purposefully manufactured so as to present a political product that appeals to a significant majority of the population. This creates an ironic scenario where the product that is being marketed is one that is purposefully modified to present it as something less than its true potential value, and individual flaws and lesser social standing are pushed to the fore at the expense of excellence and exceptionalism. This is founded largely on political pragmatism, with an ability to alter the leadership product available in accordance with perceived public demand.

This chapter addresses several issues important to an appreciation of the role of a candidate's social and economic background in the realm of political marketing. It considers firstly the theory on political marketing, and thereafter addresses the role that leadership is considered to play in shaping political marketing and popular support for candidates. It is a factor that appears increasingly important to political culture and has a significant bearing upon the type and nature of media coverage afforded a candidate. It is now also pivotal in determining the type of candidate who can advance themself as a viable contender for leadership, and determines to a great degree the extent to which they will have to reinvent themselves in order to appeal to the voting mass.

Consideration thereafter is given to a number of the variables relating to the marketing of candidates on both sides of the Atlantic. At first sight the United States has led the way in marketing candidates in an effective manner to the voter, with advancements in communications technology and market research into voter preferences playing a key role in the modern political era. Part of the reason for this was the advent of mass ownership of televisions in the 1950s and 1960s and the ability of the American voter to witness a visual image whilst also consuming material on the substance of policy. This approach to consumer culture accentuated America's progressivism, alongside the structural needs of America's presidential political system. Across time, evidence, research and experience demonstrated that the visual image and personal characteristics of the individual leader could be important in shaping voter preferences and they, accordingly, have become central features of the modern political campaign. In addition there is now comprehensive research into voter preference through conventional market research strategies and the use of focus groups to observe how the characteristics and appearance of political figures are greeted in public circles.

Political systems are significant in shaping the opportunities available to candidates when seeking to manufacture their image to suit the voter. In the United States the electoral system employed to elect the president naturally makes it an imperative that the candidate tries to appeal to a majority of voters across the nation, each individual having an ability, theoretically at least within the limitations of the electoral college system, to influence the outcome of the election within their state. In the United Kingdom the dynamics are fundamentally different. The British public do not have a direct voice in determining the specific person who will potentially be a prime minister, but rather are expressing a desire to have a constituency representative and, through that, a particular party elected to government. The leader of the party is chosen by the political party members and is not subject personally to a national election or mass popular referendum. The role of marketing in Britain is therefore directed at a different political base. It confers legitimacy upon a party choice, and has significance in symbolically selling national values through a political platform. However, there is also a contemporary move towards personification in politics where the individual is thought to encapsulate the values entertained by the political and party movement as a whole.

A significant issue with respect to candidate election is the role of the party and its membership in helping to select a candidate who generally reflects its views. The preferences in the type of candidates parties wish to have are based partly upon the historical tradition of the party, alongside the type of person who will appeal to its core membership. In determining the characteristics of the candidate, parties run risks in portraying themselves as elitist, out of touch with voting blocks or simply unattractive to the voting block as a whole. This has been an ongoing feature of British politics for some considerable period of time. In particular this has been a problem for the Conservative party which has been perceived to have an exclusive and elite identity and to have an elderly and largely aloof party membership. In the contemporary era efforts have been made to distance Conservative leadership candidates from this profile, yet this has proven difficult to achieve. In part this has arisen because the opponents and critics of the Conservatives are happy to play the class card in trying to distance the Tory party from swing voters and to portray its leaders, in particular, as socially distanced from the electorate. In America the tension, on class grounds, is marginally less apparent, yet both parties have roots and associations with voting blocks associated with ill-defined but nevertheless applicable socio-economic and demographic patterns. The Democrats are still associated with voters who have a lower socio-economic profile than the Republicans, who are in turn associated with moneyed and elite interests.[1] The introduction of social and moral issues however distorts the relationship between wealth and partisan support. Thomas Frank argues that this aspect serves to provide the backdrop for the support for the conservative movement in America, which hides its true economic intentions behind an array of value laden rhetoric, its 'leaders systematically downplay the politics of economics. The movement's basic premise is that culture outweighs economics as a matter of public concern'.[2]

An emergent feature of debate concerning political marketing is the extent to which party leaders actually reflect their party's traditional background. In an era where the centre-ground of politics is increasingly congested, and the fight for swing voters has become intense, alterations in the presentation and marketing of both party organisations and candidates has occurred. With the reinvention of the identity of both the New Democrats in America in the early 1990s and New Labour in the United Kingdom in the mid-1990s there has been pronounced alterations in political and ideological placement. Contemporary evidence would suggest that candidates still come from traditional routes in seeking the nominations of their respective parties. They are commonly wealthy (Kerry and Bush), have experienced outstanding educations (Blair and Cameron) and have social connections to the political elite in society. However, on a national stage the economic and social attributes they hold are altered to try to convey meaningful bonds with the voter. Conspicuous wealth, elite education and social contacts are suppressed, and this has been a feature for leaders across the breadth of the political spectrum. The route to power and the attributes necessary to be an eligible candidate are manifestly different to the skills considered essential to holding office and execute power, and the marketing strategies differ accordingly. Ordinariness appears to be a feature demanded of those seeking office, while exceptional political ability appears to be demanded of leaders once they have achieved office. This appears uniform irrespective of party identity, and the outcomes in politics are plainly visible. Identikit candidates, who reflect one another in the presentation of their social lives, interests and backgrounds are now commonplace in politics. This is not only a product of centre-ground congestion but also of market-based research which identifies the characteristics and appearances which are likely to have resonance with the voting public. In effect partisan affiliation is a feature which can be downplayed or minimised by accentuating leadership attributes which overtly appear to have no significant linkage to traditional class-based politics.

Political marketing and leadership: The issues

The evolution of research on political marketing is relatively recent. Its emergence has coincided with an enhanced appreciation of marketing techniques to sell commercial products, the emergence of a communications age and an appreciation of the consumption habits and preferences of voting blocks. The usefulness of marketing techniques in politics is pronounced, with the voter being considered as a consumer who will generally make rational choices based on the type of product that is available, and its appeal transcends parties, institutions and in many cases national borders. The importance of political marketing has not been lost on the political establishment, with considerable time and resources being given to enhancing research into voting preferences and habits.

At the heart of marketing is the political consumer. They drive the market, taking stock of the political products on display and making a selection based on their contemporaneous needs. Marketing research suggests some degree of sophistication on the part of the consumer, their being able to consider a large number of components when selecting their desired products. The communication of information works two ways. Lilleker and Lees-Marshment assert, 'Political marketing is the study of how politicians interface with their electorates'.[3] Voter decisions are made through retrospective evaluations and the anticipation of future political actions. However, in multiparty democracies the voter is commonly presented with a choice between competitive parties, where some degree of sophistication is required to make an informed decision about likely voting outcomes. In the context of this study, with media saturation concentrated largely on complex policy positions, party leaders are the central focus of inquiry, their prominence, encapsulation of party identity and their personal characteristics all having importance in conditioning voter response. Party profiles are linked to the identity of individual political leaders and candidates. Increasingly in the contemporary era, when the boundaries between celebrity and politics have become blurred, the nature of the character of the political leader and how it is received by the public has an increasingly important role to play. Selling candidates to the populace marries the political environment, at least superficially, with sales activity encountered in commercial activity. It is not a new phenomenon, but has been enhanced and modified across time. In 1956 Leonard Hall, the Republican National Chairman claimed, 'You sell your candidates and your programs the way a business sells its products'.[4]

A large part of the research into political marketing has advanced parties as the key vehicles through which voters shape their political identification. Historically, this is persuasive and gives a clear indication of voter choice and political ideology. In the contemporary era traditional party identities have become blurred, particularly with a concentration of politics on both sides of the Atlantic in a congested middle ground. While the absence of clear water between parties may now make political choice a challenging task, the advent of a communications revolution enhances the volume and detail of information available to the political consumer. This has gone hand-in-hand with the willingness of political leaders to expose themselves to media coverage of their personal lives, accommodating personal biographies and family experiences into the political theatre. This has added a further issue for the voter to consider at the ballot box.

Party organisations have to market their ideas and political ideology via a number of means to the mass market, to niche groups and to individuals. The materials that can be marketed are broad and include policy, political legacy and reputation, personality and identity. Given its prominence and seemingly persuasive impact on voter choice, the character and identity of leadership is one of the core emergent themes of marketing and political research. In 1990s Smith and Saunders argued that there were potential problems if there was party movement to the centre-ground in politics, specifically with respect to political marketing and the maintenance of a discernable political identity. They contended, 'The idea of product positioning also warns against the "flight to the middle ground". This will make differentiation around Unique Selling Propositions difficult to achieve.'[5] In terms of policy the case advanced may well be true, yet the advent of a concentration of party platforms and profiles in the centre makes the characteristics of leadership ever more important in the marketing framework, with a need to give distinctive identity to a party structure where the parties struggle to differentiate themselves from one another on the basis of policy or platform alone. This concept is endorsed by Billig in an analysis of the importance of political rhetoric: 'Because the ideological difference between political parties are often small and because many of the issues are highly complex, personalization can be expected. Voters are looking for leaders whom they feel they can trust and who will have the character to react well to unforeseen crises.'[6] If policy divisions are increasingly difficult to differentiate and advance to the populace then leadership can be used as an effective tool through which to levy popular support. Moreover, in addition to the identity and visual image of the political leader, the political rhetoric used by leaders has ramifications above and beyond the simple advancement of policy themes to the public. Nicholas Jones argued that the sound bites employed in the modern era are 'a highly individualistic form of expression. At their most effective they not only convey political messages but also say something about the person who utters them. The most memorable seem to reinforce already well-known personal characteristics.'[7] Furthermore Pancer, Brown and Barr argued, in 1999, 'that perceptions of candidates' personal characteristics can even affect party popularity and, occasionally, even election outcomes'.[8] If policy and platform differences are now blurred then character becomes a core vehicle through which to carry party identity, however much this might be considered to introduce celebrity to the overall democratic policy process and be detrimental to its credibility.

Lilleker and Lees-Marshment have identified a number of products, including leadership, which can be marketed by a political party to the electorate. Leadership is defined as: 'Leadership: powers, image, character, support/appeal, relationship with the rest of the party organisation (advisers, cabinet, members, MPs), media relationship.'[9] While recognising the policies and identity of a party, this text concentrates upon how this leadership has been marketed across time via an evaluation of selected political leaders. It addresses in particular socio-economic standing and efforts to present candidates attuned to the social, economic and emotional attributes of the nation they seek to represent. The evolution of leadership and the methods of presentation to the public merges public relations, media role and function, popular receipt of messages based on the perception of character, and the reinvention of the lives of candidates and leaders to suit prevailing popular moods.

At one and the same time it has a simple objective, to cater for the preferred character, leadership and emotional attributes desired by the voting mass, alongside a complex series of measures and public relations exercises through which to try and satisfy market conditions via a constructive political presentation.

There are several different types of political marketing through which political policy and identity can be sold to the electorate. These include existing concepts of product oriented marketing, sales oriented marketing and market oriented strategies.

Product oriented strategies contend that a strong political product will attract voters towards a political identity, and that the product will essentially sell itself on the basis of its lure and attractiveness. The voter is drawn to the political product on account of its merits. This model has marginal resonance with concepts and arguments based on the nature of character and leadership. In essence it argues that the selected leadership candidate or leader will have to compete to sell himself as he is, and that in a competitive market the voter will need to be persuaded, but not manipulated, towards favouring a particular individual. In this model the candidate need not gravitate towards mirroring the voter, rather the voter is expected to find the leadership skills and charisma displayed by the candidate appealing and form social and emotional connections as a consequence.

Sales oriented strategies are designed to prompt voter activity by addressing voting blocks and catering to the needs of the interested parties via strategic presentation and communication. This strategy is persuasive when considering issues of character and leadership in the modern era. Selective presentation of aspects of the leadership candidate's past, in an autobiographical context, and the highlighting of difficulties which allow social and emotional connections allows a marketing strategy based upon both mass and niche markets, and caters to prevailing social and economic conditions. The voter is presented with materials attuned to their perceived needs and expectations.

Market strategies are based largely on research and in trying to understand voter preference via the liaison between the public and the political realm and evaluating niche groups who can be persuaded on social and emotional grounds. They are at their most appealing when considering leadership, and how leaders have advanced themselves successfully, as politicians and people, to the populace. In large part this has manifested itself with party leaders seeking to portray themselves as derived from mainstream society. Parties have identified, primarily via focus groups and market research, the desired image, presentation skills and attributes which appeal to voting groups, including those closely affiliated to a party identity and those swing voting blocks necessary to claim political power. In general the market preference is identified and then the candidate is shaped to convey the desired image and express the desired views of the electorate.[10] The candidate moves to give an impression, generally a manufactured one, that they mirror the lives of the voter and that socially and emotionally they are at one with the populace.

Leaders are advanced, via marketing techniques, as possessing personal criteria which are deemed representative of the voting block, and as commodities which can be sold to the public so as to allow an emphasis on certain characteristics which appeal to market forces. Presentation of issues universally experienced by the populace are central to the matter – health, hardship, associated aspects of impoverishment, and family life coming frequently to the fore. Elitism, wealth and class division are minimised as features of a political identity.

Leadership and political parties

Marketing the person

The presentation of leadership is significant within the realm of political marketing, yet when compared with research on party and policy it lags behind. In the United States, political, academic and media concentration upon the policy orientation and election activities of the president is now a familiar and commonplace element of contemporary scrutiny. Concentration upon character as an issue which affected leadership was enhanced in United States following Barber's prominent discussion of the issue, particularly relating to the Nixon presidency, in the early 1970s.[11] In Britain too, in the modern era, increasing attention is being given to the character of the occupant of number 10, but as a first among equals the prime minister is seen to be largely beholden to the interests of the party they represent and less prone to be scrutinised as a person. Character counts but it has, thus far, been a secondary feature in the evaluation of a marketable and effective political leadership, and marginal to party politics and the advocacy of a political platform. Historically in Britain there have been muted efforts to convey character, and ordinariness in particular, as an attribute of leadership, Stanley Baldwin making it known that he lit a pipe as he gave his radio broadcasts, and Harold Wilson claiming that he put HP sauce on his food. These were tangential to political policy, but conveyed an individual personal identity as a component of leadership.[12] Even given the modern trend towards celebrity politics and the personification of politics at the expense of party politics, leaders and media commentators assert that it is policy that counts, that a beauty contest is to be avoided for the sake of the process of democracy.[13] However, as Leo McKinstry argues, '"Let's concentrate on the policies, not personalities," is the greatest piece of humbug that a politician can utter. That's like expecting bookies not to discuss form.'[14]

While there are institutional and party limits to the flexibility a leader, on both sides of the Atlantic, can display with respect to policy there are also significant variables which affect how a leader acts and how the party and populace react to them. The marketability of a leader can be exploited to suit prevailing environmental concerns or party needs. They, as an individual, can give attention to aspects of lifestyle choice, and accentuate their understanding of issues which affect the voting block. When doing so they generate media coverage which conveys the impression that they are in touch with prevailing political themes. In this context the marketability of a leader, in terms of who they are, becomes one of the great assets for a political organisation as it offers a number of presentation options and great flexibility, flexibility that is not necessarily offered in the realm of party or policy. At odds with this however is the fact that a wrong choice for a position of leadership can have an impact upon the fortunes of a party that is significant and detrimental. The Conservative party, following a crushing defeat in 1997, struggled to find a candidate who could challenge Blair and his efficient New Labour spin machine. Similarly in the 1980s the Democrats in America struggled to advance a candidate to seriously challenge either Reagan or George Bush Sr. Policy issues were a consideration but so was character. The strategic choice of a marketable candidate offers an opportunity to break out from constraints of party tradition and policy, and to unshackle, to a great degree, the burdens of institutionalised politics. Marketing strategy facilitates in making the choice an informed one, given the research into public preferences and consumption, and enhances opportunities for power to those parties which seek to maximise intelligence and prevailing popular market choice. In the contemporary era Nixon, Bush, Thatcher, Blair and current British party leaders Brown and Cameron have all adapted their personal images to reflect prevailing political marketing needs. They have relied on research and focus groups to give their respective publics the type of character and leadership attributes thought advantageous in the struggle to acquire and retain power. Much of this has been non-political in nature, concentrating on the lives, social habits and past circumstances of candidates. This has added an additional dimension to the presentation and marketing of political identities.

Political leadership and the selection of leaders is a process which does not allow a wholly unrestricted choice from a free market. As leaders are manifestations of the parties they purport to represent, and while they may display distinctive character traits and react personally in different ways to environmental concerns, they are bound and constrained by the party organisations that elevated them to prominence in the first instance. However, each leader, or aspiring leader can display an array of characteristics and skills which can differentiate them from their opponents and try to gain a marketing advantage in the electoral stakes, irrespective of their ideological disposition. Even with respect to physical appearance or social presentation an advantage may be gained, with no immediate reference to policy or ideological intent. This has been evident with the election of new leaders who received poll bounces in advance of any political proposals of note, or any prolonged critical evaluation of their leadership. A prime example is the election of David Cameron as Conservative party leader in 2005. In advance of policy directive or announcements the standing of both Cameron and the Conservative party as a whole increased notably. Opponents charged that the poll bounce relied on image as opposed to substance, that Cameron's core appeal rested on his character and its presentation, and that neither management of government or substantive policy could be legitimately bedded upon such flimsy foundations. However, as Anne Perkins pointed out in the *Guardian*, 'An engaging individual who personifies the fresh start, leading a party not overburdened by doctrine, is a strong base from which to launch a bid to capture the post-Blair era. ... He has used the long leadership contest to establish the empathetic persona of a politician who understands'.[15] In response, as Chapter 7 of this text makes clear, Labour attacked Cameron as superficial, lacking in substance and prone to change his albeit unarticulated policies to align himself with the popular mood. A 'Dave the Chameleon' advertising campaign was subsequently launched to try to exploit any popular cynicism about the politics of image and political pragmatism over the politics of ideological principle. It was critical of the onset of character-based marketing in the modern era, suggested that Cameron was elitist and stressed his disconnection from the ordinary modern voter.[16]

Leadership has been regarded as an influential factor in shaping policy direction and party ideology. Party management is undoubtedly pivotal to political success and advancement, with selection of candidates largely taking place within the party fold. In this context voter opinion on the merits of a candidate need not initially take centre stage. However it is important that the leaders themselves are seen to be part and parcel of the broader community, in terms of their appeal to both their party peer group and also to the voting segments they wish to court. Part of this emanates from their social and emotional disposition, and interpretations of who they are, and how and why they achieved positions of prominence within their party organisations. Party leaders, who may suit party needs and have the elite connections to sustain influence within party organisations, do not necessarily have the character make-up or disposition to link effectively with the public. Conversely, individuals who may court the public and be charismatic may lack the elite connections, elite credibility or party credentials to sustain a continued leadership bid. For several individuals, such as Conservative leaders William Hague and Iain Duncan Smith, and in the United States George Bush Sr in 1992, the lack of emotional resonance among the public was a problem. In Britain it was an ongoing concern that, for all the revision of policies and Conservative party reform little headway was made in the polls in an effort to unseat Blair and the New Labour government. Conservative communication strategies were altered in a significant manner, policies reconsidered and remarketed. Yet the marketing of Hague as an ordinary Yorkshireman and Duncan Smith as the 'Quiet man' failed to give the policies the launch pad they required and both leaders were unable to connect in a meaningful manner with key segments of the electorate. They were also in competition with New Labour, and its much heralded spin machine, which presented Blair as a man of the people and as the embodiment of popular discontent with the Conservative government and the ideology of the early 1990s. As the focal point of popular attention, leaders and their ability to connect socially and emotionally with the electorate substantially condition the impact of policies and the willingness of the public to embrace reform and new ideas, which might engage marginal or swing voters towards the political product of leadership.

The playing field of political marketing is littered with obstacles which have to be overcome if a credible claim of effective and representative leadership is to be made. Leaders on both sides of the Atlantic have confronted burdens which have impacted upon their ability to market themselves to the electorate as people unencumbered by the institutional trappings of politics. The convergence of party ideology with niche voting groups frequently comes into conflict with proclamations by leaders that parties are universally inclusive, and reach out to new voting groups. An inclusive communication strategy works to theoretically broaden party appeal but the party leader, through social class and traditional party connections, as well as party history, is at risk of abandoning stereotypical party roots and being perceived to have compromised the core ideology that underpins party membership and tradition. Cameron's move to appeal to a younger more progressive audience threatened to alienate the traditionalists within his Conservative party in 2005, both in terms of his demeanour and his ideological persuasion. Blair and Clinton both faced similar concerns in the 1990s. Leaders naturally run risks in this realm, yet in trying to win elections, and undertake strategic party reform, it is clearly a route that has had its benefits across time. There are also relevant issues within the socio-economic realm. The attraction of voters to party platforms and leaders that have not naturally reflected their own socio-economic backgrounds is testament to this. Reagan's ability to attract Democrats to his fold and Thatcher's ability to attract 'Basildon Man' to her Conservative party were testament to an ability, partly through the leadership skills and charismatic personal qualities, to produce unlikely deviations in electoral partisanship. Although this type of defection from traditional voting blocks is infrequent, it suggests that it is possible to limit socio-economic party associations within the electorate if policies and leadership are interwoven with emotional and social associations and marketed appropriately. Traditionally parties have attracted a core stock of voters who are influenced by party ideology, party tradition and ongoing interpretations of party strength and trust. The Republican party stereotypically safeguarded the interests of the free market and of business, and advanced the causes of substantial elements of the American middle class. Conversely, the Democrats traditionally advanced the interests of blue-collar America and minority interests. Similar stereotypes have been prevalent in the United Kingdom. The Conservative party is generally considered as being integral to the interests of the business community and upper and middle class, while Labour, particularly in its pre-Blair era, was considered to represent the socio-economic and emotional needs of the working class in Britain. The economic associations of the parties are important to political marketing. In large part they simply reflect stereotypical interpretations of party identity. There are other social associations however which cloud the picture and whether traditional economic stereotypes are still valid is open to question with the convergence of the parties in the centre-ground in the contemporary era. Republican appeals to moral considerations and social themes beyond the realm of economic interests have forged a complex voting coalition which is now only partly based on economic criteria. The presentation of the Democrats as the product of a cultured eastern liberal elite, removed from the trials of American working-class life also clouds the picture of the party model as being simply rooted in economic grounds. Social and moral considerations interwoven with populist rhetoric have come to characterise a more intricate electoral backdrop in the contemporary era.

Images and candidate portrayal

The importance of an image, both physically and in terms of making symbolic connections to the voter, is obviously key in terms of coming to an understanding of how wealth and social standing are manipulated by candidates and leaders to embrace voter needs. Part of the image presented will indeed be a true one, a manifestation of the best characteristics that a candidate can offer. However, in large part the modern presentation is a compilation of what can be offered by the candidate and what is desired by the voter. Because of the desire to shape voting behaviour the presentation is played out on a public stage, giving maximum contact between the voters' minds and the presentation of a preferred candidate image. Kernell suggests, with specific reference to the American presidency, that leaders now go public and utilise popular opinion as a core tool in the advancement of not only their chances of election or re-election, but also to influence others in government. Image has become a core political weapon in establishing influence, power and credibility in the legislative process.[17]

Attention to visual image and branding has become a necessity for political leaders, replete with rhetorical devices to create a manufactured identity which encapsulates the political product. This is important to the manufacturing and cohesion of political communities and the identification with political groups which might be pivotal in the creation of workable majorities. Huddy argues that political cohesion 'can be influenced by the political environment and manipulated by political rhetoric, to constitute an additional powerful ingredient in the development of group loyalties and their political manifestation'.[18] Of key note for this study are the connections which try to emphasise close social and emotional associations between the candidate and the voter, particularly those which transcend narrow voter segmentation on class or socio-economic grounds. The identification on a personal basis is important because it creates a linkage that can transcend both personal identification and thereafter have ramifications into the realm of policy. Thomas, Sigelman and Baas argued, as far back as 1984, that, 'The idea of presidential identification holds that, consciously or not, most citizens harbour deep-seated feelings of a personal – possible even an emotional – nature towards the nation's most visible leader. The feelings can be compared with parallel representations of how one "would like to be personally in an ideal sense."...presidential identification betokens a sense of "psychic proximity" between citizen and president. As such, its implications are straightforward: the greater the identification with the president, the more likely that his performance will meet with approval.'[19] Newman has identified two core areas which give political leaders an opportunity, with great inherent flexibility, to influence how they are perceived by the voter. Firstly, there exists a social connection with the voting block. Leaders seek to cast themselves, primarily in the realm of socio-economic identity, at one with the core voting blocks in the electorate. This is achieved through an identification with general and ill-defined socio-economic group memberships and the cultivating or deflecting of party associations that are wealth related, with an objective of appearing to be similar to a desired target audience. The foundation of this strategy, as this text identifies, has been to plead impoverishment and to downplay any suggestion that the candidate has achieved office on account of wealth or privilege. Associations are made with respect to hardship, financial adversity and aspects of a candidate's life where impoverishment can be accentuated. These are presented as central to a political identity. Two aspects of the presentation of an ordinary existence are important to mention. The associations between elector and elected are formed through a number of bonds, some of which are grounded on impressions of the political standing of the candidate. Importance is given to authenticity, that the candidate is actually who and what they claim to be. A lack of authenticity, or the exposure of its use as a mask of reality has undercut the marketing efforts of many candidates, exposed as having fabricated their past for political gain. William Hague, as discussed in Chapter 5, was compromised after having made claims of his Yorkshire past which did not hold up to scrutiny. In a political theatre replete with an abundance of information about policies, parties, ideology and intrigue, the simplicity of a perceived personal association between the candidate and the elector is important. Ordinariness and the experience of the mundane are issues that the voter can associate with, irrespective of their subjective economic position, or their ability to understand and decide on policy considerations. As a consequence, the importance of the creation and presentation of ordinariness gives a bond that is, in theory, universal, classless and allows all voters to create a relationship with the candidate on grounds that they can understand. The politician and leadership candidate does not have to promise any policy in this area or cultivate a progressive or insightful ideology. Rather they simply have to be 'themselves', demonstrate that they are part and parcel of mainstream society and highlight that they understand and can market ordinariness. In large part, because of the contradictions between the platform needed for the elevation to political leadership, and the social origins of the candidates who acquire leadership, marketing strategies are needed to enhance the presentation of the candidate as an ordinary person. There is also a contextual aspect where leaders and candidates can use environmental circumstance to further endorse their claims of authenticity. Recessions, for example, invite associations with the plight of those adversely affected by economic conditions, a fact not lost on leaders such as Clinton in 1992 when he shared the 'pain' experienced by the voters, or Thatcher in 1979 who exploited the winter of discontent. A core problem for most candidates is that they possess significant wealth, and occupy a socio-economic position far above that of the general populace. This in itself is not harmful within elite political circles, but can be used to suggest that candidates are out of touch with the experiences and day-to-day lives of ordinary voters. As a consequence embellished or manufactured impressions are necessary to suppress popular interpretations of elitism.

Newman's second component of note when marketing the character of a leader is the construction of an image which suggests a sharing of feelings and emotions with the electorate. Newman suggests that 'the candidate emphasises his personality traits to reinforce an image in the voter's mind and, by doing so, makes an emotional connection with the voter'.[20] This offers the opportunity to either complement or, if necessary, bypass any problems with socio-economic standing and to empathise and sympathise with the mindset held by voters. The issue of personal wealth is minimised and aspects of personality are maximised. The candidate can portray oneself as one with a broad selection of voting blocks, depending upon the type of psychological association that is deemed necessary and appropriate. Drew Weston captures the spirit and importance of the emotional appeal to the voter: 'Winning elections requires crafting messages attentive to the disparate emotional meaning of words, phrases, images, and symbols to different emotional constituencies.'[21] Additionally he believed that it was the Republican party which had captured this spirit in the modern era, accentuating emotional attributes at the expense of rational policy objectives, and for good reason. 'Republicans understand what the philosopher David Hume recognized three centuries ago: that reason is a slave to emotion, not the other way around.'[22] The advent of new media has enhanced the opportunity for political figures to go on talk shows and discuss their personal lives, as opposed to their political positions, with an emphasis on who they are rather than what they stand for. Again, little political knowledge on the part of the voter is required. Commonly issues advanced are devoid of specific socio-economic meaning, such as health issues, relationship themes and the challenges faced within the modern family unit.

There are prominent issues in this regard with respect to socio-economic status and the position of the individual voter as both the creator of the market through perceived demand, and the recipient of its political product. One of the core problems is how socio-economic status interplays with party support and identification with leadership. Traditionally this has historically been manifested in party support for class positions, with Labour and the Democrats perceived to be supportive of working-class issues and Republicans and Conservative parties thought to be defenders of moneyed interests. However, there are additional issues of note. Increasingly the rhetoric and personal recollections advanced by political leaders has been directed at voters in a classless context. Issues of presentation are purposefully inclusive, earmarking the character of the candidate as transferable across social groups. This furthermore allows an appeal that transcends traditional party divides. A core theme which assists in understanding why a concept of ordinariness is important in political marketing of candidates and their wealth is self-identification. Voters appear to place themselves in self-appointed positions, which do not necessarily represent their economic status. As indicated by Sears, Huddy and Jervis, 'When respondents were asked whether they identified with the middle, lower working or upper class, their sense of subjective identification was a far more powerful indicator of their conservative-radical orientation, position on socioeconomic issues, and voting preference than objectively determined membership in a socioeconomic class based on factors such as income and occupation.'[23] This assists in an understanding of why political leaders appeal to a sense of ordinariness. It can be a very potent political tool. Irrespective of their true wealth, or identity as working or middle class, many individuals consider themselves as 'ordinary', giving the concept of ordinariness a breadth of appeal with great cross-class flexibility. Thereafter, there is an emotional aspect which gives an additional bond to the impact of self-identification. Tajfel argues, for example, that a social identity involves an individual's 'knowledge of his membership in a social group (or groups) together with the value and emotional significance attached to the membership'.[24] The modern marketing of the political candidate revolves around two core concepts. Firstly, the eradication of a specific class-based appeal can be achieved through a campaign directed at the 'ordinary' voter. This exploits self-reference criteria used by the voter. Secondly, the interplay across an appeal devoid of class specifics and the advancement of an emotional discourse creates the opportunity for further bonds with an expansive and flexible mass audience.

The social and emotional issues most frequently advanced are those which have high salience factors, health, emotional trials and tribulations, and if those have not been experienced by the candidate personally, then family members or friends can be utilised to fulfil the necessary emotional connections. The outcome of this type of candidate presentation has several consequences above and beyond the mere highlighting of the personal experiences of candidates. Firstly, the type of leader desired by the electorate hinges upon perceptions of the background of the candidate as opposed to the political skills or diplomacy that a candidate may entertain. Secondly, in pushing forward this type of association an emphasis is frequently placed upon the candidate as a product of social and emotional adversity. Indeed it appears preferable politically to have been subjected to adversarial circumstances, to having had a smooth and seamless transition to a position where one can challenge for power. Thirdly, candidates with no adversarial concerns which can be marketed socially or emotionally are prone to create or manufacture such problems. Given the stock from which political elites are garnered this can prove problematic and lead to accusations that candidates are deceitful when advancing a public face which does not equate to the true context of their personal and historical circumstances.

In the contemporary political environment the private realm of the politician is now advanced as a core element in creating a politically beneficial asset in the public realm, and an individual's autobiographical past is now part and parcel of the public domain. Concentration on a number of issues which seem tangential to serious politics are to the fore in popular discussion. In particular, presentation and rhetoric tends to highlight how an individual has overcome poverty and has risen to a position of prominence. At the same time candidates entertain the idea that they have not lost touch with the mundane and the challenges of hardship and impoverishment. This is particularly true of candidates in the 1990s and onwards. Clinton advanced his personal problems, and those of his family, as issues which gave him additional connections with the economic and emotional trials endured by American voters in the run-up to the 1992 election. In 2000 George Bush Jr emphasised the problems posed by the classless affliction of alcohol dependency. In the United Kingdom Blair emphasised the problems he faced as a parent, although not always successfully, and accentuated his tenuous connections to working-class Britain through discussion of his pastimes and his non-political interests, particularly in music and sport. In the contemporary era in Britain, Brown and Cameron have played an emotional chess game, both emphasising their involvement with aspects of the British health care system as evidence of their understanding of its practical and symbolic importance. This emerged on account of their experiences with it as individuals and parents. All portrayed themselves as being in touch, as individuals who could empathise and sympathise with the membership of target voting blocks on universal and salient issues, and thereby demonstrate demographic inclusivity. Increasingly the political context is one where candidates are considered victims of circumstance and through the overcoming of adverse conditions social connections are established. Again, wealth, particularly personal wealth, is not perceived as an issue or a topic for debate unless claims of impoverishment can be advanced.

A feature of importance in the marketing of leadership is to be perceived as ordinary rather than exceptional. This is itself is an unquantifiable aspect of political image and presentation, but its strength lies not in being able to specifically pinpoint what ordinary or average is, but rather in the flexibility of the notion of what is ordinary in political theatre. The ordinary factor of politics, or as expressed in the United States the notion of being 'regular', is a voter centred issue which has evolved into an essential component of political marketing and in shaping the characteristics of leadership. In *Policy Today* Aker assessed the nature of the American political character and the concept of ordinariness as a politically beneficial facet. 'At the very least, among politicians, appeals to ordinariness sound pretty familiar. How many public officials work harder than their opponents every election season to present themselves as just like everyone else? In 2004, for instance, John Kerry wind-surfed, snowboarded and rode Boston ferries in a struggle to craft himself as an ordinary guy. This, in response to George Bush's powerfully crafted persona of the wood-chopping, brush-clearing, pickup truck-driving rancher. The legacy of this "ordinary people" idea ... is that it has become one of the most important for crafting our sense of the American character, and we want our leaders to be ordinary as well.'[25] This is not merely restricted to the two countries discussed in this work. In European politics similar dilemmas have existed for political leaders. French President Valéry Giscard d'Estaing was accused of being too 'grand bourgeois'. In response he tried to change perceptions of his image by learning to play the accordion.[26] However, when asked, he was unable to give the price of a Paris metro ticket, signalling to the media that he was not in touch with the day-to-day activities of ordinary people. This perceived detachment and a lack of commonplace knowledge was considered detrimental to his political standing. A similar concern existed in 1976 for Swedish Prime Minister Olaf Palme, who was unable to state a reasonable figure for an average flat rental.[27] No justifications were advanced as to why a political leader should know facts such as these, nevertheless the lack of a precise response was considered to be a negative mark against credible leadership. Swedish politics offers a further, more contemporary, indicator of the power of the ordinary in political life. In the mid-1990s a prominent female politician, Mona Sahlin, who had enjoyed political success partly on account of perceptions of her ordinary identity, faced challenges to the image she had conveyed. She was challenged over discrepancies in her financial standings and alleged abuse of government finances. She had previously made great play of her connections to mainstream Swedish society, 'Filling the attractive image of a modern handsome young mother, she managed to transform politics into something which most people could recognise as relevant to their own lives. This was accomplished successfully by using the language of everyday life, especially the communicative idiom of young urban mothers.'[28] However, the exposure of the nature of Sahlin's personal finances drove a gulf between the conveyed, and desirable, political image of ordinariness and her popular image. She played to the image of her being the mother of four children combined with a heavy workload to try to explain the charges of financial impropriety, but with little success. The image of her ordinariness had been undermined by the 'inherent mismatch' between her claims of being so, and the allegations concerning her misuse of her wealth. This proved detrimental to her political position.[29]

Poll questions frequently ask voters about whether the candidates understand the needs of, or can associate with, ordinary people. This suggests that to both candidates and voters, expectations and perceptions of ordinariness are important. Similarly, candidates in American presidential election races are asked about whether, if they have not experienced them, they can understand how ordinary or regular people are affected by the problems in society, as highlighted in Chapter 4 of this text. The stereotypical questions in this context are normally whether a political figure knows the price of everyday commodities, and whether they are in touch with the day-to-day experiences and mundane aspects of life. The perception and portrayal of ordinariness is not without its problems. On account of its being ill-defined, but much used, it has become entwined with political stereotypes and is now part and parcel of the public relations machine of politics. It does however impact more heavily on one side of the political spectrum than the other. The core problems have been faced by political parties on the centre-right. Both the Conservative party in Britain, and the Republican party in the United States have been historically portrayed as parties which have preference for, and have been supported by, those in the higher income brackets. Candidates who have been forwarded by those parties in the modern era have frequently been accused of being out of touch and lacking the connections with ordinary people to allow them to make emotional or socio-economic bonds. This has presented problems in marketing candidates who have strong associations with privileged elites and higher social class standing. At the same time they are asked to show, in order to market themselves effectively, that those connections are minimal, and that the pitfalls of an ordinary existence are part and parcel of their upbringing and make-up. Nevertheless, in the United States it has been the Republican party who have success-fully embraced the concept of forging social and emotional bonds and minimising the impact of the perception of wealth and elitism. Frank Rich, writing in the *New York Times*, pinpointed the cultural pitfalls facing leaders who desire to run for office, and need considerable wealth to do so: 'Our conflicted attitude about money, old and new, runs deep. There is nothing more American than piling up wealth, and yet nothing more un-American than showing it off.'[30] This has proven to be an issue where there is hard evidence in the form of opinion poll statistics which highlight how party stereotypes play a role in conditioning individual interpretations of candidates.

One of the central aspects which characterised this feature is the idea of political life as being distanced and removed from the experiences of the ordinary person, and this has further ramification with the idea of political party placement. In 1986 William Schneider argued that anti-establishment populism was 'the most important feature in our politics in the last twenty years'. Furthermore he claimed, 'It is ideologically ambivalent. And it has displaced progressivism as the dominant motif of

American politics. Elites tend to be rich and well-educated, hence, economically conservative and culturally sophisticated. Populism is anti-elitist and therefore just the reverse – left-wing on economic issues and right-wing on social and cultural issues.'[31] This poses a clear challenge to those who aspire to power, with this inherent contradiction at the heart of the marketing challenge. Several politicians of the modern era have advanced populist messages and presented themselves as representative of grassroots society despite their significant personal wealth. Reagan argued in favour of powerless elements of society against the institutions of government for example, as outlined in Chapter 4. However, in the main, populist declarations have been varied in their impact and their scope in the contemporary era. Part of the reason for this is that they still maintain a class-based element in their construct and the main thrust of modern political marketing concerning the individual has been to minimise class-based political perceptions, certainly with respect to leadership portrayal.

A further consideration of leadership, which is discussed in further depth when the contest between Clinton and Bush Sr is discussed in Chapter 4, is whether the perception of ordinariness is actually a prerequisite for election to office. In essence the voters appear to desire a candidate drawn from their own ranks, and consequently the candidate is theoretically better placed to understand the policy needs of the electorate. However, this argument is grounded on a flimsy assumption that in order to cure social ills it is an asset to have possessed those ills in the first instance. As President Bush argued in 1992, it erroneously suggests that to cure an illness doctors must have had the illness themselves, so as to properly understand and appreciate it. While there was logic in Bush's response and an appreciation of a specific interpretation of leadership, it lacked both a social and emotional connection and was used by the media, as well as by Bush's opponents, to suggest that Bush was out of touch and could not empathise with the plight of those affected by recession.

Preparation and presentation

The presentation and branding of candidates as ordinary is advanced via a number of platforms. It is manifested through the presentation of leisure and social habits as a facet in demonstrating that the hobbies and pastimes of candidates are similar to those of the population as a whole. Pastimes perceived as elite or exclusive in nature are removed from popular view. Candidates such as David Cameron, Tony Blair and Bill Clinton accentuated their preferences in sports, music and personal interests so as to demonstrate that they were in tune with contemporaneous social preferences and interests. Again, although tangential to the formation and execution of policy, it gives each voter, irrespective of their preferred political ideology or personal wealth, an opportunity to associate with candidates on a personal level, and to form the strong bonds of a relationship which transcends political party affiliation. This issue can also have social and visual foundations. For example, Newman points out that in 1992 'Clinton and Gore generated images of themselves as ordinary people by surrounding themselves with average looking voters on their bus trips in small towns around America'.[32] Political knowledge was not required, or necessary, to form bonds with the candidates.

The adoption of an ordinary or regular profile when gaining identification with the voting block is not accidental, but is in large part based upon research into the type of candidate who will appeal to the mass, and the type of voter who can be swung behind a party, platform or individual. In America both the Republicans and Democrats have extensive information on voter characteristics which allow detailed understandings of the preferences of each voter on an individual basis.[33] The socio-economic make-up and lifestyle preferences of voters can be analysed to determine a profile of the type of consumer the voter is likely to be. Thereafter a political message which adheres to the voter preference can be delivered to suit their personal political and emotional needs. There are however concerns that this creates a political environment where political needs are satisfied, but not in a fashion where the voter is asked to actively contemplate a spectrum of political ideas or options. The outcome is that the public, when defined as ordinary or when they perceive themselves as such, can and will receive simplified messages which portray a candidate in a similar fashion. Political knowledge and understanding is not a necessity on the part of the voter. Character-based marketing creates a political environment where perceptions dominate over substance, as through active research and understanding of the electorate each candidate can portray oneself as ordinary to any given audience. The presentation of the candidate is, theoretically, always attuned to the needs of the voter.

There is a difference between campaigning for power and actually administering a leadership position. On the one hand candidates in pursuit of office must assert authority and leadership, and prove themselves politically fit to lead the nation. However, at the same time there has to be a sense that leaders are derived socially from mainstream society and that they, in large part, demonstrate the same values and characteristics as the voting block. There appear to be values that are considered common to the elected and the elector, and some that are enhanced or are the preserve of the political leader with respect to the exceptional characteristics. As Bruce Miroff says of the American president, 'The president's character must not only be appealing but must also be magnified by the spectacle. The spectacle makes the president appear exceptionally decisive, tough, courageous, prescient or prudent. Whether the president is in fact all or any of these things is obscured. What matters is that he or she is presented as having these qualities, in magnitudes that ordinary citizens can imagine themselves to possess. The president must appear confident and masterful before spectators whose very position, as onlookers, denies the possibility of mastery.'[34] In simple terms the American President, and in essence the Prime Minister of the United Kingdom, must play to two political audiences at the same time, one that is exceptional in the political realm and one that is ordinary in the public realm. Mary Stuckey underscores this when discussing the American President, 'They must appear to be of the mass and, at the same time, above it'.[35] This is the marketing challenge that faces those intent on refining the image of candidates, and in essence it is one that has been addressed successfully across time. Writing in the *Independent* newspaper in Britain, Peter Wilby observed the challenges of modern leadership: 'In theory, we should be looking for the things that make them [leaders] special: magic and mystery among the Royal Family, wisdom and foresight among presidents and prime ministers. In fact, we want to feel that, underneath, they are just like us...in our democratic age, we want a president, a prime minister or even a monarch to be what the Americans call a regular guy. So we were thrilled to learn that the Queen can make tea, that Bill Clinton went on camping holidays, and that the teenage Tony Blair wanted to be a rock singer.'[36] The British media also picked up on the transference of the idea of ordinariness from popular culture into the realm of politics. 'Today it is more important to be "grounded" than to have ideas....Ordinariness wins votes; it makes the ordinary feel better about themselves. When someone on a reality TV show is revealed to be more than normally dumb...the public immediately warms to him. It is no coincidence that the most spectacularly gormless of Big Brother contestants, Jade Goody, is the one who has effortlessly attained celebrity status.' Furthermore, 'Authenticity suggests a person uncontaminated by excessive knowledge or educational overqualification. Those with above-average knowledge and intellect are deemed to be essentially inauthentic and therefore not to be trusted – it was the reason why

David Willetts and Oliver Letwin were quickly ruled out of the [2005] Tory leadership contest.'[37] Conventionally this quandary, between the presentation of elitism and ordinariness, has been addressed by dividing the marketing strategy of leadership into two distinct parts, which address where a candidate has come from and, thereafter, how their experiences are manifested in the active or potential practice of their leadership. The hardships and ordinariness of the candidate's early years are the foundation for the promise of both informed and exceptional leadership in later years. Rich argues, 'faux populism has become de rigeur among the wealthy in the public eye. We are awash in ambitious rich people, from the political arena on down, who play up their humble roots and home-down habits, however few or fictional in reality, to sell us products or themselves.'[38] This allows the marketing strategy to address the interests of a range of voting blocks, and gives candidates the leeway to be selective in pinpointing the issues and aspects of their past that are best suited to demonstrate the salient themes which allow connection with the voter. It also allows a separation of the candidate from the electorate when political issues demand that the leadership skills they possess are utilised. In those instances candidates can both be ordinary, but can also become exceptional. Furthermore, it allows candidates to retain the elite associations essential to the informal and internal workings of government.

Leadership, marketing and the media

The media are instrumental to the portrayal and marketing of candidates in the modern era, and changes in media presentation and media activity have had a significant influence upon how the political marketing of candidate wealth has been conducted. In part the media, and its ability to disseminate information to both mass and niche markets, explains why political marketing is now fundamental to the conduct of politics and explains why there have been changes in perceptions of voter preference with respect to leadership, political marketing and identity. It appears that in the modern era a greater importance has emerged with respect to the weighting assigned to a candidate's image and character. This is partly shown via research undertaken by Scott Keeter who looked at how voter activity influenced preference for candidates. He compared how television watchers and newspaper readers evaluated candidates' personal qualities. Addressing a number of variables, important in political marketing, such as attitudes towards parties, age, education and income he found that those who derived their political news from television gave a greater weighting to the individual characteristics of candidates than those who derived their political news from printed mediums. Additionally this appeared to be an enhanced feature in the 1970s as opposed to the position in the 1950s.[39] He found that 'voters choose as best they can. Television makes information about candidates' personal qualities cheaper to obtain than information about issues. And regardless of its accuracy, such information obtained through television seems more credible.'[40] This is not to say that personal characteristics were, or are, deemed to be singularly pivotal to voter assessments of candidates, but rather that across time the visual image and characteristics have become more accentuated in shaping voter opinions. Character counts and, it appears, as image has come to play an influential role in politics, it has become an increasingly influential factor.

In a study of leadership traits undertaken by Ohr and Oscarsson in 2003 attention was directed at how political performance related criteria were perceived by voters and how personal attributes and physical image impacted upon voter choice. They identified that politically relevant issues and characteristics had received more attention, and were considered more important, than personal criteria such as family life or physical appearance. However, their study uncovered several points of note when comparing a number of parliamentary and presidential systems of government and how political leaders were perceived. With respect to the emotional connection between elector and elected that is central to this text, they found that ' "empathy" is a stronger determinant of a leader's overall judgement than "trustworthiness" '.[41] They also found 'performance related leader traits such as leadership qualities, trustworthiness, reliability, and empathy clearly have a discernable impact on the voting decision in Western democracies'.[42] What appears to be increasingly clear is that the attributes of leadership and the personal presentation of candidates, in both parliamentary and presidential political models, are of note in how the leaders are perceived and that changing habits in communication enhance these factors. Ohr and Oscarsson found that for German leader Gerhard Schroeder there was a 'strong effect of his family life on his overall judgement, a trait which is not directly performance related'.[43] This however was not considered to be a strong or universal determinant of voter choice or bias, although the political situation in Germany appears to be changing somewhat and was becoming more reflective of the interweaving of the private and the public found in other liberal democracies.[44] Nevertheless, while Ohr and Oscarsson cast doubt on ideas that voters make assessments and judgements based on perceptions of the lifestyle and social habits of political figures it appears clear that there are two issues which arise from their study and are of relevance to this text. Firstly, there are emotional traits which appear to have resonance with the voter, particularly empathy, and an ability to be seen to understand the emotions of the voting block. Secondly, although potentially less important, the personal characteristics of candidates can play a role in how the political figure is entertained as a political leader. The political marketing of leaders, across political systems increasingly plays heavily on personal characteristics which are important to leadership, such as trust and emotional connection. Whether this is futile when contrasted with policy and party considerations, in terms of the acquisition of votes, is open to question. Nevertheless, as this text makes clear, this has not restrained political figures or their advisors from presenting personal lives and character attributes as important to an understanding of candidates and how they can interact and appear genuine and authentic to the voter.

In undertaking a comparative study of candidate portrayal on the grounds of wealth and leadership, the nature of the media in both the United Kingdom and United States has to be acknowledged as its style and approach to political issues has some bearing upon how voters gather information. In the modern era, the voting public, of all social classes and backgrounds, have widespread access to both old and new media devices. While the volume of political material available to enhance political understanding increases, the breadth of credible and legitimate political options appears at the same time to be decreasing with the congestion of parties in the centre-ground of politics.

There are aspects of media presentation worthy of consideration with respect to candidate wealth and its portrayal. The British tabloid media are deemed, more often than not by themselves, to be important to the outcomes of elections and instrumental in shaping popular thought about candidates and parties.[45] This in true in as far as they are influential in presenting politics to specific social groupings and have an impact on how elections are viewed, as the consumption of the written tabloid media is essentially class based. The tabloids are also largely consumed by the politics of sleaze and a large part of the political coverage is based upon the portrayal of political figures in an unflattering and simplistic light. This further emphasises a concentration upon political figures based upon personal conduct rather than institutional activity. While it is not suggested that wealth and corruption are the sole focus of the sleaze enquiries by the 'gutter press' it nevertheless accentuates the political figure as an individual whose character is pivotal to the impressions that they create socially. There are, naturally, political leaders whose identity is shaped by the tabloid press or by the strategic manipulation of the media so as to construct a positive political image. Margaret Thatcher's identity as the Iron Lady is a prime example, testament to her strong and resolute political character. However, in a similar ilk John Major suffered in the United Kingdom as a consequence of being portrayed, in the tabloids and through other media outlets, as a grey and characterless figure who lacked political charisma.

Similarly, wealth is a salient topic of note for the media, with a focus on the issues which might cause disparity between electorate and elected. In the contemporary era much play has been made of the education, family background, wealth and standing of the vast majority of candidates emerging to contest party leaderships on both sides of the Atlantic. Much was made for example, in the United Kingdom of Conservative leader David Cameron's education at Eton, one of the most prestigious public schools in the United Kingdom. In a similar vein however, Blair attended a school in Scotland of comparable elite standing. This type of social background was picked out in a story by the BBC which examined a report on education by the Sutton trust. This report is discussed further in later chapters. It argued that the educational attainment and background of MPs was different from that of the population as a whole. The trust's chairman argued that there existed an 'educational apartheid' and that the education of the political elite was based on an ability to pay. Sir Peter Lampl stated 'The education profile of our representatives in Parliament does not reflect society at large'.[46] Why it should have mirrored society was not made clear, but the profile and tone of the story was symptomatic of a wider suggestion that both a social and socio-economic gulf existed between representatives and those represented. In a similar vein, virtually all of the candidates standing for the American presidential primaries in 2004 shared similar characteristics. The uniformity of their wealth and prestige contrasted significantly with the socio-economic and demographic make-up of the electorate, a point seized on by the media and one addressed prominently and defensively by the candidates. These issues, highlighted by media interests, were components which formed the basis for discussion in both the mass and elite media during periods when candidate and leadership selection was ongoing. During the 1992 presidential election George Bush Sr and Dan Quayle were criticised for being seen as aloof from the prevailing recession on account of personal wealth and family standing.[47]

In the United States the value and impact of tabloid style media coverage is less pervasive and prevalent. However in the realm of new media, Internet coverage of leaders and their campaigns has opened up new avenues of political marketing which can be exploited to try to entice voters to a candidate. This, as explored in later chapters, is a double-edged sword with respect to the positive portrayal of candidates based on their social class. On the one hand the new media offers an opportunity to portray a candidate in a direct and unadulterated fashion to the electorate. This allows concentration upon aspects of candidate characteristics selected by their campaign team. Clinton was particularly adept at exploiting this format via confessional performances on talk shows. The Internet also allows for the marketing of the political candidate, but allows intrusion into the personal lives of candidates that can prove to be destabilising, alongside an opportunity to research candidate wealth. Naturally negative advertising exists in a format similar to that traditionally displayed in the written press and on television, and web sites can enhance the dissemination of these types of messages. However, in addition to this there now exists the opportunity for the voter to actively investigate the past, activities and families of candidates so as to see whether the image advanced is indeed a genuine one. Personal recollections, weblogs and investigative journalists allow for the comparison of the presentation of the political identity of the candidate with alternative viewpoints and factual material that can call into question the authenticity of the message. This serves to cloud understanding and complicate the process of the marketing of an individual political identity.

Conclusion

Contemporary party leaders read off a common hymn sheet. In virtually every modern case study all candidates, whether they possess an ordinary or elite background, accentuate their humility and ordinariness rather than portray themselves as socially exceptional or divorced from mainstream society. Across time the marketing techniques associated with character and the portrayal of wealth have become more refined and a uniformity has emerged. Political candidates advance interpretations of their pasts as being laced with impoverishment and social attributes which suggest forms of hardship. However this uniformity in social and emotional presentation has also coincided with a period when the major parties in Britain and America are competing for a congested centre-ground in politics with respect to policy. As a consequence, the fight to advance social characteristics which may appeal to the voting mass is important, for it serves as an additional outlet through which to offer party and political differentiation and enhance political choice.

Clearly political marketing deviates from commercial or business marketing. While in commerce weight is placed on presenting the populace with the best product available, and one which will at the least satisfy the needs of the consumer, character-based marketing and the portrayal of wealth and elitism is an altogether different product. Rather than offering a pristine and flawless product, the recent evolution of character-based marketing has sought to provide the public with political leaders eager to accentuate a number of issues which show them in a less positive light, and accentuate the mundane. The majority of the problems come from experiences that have been overcome and cast aside, albeit with some difficulty. Family problems, alcoholism, the pressures of bringing up a family, disability, impoverishment; all are political tools through which to connect to the voting mass and suggest that emotional and social connections can be forged to give an identification with a candidate. The resolution of these problems largely confirms a merit for office. Exceptionalism in office can then be used to provide a mandate for continued leadership. Sophisticated political knowledge on the part of the voter is not a necessity. Images and identities can be created to give appeal to a candidate, devoid in large part of their political ideology or standing. Naturally, in the main, the marketing of candidates as socially and emotionally in tune with the populace goes hand-in-hand with the presentation of policy and party ideology. Nevertheless the increasing focus on the private lives and social attributes, and how these interplay with the activities of the ill-defined 'ordinary' person has taken an increasingly central role in political presentation in the modern era.

In the 1960s Kennedy portrayed his administration as one composed of the best and the brightest, one where excellence was deemed to be essential in shaping popular perceptions of government. Although aspects of Kennedy's character and private life were hidden from public view, and he emerged into politics from a position of elite standing, the general objective was to advance him as the best candidate available to the American public at that time irrespective of his background. His wealth was portrayed as a feature that conferred on him celebrity status. There were attempts to market him positively, particularly with respect to his military record, but his elite family position, wealth and social relations were not considered an impediment for office. Fundamental changes have occurred across time in this area. Candidates now seek to obscure perceptions of elitism and reinvent their image to be more attuned to popular sentiment. It is clearly debateable as to whether this is advantageous or problematic for democracy. While the consumers, across time, now receive portrayals of the candidate they are deemed to want, the impression is that a large part of politics is now founded upon simply presenting candidates tailored to identified social profiles, irrespective of their true origins or their social and emotional under-standings of the electorate.

2
Cloth Coats and Camelot

The evolution of political marketing with respect to political identity and socio-economic status originated before the onset of the communications age and the advent of mass communication in American politics. Although its pace accelerated considerably, and it has been refined substantially in the contemporary period, in the post-Second World War era there was already an appreciation that divisions between a political elite and the voting mass might be perceived as a political liability. Spin control and public relations techniques were present and considered important to conveying an image of candidate ordinariness to the public, replete with a press corps that were largely respectful of political wishes and intent. Franklin Roosevelt's disability and its masking from public view is testament to the pretelevision understanding that image might be considered important when presenting a political identity to the public. Nevertheless the advent of television and the introduction of marketing and advertising techniques into the realm of politics was to bring about changes in the format and portrayal of political figures. This was not restricted to the physical image alone, but also with regard to the concept of privacy and the slow exposure of political biographies, families and private pastimes for public scrutiny. Associated with this of course was an understanding of the lifestyle habits of the political class, with opportunities to observe class and social disparities between those elected to public office and the voting mass.

Through the nineteenth century the emergence of political identities rooted in the log cabin to White House myth was prevalent and celebrated in popular culture and embraced by presidents from both political parties. Political leaders were keen to be seen to be of the masses, and embraced both wealthy backgrounds and a public presentation of a mythical and rustic America, suitable for public consumption. There were also several presidents in the twentieth century who embraced the idea of ordinary backgrounds and tried to convey images of ordinary lifestyles and backgrounds, several of whom are discussed in this text.

This chapter considers how political marketing and the creation of a political identity was undertaken by Nixon and Kennedy. Other political figures adopted strategies reflective of these two significant figures in American politics; however, given the available space and the media coverage afforded both Kennedy and Nixon it is appropriate to primarily consider how they approached the issue of wealth and cultivated social and emotional associations with the voting block. At the centre of the debate is the effort to convey, on the one hand, a sense of social and emotional communication with the voting block and, on the other, to market social and socio-economic origins as deemed necessary to advance an image beneficial to the politician's interests. This was practised via the advancement of personal issues, the identification of the type of candidate desired by core voting blocks and market research to define contemporary voter needs. Although somewhat haphazard in its early evolution there was a clear effort to portray candidates as being at one with the voter and to be seen to be associated with their needs. The efforts by Nixon to refine and advance a political identity rooted in the ordinary are first considered. Nixon had difficulty in the latter stages of his political tenure in separating himself from his earlier political career and this proved to be a challenge for his aides, ultimately culminating in the reinvention of Nixon's identity in the 1968 election campaign. Kennedy's position is less clear cut. Although his wealth and elite status is, and was, well known it was not an issue that was shielded from public view to any great extent. Rather other issues, including his religion, were considered to be a greater potential liability than the Kennedy family wealth. While others charged that Kennedy's wealth was an impediment to his electoral credibility his own embrace of Camelot suggested that the candidate and the media thought otherwise.

Nixon: Ordinary and exceptional

The emergence of advertising was important to Eisenhower's 1956 campaign but, at the time, was not considered to be a critical component in the arsenal of weaponry needed to win an election. Eisenhower turned to Walt Disney to assist in producing an advert which had a simple message, one grounded in commercial branding. The message was 'You like

Ike, I like Ike, everybody likes Ike'. No message was conveyed concerning Eisenhower's wealth or social position, his policies or ideology; rather an objective position was adopted to give universal appeal and voter coverage. As Eisenhower was reluctant to appear in advertisements personally, slots were created where he could be seen to answer questions from the public regarding his leadership and policies. Roster Reeves, who created slogans for M&M, among other brands, created an 'Eisenhower Answers America' slot. An evaluation by ABC of the advertising used argued that 'Those ads attempted to show Eisenhower as a man of the people who cares about the people'.[1] When Nixon and Kennedy became involved in politics in the post-war era they became entwined in the already existing political sphere of advertising, marketing and personal presentation. Although Nixon was credited with reforming the realm of political communication during his time as President between 1968–74, and for having altercations with the media corps on a number of prominent occasions, as he arrived onto a national political stage the core essence of political marketing and the selling of the individual politician as a marketable commodity was already in place.

Nixon could approach post-war American politics from a position of political strength. He was widely regarded as an earthy individual who had endured a breadth of experiences and was not derived from an elite political stock. This was important as it allowed him to play a populist card and argue that he stood firmly against an eastern liberal elite, against whom he would struggle for much of his political life. Nixon's early life was removed from elite society and this gave him a pronounced political asset when running for office. He could portray himself as a person in touch with the problems encountered in towns across America, and fought hard to retain this image as he ascended the political ladder. Theodore White, in *The Making of the President 1960*, captured the core essence of Nixon and his past: 'Poor from boyhood, able, intense, dark and watchful as he surveys the world about him, Richard M. Nixon has brought from his impoverished middle-class youth many strange qualities. ... He has had to realize how vulnerable a naked man, without money or family prestige, can be in a hostile world that over and over again savages him for no reason he can define.'[2] Although a somewhat romanticised notion it conforms well to Nixon's general profile as a person removed from the wealthy and elite, and as a man who had to fight to get an ordinary voice heard in politics. Nixon himself, in his memoirs, relates an upbringing and a childhood classically in keeping with the log cabin to White House stereotype. His life in Yorba Linda, California was 'hard but happy'. He also attributed his success and values to the lessons he learned observing his father, particularly with respect to a populist oriented conception of America. Nixon argued, 'My father had a deep belief in the "little man" in America. He opposed the vested interests and the political machines that exercised so much control over American life at the beginning of the century.'[3] In later years political figures would routinely use the family, and particularly the instructions received from parents to justify and shape their political ideology. For example, in Britain both Thatcher and Brown commonly used the instructions received and the moral lessons gained from their fathers to highlight the underpinnings of their personalities and political ideologies. Nixon also endured the loss of several family members when young, and went through a number of life trials and challenging circumstances, although unlike contemporary candidates he did not seek to overtly exploit this as a feature which would underscore his emotional credentials.

Nixon's career was founded on strong political principles, and strong moral values, derived from his Quaker upbringing. Following election to the House of Representatives he made his name through strong anti-communist measures and took a prominent role in the House Committee on Un-American Activities. He was later elected to the Senate and was chosen to be Eisenhower's running mate in the 1952 election. Nixon's career appeared to be on the rise with an emergent national profile and a golden opportunity to assist Eisenhower in the White House. The transition from ordinary person to political figure, in keeping with the core thrust of this text, was one based on a perception of the mix of the ordinary and the exceptional, as related in a 1969 reflection on the 1968 election. 'If it is true that the ideal politician is an ordinary representation of his class with extraordinary abilities, Richard Nixon was never more exemplary of the thesis than when he finally "made it."'[4] Although in 1952 Nixon's standing appeared to be strong, it threatened to deteriorate on the grounds of questions about his personal wealth and how it might impact upon both his moral principles and how he related to the electorate. Nixon was accused of using campaign funds for his own personal use, and of amassing a secret fund to support a comfortable lifestyle. This went against the grain of a political figure who portrayed himself as an ordinary American, yet the media headline of the *New York Post* gave an alternate impression. 'Secret Nixon Fund! : Secret Rich Men's Trust Fund Keeps Nixon in Style Far Beyond His Salary'.[5] Nixon was aggrieved that the story had been run, and alleged that the funds his campaign possessed had been misrepresented. Further, he contended that his Democrat opponents tried to give the story added credibility so as to make him appear both corrupt, living in comfort on money that was not rightfully his, and an electoral liability. Calls were made in the media for Nixon's resignation, amidst internal queries from fellow Republicans that he was sapping strength from the campaign by not taking a decisive step and resigning. Nixon resolved to fight the allegations, on the grounds that he believed them not to be true and to have given way to the media and Democrats would have been personally and politically catastrophic. Seventy five thousand dollars was advanced to purchase a half hour slot on national television for Nixon to address the allegations of wrongdoing.

In preparation for the address Nixon pinpointed several topics to counter the allegation of corruption and to sell himself as a person who lived to his means and was attuned to the American people and the national mood. He considered a scandal endured by the Truman administration where a $9,000 mink coat had been given to a secretary and considered how public funds should be properly managed. Thereafter, he considered ways to relate to ordinary people, thinking 'I made a note to check out a quotation from Lincoln to the effect that God must have loved the common people because he made so many of them.'[6]

Nixon approached the presentation by associating himself with his wife and creating a family oriented experience. His wife Pat accompanied him onto the stage and became part and parcel of the presentation. The televised presentation was a risk. While it tried to address the allegations of financial mismanagement directly, in part it lent credence to the attacks from the Democrats and sections of the media. Moreover, Nixon was taking his message to the entire American people, and additionally in 1952 television presentation was not a well-practised political art and Nixon consequently would expose himself to a decisive blow to his political reputation if it were to go badly. Nixon rebutted the allegations of corruption and set clear guidelines for what was acceptable and what might be considered unethical with respect to campaign finance. Thereafter he considered aspects of his own personal finance. Although this occurred in the era before political marketing strategies with respect to wealth and socio-economic standing had matured, it nevertheless indicated that Nixon was earnestly aware of how he might associate closely with the populace, and thereafter distance the viewing public from the allegations advanced by his accusers. Nixon addressed several questions relating to political business, stated that there were ways that money could be used to advance individual interests, and then rebutted allegations by stating 'The first way is to be a rich man, So I couldn't use that.' Secondly, Nixon discussed his wife, conveying a social bond between himself and Pat Nixon that appeared to suggest that they, as a team, were above corruption. Thirdly, Nixon offered to be open about his finances to display to the public that he was not wealthy, suggesting that this was a move of unprecedented significance, 'And so now, what I am going to do – and incidentally this is unprecedented in the history of American politics – I am going at this time to give this television and radio audience, a complete financial history, everything I have earned, everything I have spent and everything I own, and I want you to know the facts.'[7] Nixon then related his humble origins, his family wealth and his marriage to Pat. The objective of the narrative was simple. Nixon appeared to be of the same stock as middle America, had endured the same life experiences and had worked honestly to get himself into a position from which to run and compete for political office. He sought attachment with the electorate on social grounds, and related the tale of how the family received a pet dog, Checkers. It was from this reference that this specific televised address received its nickname. 'It was a little cocker spaniel dog, in a crate that he had sent all the way from Texas, black and white, spotted, and our little girl Tricia, the six year old, named it Checkers. And you know, the kids, like all kids, loved the dog, and I just want to say this, right now, that regardless of what they say about it, we are going to keep it.' This had little to do with allegations in the national media of corruption, however, it made Nixon look like a caring and ordinary person, more in association with his family and children than a man beset by detailed campaign finance concerns.

When discussing the family wealth and finances Nixon alluded to specific detail regarding the history of his own and his family's finances. In particular he portrayed himself as largely a person who had no significant wealth. As a way of branding his wealth, personally and politically, he pointed out the contrasts between wealth and the position of the ordinary American, 'Well, that's about it. That's what we have. And that's what we owe. It isn't very much. But Pat and I have the satisfaction that every dime that we have got is honestly ours. I should say this, that Pat doesn't have a mink coat. But she does have a respectable Republican cloth coat, and I always tell her she would look good in anything.'[8]

The television audience for the Checkers speech was the highest recorded for a political broadcast, with approximately 60 million viewers, until it was surpassed in 1960 by the presidential debates between Nixon and Kennedy.[9] Nixon's speech was greeted enthusiastically by those in the Republican party, and although there were reservations at first, was considered to be sufficiently satisfactory to Eisenhower so as to convince him to retain Nixon as his vice-presidential nominee in 1952.[10] Nixon saw himself as an ordinary person fighting against conspiratorial forces which would dog his entire political career, the elite media from the East coast and Democrats determined to undermine his character. Part of Nixon's skill in advancing himself as a person as well as a politician was that he accommodated ideas of other politicians, among them Roosevelt and Truman, and assembled a text which tried to evoke the necessary public and political support. Although some authors, such as Bruzzi, have expressed a critical evaluation of Nixon's speech and its hollowness, it was greeted, both by Nixon and his contemporaries as a mark of esteem and a signal that Nixon could fight his corner in elite political circles.[11] It also suggested that emotions had a resonance among the public, as recited in *An American Melodrama*, 'The emotional tone of the Checkers speech has clearly stayed in people's minds longer than the facts – such as they were – about the fund. Perhaps it was assumed that emotion, in the unyielding interrogator of Alger Hiss, must be synthetic – but there is much testimony that Nixon, for all his normal containment, is full of emotion. It is sometimes thought that emotions long pent up must be of the grander kind, but they may be something as commonplace as self-pity, which was the dominant tone of the speech.'[12] The lesson of the Checkers speech for Nixon, and for the relationship between the elected and the electorate, was that emotional bonds and relationships could be used to obscure factual issues. To be seen to be part of wider society was possible through considered selling of a message based on issues tangential to the central charges laid against a candidate. That Nixon, an individual ill at ease with the media could create associations of this nature was notable as it suggested that opportunities to build upon a non-policy agenda and to divert popular attention to issues of an emotional content existed.

When approaching the 1960 election Nixon was aware of his personal standing in national circles with the electorate, but he also had had a career parallel to that of Kennedy. Both entered politics in the post-war era, both had waged successful political careers, and both were strong individuals who demonstrated political ambition. In shaping coalitions of voters both anticipated that specific demographic groups might be pivotal in getting them elected. For example both avoided explicit criticism of Senator Joseph McCarthy for fear of alienating his supporters. Although Nixon was known for his strong anti-Communist stance, McCarthy's crusade was left to falter under its own momentum.

When approaching the 1960 election Nixon was aware that Kennedy possessed considerable strength in contesting the campaign. According to his own memoirs Nixon 'considered Kennedy's biggest assets to be his wealth and the appeal of his personal style'.[13] As related later in this chapter the wealth held by Kennedy was as much about the family resources and connections as it was about available campaign finance. Nixon recognised the threat posed to his campaign by Kennedy, and the risk entailed by agreeing to take part in the much written about presidential debates of that particular campaign. In the first instance Nixon had much to lose as he was in a position where he would have to defend his position in the aftermath of his tenure as vice president. He was in essence the incumbent of the White House and the attendant risk in participating was greater for him than it was for Kennedy.

Nixon, in seeking to address the needs of the nation, made several errors in the conduct of the 1960 campaign. He agreed to visit every state in the Union in his election campaign, and following a knee injury found himself to be tired and ill in the run-up to the debates. As is commonplace knowledge Nixon found that politics had entered a new era with the debates. He recognised that Kennedy's appearance had a bearing on the campaign presentation and that in preparation for the first debate 'Kennedy arrived…looking tanned, rested, and fit'. Nixon, by contrast, came over badly on the television, conveying a sense of unease. This had a significant impact upon who he could appeal to and shaped perceptions of his political identity. Although much is made of the fact that those who listened on radio thought Nixon a more convincing performer, the fact remained that more Americans watched the debate on television and the audience figures reduced significantly as the second, third and fourth debate progressed. Nixon pointed out that the poll statistics did not move markedly in the aftermath of any of the debates and they worked as a visual spectacle, rather than as a method or means for the persuasion of the mobile or swing voter. They served to consolidate opinion rather than alter it. In this sense, the singular presentation of the candidates was not a feature that gave a distinct advantage to one candidate over another. Rather, after 1960 it became a necessity to consider physical appearance as an issue which might, although not perhaps turning voters to a candidate, be sufficiently impressive so as not to turn voters off or alienate them. Nixon, reflecting on the overall experience of 1960 saw it as a transient period for political presentation. He commented, 'As for television debates in general, I doubt they can ever serve a responsible role in defining the issues of a presidential campaign. Because of the nature of the medium, there will inevitably be a greater premium on showmanship than on statesmanship.'[14] He also felt that there was a shift in control, away from campaign managers and the candidate to the media, commentators and producers. This invariably changed the nature of political marketing. From the 1960 election onwards the direct personal link between candidate and voter, as spurious as it was, was fractured and Nixon's promise and attempt to visit all 50 states to reach out to voters became a feature consigned to the history books. Thereafter the point of contact between candidate and voter was largely in a stage-managed environment or via electronic communication. Marketing was not closed however by Nixon's 1960 experience, rather the nature of the target audience was altered, and the mass audience was, in Nixon's mind at least, to be reached through more subtle means. An accentuation on the social and emotional position of the candidate was needed, and the creation of an autobiographical narrative to which the audience could relate.

Nixon's approach to selling himself as an individual encountered mixed fortunes as he considered his political opportunities in the aftermath of the 1960 loss to Kennedy. He had clearly understood how to convey himself as a person on a number of levels, from Checkers through to the most narrow of defeats against Kennedy, but he understood that problems existed with his image, particularly in the aftermath of the defeat for the Governorship of California in 1962. In the prelude to the decision on whether to run in the 1968 election he considered the problem of the 'loser image' that now cast a shadow over his campaign and his personal political identity. However, Nixon appeared to learn the lessons from past defeats and was given advice by a former advertising agency worker, Bob Haldeman, who would later form part of the Berlin Wall with John Ehrlichman, that would shield the future President from unwanted intrusions into his working life. The marketing and presentation of the individual would now hinge upon the interpretation and intervention by individuals adjusted to commercial selling practices and entertaining customer preferences. As such, the pressure was now for the candidate to shape their personal position to suit that of the voter, and be less inclined to try to persuade the voter to move to their position.

In an internal memo to Nixon, Haldeman argued that the strategies that had been pursued thus far were ill-disposed to bring about the type of political control that might be needed to address the chaos that existed, according to Haldeman, in the political arena. This marked a more pronounced effort to exclude criticism, both personal and political of the candidate in question, allow the candidate to convey a message on their own terms and thereafter exert control over presentation, particularly given the personal experiences of Nixon's past. Haldeman advised Nixon, 'The time has come for political campaigning – its techniques and strategies – to move out of the dark ages and into the brave new world of the omnipresent eye'. Casting a critical eye over the advertising, marketing and presentation of candidates Haldeman further remarked, 'No wonder the almost inevitable campaign dialogue borders so near the idiot level'.[15] The impact of Haldeman and others trained initially in advertising, rather than politics, brought about a revision of marketing in American politics. Much has been made in literature of the 'selling of the President' and the emergence of a manufactured image following Nixon's election in 1968. It marked the emergence of presidential candidates sold on who they were, the 'new' Nixon in this instance, as much as what they stood for. Nixon embraced the reinvention of his character and political persona, assisting in identifying how he performed best, the preferred forums for clarity of message, how his family and personal life could best be sold to the public, and how strategic research of opposing candidates might make it hard for them to follow suit. Other factors were important to the reinvention of Nixon, and the consequent selling of a candidate who went on to win comfortably in 1968 and then by a landslide in 1972. Internal campaign memorandum confirmed to Nixon that politics in the 1960s had changed. Gone were the smoke-filled rooms and mass appeals to a universal voting mass. Nixon invited a reconsideration of how he might be made more appealing to a variety of demographic groups. Accordingly his willingness to understand but not always accommodate change, placed alongside his experience of political loss, and the involvement of individuals who were initially engaged in marketing and advertising rather than politics created a potent mix which assisted in catapulting Nixon to the presidential office.

The emergence of a new Nixon, suited to the political 'arena' – one of Nixon's preferred gladiatorial terms, was directly linked to changes in the nature of communication. Although Nixon remained sceptical of media in virtually all its forms, part of his political aptitude was to allow others, better versed in the subject than he, to assume command of the variety of mediums and mount a concerted challenge for political power in the late 1960s. Far from being a person who failed to grasp the nature of television, a charge laid at Nixon's door following 1960 and 1962, Nixon appeared to be a political candidate suited to accommodating a variety of different mediums and, prior to Watergate, exploiting them in a successful manner. One of the key texts which addressed political marketing was *The Selling of the President* by Joe McGuiness. He dissected the Nixon campaign of 1968, giving praise and cynicism in equal measure to a transformation in politics and how candidates were marketed to the populace. McGuiness argued that the Nixon election team were well versed in the changes in presentation across the 1960s and 'once they recognised that the citizen did not so much vote for a candidate as make a psychological purchase of him, [it is] not surprising that they began to work together.'[16] The fusion of advertising techniques and popular interpretations and consumption of a candidate created a position where personal emotions counted. Rather than intransigent political and ideological positions coming to the fore, the post-1960 era witnessed a fundamental change in the consumption of politics, one based primarily on the visual, as opposed to the written, exchange of information. In large part this was attributable to increased concentration on the person, alongside consideration of a slow decline of political party identification. An acceleration of the personification of politics entailed a move from the selling of policy to the selling of an individual character, one removed in part from strong bonds of socio-economic party affiliation. Additionally, a marketable political character had to be seen to be derived from the populace and not as a person who stood above the fray and observed the problems besetting society from afar. Anticipating Nixon's effort to contest the presidency in 1968 Marshall McLuhan argued, 'In all countries the party system has folded like the organizational chart. Policies and issues are useless for election purposes, since they are too specialized and hot. The shaping of a candidate's integral image has taken the place of discussing conflicting points of view.'[17] Nixon's position as a person, in conjunction with his physical image and managing his legacy, became central to the election effort. It became a feature of the campaign, with Nixon pinpointing who he wanted to identify with, how he wanted his personality to be conveyed, and how the selective audiences chosen for his interactive liaisons and debates would represent the target markets in the United States.

The problem for Nixon's campaign staff in 1967–68 was that he had a track record by which he could be judged both politically and personally. His entry into the 1968 race was conducted against the backdrop of his past successes and failures. While he could not be charged with entering the 1968 contest with a lack of political experience, his image and its reinvention was hard given his prior political prominence. As mentioned earlier in this chapter with respect to the Checkers episode, he had already advanced his personal credentials in the 1950s, however that episode was sufficiently far behind him that there were new voters and new coalitions to appeal to in a different political environment. While Checkers had saved Nixon's career in 1952, in many respects it had little influence in dictating the outcome or conduct of 1968. Nixon was to be reinvented for 1968, presented as a person largely disconnected from the past and refreshed for a new political fight. He was presented as having the experience needed for office, and as having an earthy quality which allowed him to relate to, as Kevin Phillips termed it, the emerging Republican majority. Prior to his remodelling Nixon was viewed as a political individual who, in stark and unmodified terms lacked the resonance to relate to the public and the ordinary American. McGuiness argued that as 1968 approached 'Into this milieu came Richard Nixon: grumpy, cold, and aloof'.[18]

The reinvention of Nixon was in large part about marketing a Nixon that America was thought to want. He played off and exploited racial and urban tensions in society, cast audiences that mirrored the demographic sensibilities of America, and cast himself as an individual who, through a number of stock answers, understood the issues of 1968. Discussion largely centred on whether there was a new Nixon, who accommodated a broad cross-section of social interests, or whether the main thrust of 1968 was mere packaging and that the Nixon of 1960, with both his strengths and faults, existed. A large part of the concern within the Nixon team, and an issue of tension between his political and media advisors, was whether Nixon could be portrayed as a emotive and warm person, rather than merely as a political figure who had a number of policies which might appeal to the public. This marked a change from the past and tried to take an experienced politician and transform him as a person who could be sold as a political commodity. Politics by 1968 was rooted in perceptions of individuals and Nixon, for all his skills and political experience, appeared to be challenged when conveying a personal association with the electorate.

One of Nixon's media advisors and a core architect of Nixon's campaign strategy, Gene Jones, argued 'My one qualm about Nixon is that I'm not sure he's got the sensitivity he should. To Appalachia, to the slums, to the poverty and destitution that reside there. I don't know whether as a human being he's actually got that sensitivity.'[19] One of the reasons for the concern was that although Nixon could refer back to the ideal of the cloth coat, his political associations had seemingly created a gulf between himself and the voter. As part of the campaign literature of 1968 Nixon's authorised biography emphasised his elite relations and connections, citing that 'Nixon belongs to impressive in-town clubs – Metropolitan, Links, Recess – and fashionable country clubs – Blind Brook in Westchester, Baltusrol in New Jersey.' This of course emphasised his association with elements central to his fund raising and status. The paradox between the elite standing of the political figure and the need to associate with the ordinary voter was clear. Joe McGuiness was highly critical of Nixon's campaign which appeared to pretend to befriend the impoverished and the needy, when it appeared to him that socio-economic relations between candidate and the electorate were strained: 'And now this Nixon came out of his country clubs which he had worked so hard to make and he waved his credit cards in our face.'[20] In keeping with the overarching argument of this text, efforts to recast Nixon as a person who was the product of mainstream society were clearly strained. This was exacerbated in the spring of 1968 by the campaign of Bobby Kennedy who appeared, irrespective of his own personal wealth, to represent the cause of those at the lower end of the socio-economic spectrum. This underscored questions about who Nixon really stood for and where he considered his voting base to be. In particular this was even more problematic because of the racial tensions of the era and the challenge posed by George Wallace in the South. As a consequence many of Nixon's portrayals in sensitive areas such as race were non-committal and allowed a subjective interpretation on the part of the recipient. Although poll after poll showed that Nixon had a healthy lead in the campaign when facing Humphrey, there remained an undercurrent of discontent that he, for all the communication and revision of his image, was still socially and emotionally distanced from the voter. Nixon may have possessed appealing policies, but he frequently was perceived to have had lacked the warmth needed to convey a sense of emotion needed to connect to the American voter.

This was emphasised in the realm of the political campaign commercial. Nixon's advisors had toyed with a number of different formats through the campaign and had achieved success with most of their presentations – including the overlaying of the candidate's voice on top of a collection of photographic stills, to emphasise a connection between the visual image and the candidate's beliefs. Intensive examination of the reaction of focus groups and internal criticism led to refinement of the material and how it might be interpreted by the populace. In essence market research had engrained itself into politics. Consideration was given to accurate assessments of Vietnam and undermining the Democrats while defending the national interest, and being seen to be supportive of the armed forces. The underlying problem with the campaign communication appeared to be Nixon himself.

His advisors were disappointed that he failed to watch his own perform-ances in order to learn from his strengths and weaknesses, and would not use an autocue for presentations. He was personally quite adverse to the reformation of his own personal position arguing, 'I'm not going to have any damn image experts coming telling me how to part my hair'.[21] Poll statistics were gathered to further intelligence and research, and to try to 'discover how Nixon's image differed from Humphrey's'.[22] However, even though Nixon wanted to know the findings, he did not wish to wholly sacrifice himself to the image makers whom he had brought to his political team. Although communications strategies were modified, they could not, it appears, modify Richard Nixon's personal-ity to any significant degree.

By way of direct contrast his opponent Hubert Humphrey was thought to have a folksy personality, but his position was undermined by internal party disorder and policy indecision which, in effect, undermined his candidature for office. Naturally there were concerns that Humphrey was not the ideal candidate for the Democratic party. The decision of Johnson, in March 1968, not to contest the presidency, alongside the assassination of Bobby Kennedy, left Humphrey as a default candidate, left to deal with national rioting and the increasing problems posed by the Vietnam conflict.

The Nixon campaign team encountered problems in 1968, but problems unexpectedly posed by the use of marketing techniques to advance the cause of their candidate. As addressed in Chapter 1, a dis-tinction between commercial marketing and political marketing is that the candidate is not necessarily advanced as a person who is faultless. The Nixon campaign was guilty of, if anything, over-glossing the image of their candidate. 'The American people had been presented with the supercandidate, the supercampaign, yet – even faced with the sweaty, babbling alternative of Humphrey – they showed signs of discontent.' Humphrey's team produced a half-hour campaign commercial entitled the 'Mind Changer'. It concentrated on Humphrey as a person, and cast him as an ordinary individual who enjoyed pastimes of a similar ilk to many across the American nation. While the commercial was flawed in many ways, it is also notable as its themes, content and the emotive tone have been replicated, on both sides of the Atlantic on a number of occa-sions, as later chapters of this text make clear. McGuiness observed that 'It showed Humphrey wearing a stupid fisherman's hat and getting his lines snarled on a lake near his home and it took shameless advantage of the fact he has a mentally retarded granddaughter. It was contrived and tasteless. But it was the most effective single piece of advertising of the campaign.'[23] This, although quite distinctive, presented Humphrey as being accomplished in conveying a sense of ordinariness, one that was both accessible and authentic. In contrast to Nixon however, he was perceived to be lacking the core element of political exceptionalism that was also needed to successfully challenge for power. This had been a problem in the primary races for Humphrey in 1960 and was a feature which suggests that the creation of a political identity requires both popular perceptions of ordinariness and exceptionalism rolled into one political character.

The lessons derived from Nixon's portrayal of his candidacy across time are many. At an early stage of his political career Nixon understood the need to exploit his social standing and to accentuate his ordinariness, with respect to wealth and his social habits. However, this on its own, as communications evolved, was insufficient to propel him to the White House. In the latter stages of his political career he resolved to present a New Nixon to the populace, one based as much on a reformation of presentation techniques as a reinvention of the individual's political character. Nixon, as a politician, was portrayed as being connected to the policy needs of the nation, and as a person was more comfortable with the political environment. That said, he remained uncomfortable with attempts to alter his political character. His contribution to the marketing of politics in the realm of wealth was important, particularly as the Checkers speech suggested an importance to the downplaying of wealth and how television might be used to give this image. Thereafter, although increasingly a wealthy individual, the task for Nixon was to maintain the impression that he was derived from the populace and had not abandoned his social origins. Although largely in its infancy with respect to the communications age, this was achieved through presentation strategies and gave the populace, particularly in 1968 the type of candidate it was thought to desire as pinpointed by market research. Nixon, unlike the folksy Humphrey, combined political experience and exceptionalism with elements of ordinariness, and this combination would, in time become a potent mix and a great asset in the pursuit of the presidential office.

John F. Kennedy

Kennedy, as a person and a candidate, is important to an understanding of wealth and how it impacts upon perceptions of a political leader. The grandeur of Camelot and the public understanding of the elite nature of the Kennedy family contrasts with the modern convention whereby elite leaders seek to play down and diminish the consequences of their economic standing. Although conferred with great wealth, and attacked, as discussed later in this chapter by his opponents on those grounds, Kennedy accentuated other issues in his candidacy and was cast by media observers as someone who could, despite his social standing, understand and address the issues facing the United States.

Kennedy's victory in the 1960 election witnessed a change in the nature and conduct of the presidency. It was considered that it contributed to the ability to 'substitute image for substance' and to advance messages which were spun to the American public.[24] Moreover, he contributed to an altering of the nature of the presidential office, whereby the character of the leader became a feature to which the electorate could more easily relate, the 'personalization of the presidency'.[25] This was not merely about Kennedy, but came hand-in-hand with the advent of new developments in communication and media practices. There were however notable features that differentiated the Kennedy presidency from others that would follow when marketing is considered. Kennedy's personal life was not open to scrutiny in the way that later presidential candidates would experience. While aspects of Kennedy's relationship to his wife were publicised and his autobiographical past was exploited to demonstrate his patriotic duty to his country, the episodes chosen for election purposes were specific in nature, and media respect for more sensitive areas of the President's life were, contemporaneously at least, shielded from public view. The President's health, specifically that he suffered from Addison's disease, and that he strayed from his marriage were issues that only belatedly came into the public sphere and were subject to popular debate. His marriage had to be carefully managed, although Jackie Kennedy was able to create her own political identity both in a domestic and international capacity. As a senator, a presidential candidate and finally president, his ill-health was shielded by a number of protective claims, including that he had flu, suffered from malaria, and that he 'injured his back on some rocks while swimming off Cape Cod'.[26] Part of the reason for the acceptance of information that may not have squared with the truth may have been the perception, certainly among his Republican opponents, that he was given positive and sympathetic press coverage.[27] Even given the belated exposure of many of Kennedy's personal issues he has retained his standing as one of the most popular presidents when polls are conducted to evaluate the historical context of leaders.[28] Kennedy had an 84 per cent approval rating in a poll taken in 2006, 13 per cent higher than his nearest challenger.[29] This suggests, perhaps only superficially, that although preferences have changed with respect to the presentation of socio-economic identity, the allure of Camelot, and a president clearly divorced economically from the rest of the populace, can be seen as an issue which is not necessarily a liability.

Kennedy's attempts to push himself to the fore as a political candidate rested upon a number of issues related to the marketing of his personality and the identity he conveyed. One was his wealth, his family fortune allowing him a lifestyle far removed from that of mainstream America. In contrast to other candidates discussed in this text, and certainly with the marketing of wealth and political identity in the contemporary era, Kennedy was quite forthcoming about the financial standing of his family, even during the election year of 1960. When asked by a *Time* journalist about the impact of the Great Depression Kennedy responded by stating, 'I have no first-hand knowledge of the depression. My family had one of the great fortunes of the world and it was worth more than ever then. We had bigger houses, more servants, we travelled more. ... I really did not learn about the depression until I read about it at Harvard.'[30] Secondly, there was the issue of religion. Kennedy's Catholicism was perceived to be, by his own camp in particular, an issue which might condition the votes of a number of key states and so shape the primary races, and thereafter give his opponents a prime target during the national campaign. His father Joseph P. Kennedy argued, 'Let's not con ourselves. The only issue is whether a Catholic can be elected President.'[31] Kennedy used television to offset potential doubt about his religiosity and challenged negative perceptions: 'There is no article of my faith that would in any way inhibit – I think it encourages – the meeting of my oath of office.'[32] He also asserted, 'I am not the Catholic candidate for president. I am the Democratic Party's candidate for president who happens also to be a Catholic'.[33] However, while it dominated internal considerations and concerns within the Kennedy camp, it partly shielded other issues, including the wealth entertained by Kennedy personally and the means he could use in order to advance his campaign agenda.

Part of the allure of Kennedy as a political candidate, at all levels of his political career, was that he advanced himself and his political position to be one where he as a person mattered. Policies were significant, and he was wholly able to advance his cause in this regard, but who conveyed them did too. Kennedy has been identified by Newman, a key writer on the marketing of political figures in America, as the first 'celebrity president'.[34] He received a media coverage and popular standing in keeping with that enjoyed by music and media figures of the time, partly obscuring weak job approval figures as his presidency progressed. Kennedy's presidency, once he had settled into office, was one of grandeur and one where 'the coming together of vast media coverage, inflated popular expectations, and talent at producing spectacle began'.[35]

In the overall context of this text the Kennedy period, and his candidacy, appeared to mark the closing stage of an era where candidates could easily accommodate elite social origins as part of their political candidacy. In later elections candidates emphasised how their humble origins prepared them for office, and political aptitude granted them political opportunities based on merit. In White's *The Making of the President 1960*, which provides an all-encompassing narrative of the 1960 contest for leadership, he evaluated how Hubert Humphrey, discussed earlier in the context of the Democratic campaign of 1968, appeared to have the personal attributes to relate to the general populace but lacked elite credentials which separated him from the mass, and thereby undermined his credibility to lead. 'What spoiled the Humphrey campaign – apart from the underlying fact that this country, Democrats and Republican alike, was unwilling to be evangelized in 1960 – was the very simplicity, the clarity, the homely sparkle he could bring to any issue. He could talk on almost any subject under the sun – to farmers, to workers, to university intellectuals. And when he finished there were no mysteries left; nor was he a mystery either. He was someone just like the listeners. There was no distance, no separation of intrigue, none of the majesty that must surround a king.'[36] Humphrey appeared to be a candidate who was before his time. His ability to communicate across social groups and to be of the masses was a skill and an aptitude that was later replicated by candidates such as Clinton and George Bush Jr. However, although in the 1990s a folksy approach was seen to be a pronounced asset to a campaign, in the 1960s it was considered problematic. The passage of time and the increasing transparency of candidates' lives accentuated the ordinary at the expense of elite considerations, and Humphrey largely set a tone that, although not successful at the time, would be a profitable strategy to employ in future decades.

The perception that personal wealth created a gulf at the elite level as well as on a personal level was evident with the involvement of Kennedy in the 1960 Democratic primary race. Although in modern politics the employment of vast campaign funds and resources is commonplace, particularly when individuals such as Ross Perot could employ their own personal fortunes, in the 1960s campaign management and finance were by contrast simplistic in their construction. Humphrey found that paying for television commercials stretched his finances and that he struggled to challenge Kennedy's financial bandwagon. Humphrey argued that it was like a 'corner grocer running against a chain store'.[37] Theodore White believed that it was not simply down to money that Kennedy could have a better campaign organisation with more offices in key voting districts and more staff to advance his campaign agenda, but also because 'the long-established connection of Kennedy's friendships and social background that provided his [campaign] with the talent'.[38] The portrayal of Kennedy during the primaries was that of a candidate who was accomplished on many fronts, his elite standing bestowing him with several advantages in the political arena.

Kennedy was subject to media criticism about his wealth and queries about how much he was actually worth. This came largely in the aftermath of the 1960 election and had little bearing on discussion during that particular contest. As the Kennedy family kept the exact nature of their wealth private, much of the discussion rested on speculation rather than established fact. One such discussion was entertained by *US News & World Report* in an article entitled 'The Richest President, How Much He Has, How Much He Gets'. Kennedy's aide Ted Sorensen claimed that Kennedy was not prone to read that particular publication.[39] Additionally, when in office Kennedy offset charges about his wealth, giving his salary for being president to charity and giving the royalties from his writings, particularly for *Profiles in Courage*, to other similar organisations. Although not flouted as an issue which could be considered as an asset, wealth, and its relationship to politics was something that was central to the impression of political success for the Kennedy family. A cousin of Kennedy's father, Joe Kane, who introduced Kennedy to politics in Boston, observed: 'Politics is like war...it takes three things to win – the first is money and the second is money and the third is money.'[40]

Kennedy was attuned to many of the political marketing techniques as practised by other politicians of his time, and in key areas which were to be enhanced and expanded by others in future years. In polls his team looked to enhance his position by identifying the type of policies which would be popular and the type of person who might be swung behind his particular cause and ideology. In using Louis Harris to provide information and accelerate the onset of a sophisticated political marketing machine the Kennedy team tried to pinpoint how and why individuals voted for them.[41] Political marketing rested on internal understandings of voter desire. This was replicated by the Republicans, who employed Claude Robinson to aid Nixon. The research was utilised by each party. Indeed the opponents secretly traded poll research information to allow internal results to enhance their intelligence. Although cast as fractious opponents each side realised that the majority of the core voting groups they sought to persuade were rooted in specific camps and that information might be traded for mutual benefit.[42]

Kennedy was considered to be both ordinary and exceptional by his aides. In an enlightening and informative book on Kennedy by his Special Counsel, Ted Sorensen, a subjective interpretation suggests that in terms of the conveyance of social and emotional information Kennedy transcended the problems posed by perceptions of Camelot. Appropriately, Sorensen began his text with the marriage of the ordinary and the exceptional, ' "The truly extraordinary man is truly the ordinary man." The first time I met John Kennedy I was immediately impressed by his "ordinary" demeanour – a quality that in itself is extraordinary among politicians.'[43] Kennedy did not advance himself publicly as a victim of circumstance in an overt manner, his family having had a number of bereavements and one of his sisters being confined to an institution on the grounds of her mental health. He was considered, by Sorensen at least to be able to make a connection with the voter, personally and politically. Sorensen argued that 'When I first began to work for him, it seemed we had nothing in common. He was worth an estimated ten million dollars, owing primarily to the vast trust funds his father had established many years earlier. ... My own background was typical of a middle-income family'. Thereafter there were differences in education too. 'He [Kennedy] had attended the exclusive Choate Preparatory School for boys, graduated with honors from Harvard, and studied briefly at Princeton. Stanford and London School of Economics. My [Sorensen] total tuition in six years at the University of Nebraska, from which I received my degree in law, could not have paid for a single year at Harvard.'[44] That Kennedy was not, in material terms, an ordinary person was clear. He was from an elite social group in the United States, had been pushed to the fore in the realm of politics by his father and enjoyed a lifestyle that was removed from the mainstream of American society. Although he had served in combat in Second World War and was clearly a patriotic American willing to serve his country, other factors particularly his religion appeared to pose problem of an association between candidate and electors.

Sorensen thought that the issues which might potentially prove divisive were not ones that posed problems for Kennedy as a person or candidate 'Yet all these differences made very little difference in his attitude. He was not simply a sum of all the elements in his background – a Catholic war veteran from a wealthy Boston family who had graduated from Harvard. His most important qualities he had acquired and developed on his own, and those who attempted to pigeonhole him according to the categories in his case history were sadly mistaken.'[45] Although Sorensen considered Kennedy's wealth to be a minimal issue in the campaign, it was largely this way as a consequence of a focus on his religion and policy, and his opponents were unable to push the issue of wealth to the fore as an issue of social and emotional division, and exploit it to their own gain.

Through the primary campaign Humphrey tried to press Kennedy on the perception that personal wealth created socio-economic divisions between the candidate and the electorate. Sorensen argued that 'Humphrey, meanwhile, asserting desperation for funds despite his continued confidence of victory, pushed the poor boy vs. rich boy theme to new heights. He went beyond stressing his own humble origins and Kennedy's wealthy background and began charging the Kennedy's with illegal acts.'[46] Ultimately Humphrey failed to get his message to resonate. Media and political commentary upon the wealth of the Kennedys appeared to be more an issue of celebration than condemnation, and was a feature of the Kennedy family aura that was later magnified as the 'Camelot' myth once the candidate had reached the presidential office. Kennedy's need to present himself to the public in a particular way is clear from the approach his campaign team adopted in the election campaigns he engaged in. The emphasis on religion presented his opponents and the electorate with the predicament that to address the issue directly was to suggest that it mattered, and hence to avoid it was to suggest, as the Kennedy team desired, that religion had no bearing on the debate concerning the election.[47] Kennedy used events to popularise himself and his campaign and to create the necessary image to engage with the electorate on an emotional level. His 1953-wedding was presented as a 'storybook' event with guests from all political positions.[48] It was portrayed as the union of two historic families and the creation of a realm of monarchical proportions.

The lessons from the Kennedy experience were that wealth could be considered an issue that was not a pronounced problem for a political candidate. In keeping with many of the political leaders in the United States in the twentieth century Kennedy was from an elite background, with a lifestyle far removed from the mainstream of that society. While muted in its profile during Kennedy's campaign, his wealth and the chic it brought to the White House once elected was openly celebrated in the media. Caution must be exercised however when simplifying Kennedy's overall position. The Kennedys did not openly disclose their wealth and his religion was seen to be more of an impediment to office than financial acumen. Kennedy's wartime exploits were accentuated to highlight his patriotism and his commitment to American values. However, Kennedy was perhaps the last president who could view wealth as an issue which would not be problematic when entertaining a candidacy for the White House. Following his tenure wealth was gradually considered to be a handicap. It still was an essential aspect of mounting a campaign, with personal and campaign finance in abundance, but it could no longer be considered to be an element that would be beyond critical media scrutiny or that could be used to provide emotional associations with the electorate. Across time, it became imperative to show that even if a candidate had enormous wealth, it was not an impediment to their understanding of and social awareness of the plight of the ill-defined 'ordinary' person. Camelot appeared to be, for the contemporary era at least, the last time a President could appear to live differently from society and be celebrated for doing so.

Conclusion

The experiences of Kennedy and Nixon in the 1950s and 1960s showed that while there were a number of areas of political marketing that were established, candidates had different fortunes in trying to advance their positions. Clearly both came from vastly different social backgrounds, but notably neither tried to mask their origins to any great extent. They sought, while accentuating their different respective strengths, to convey their worthiness for election to office and to accentuate and utilise their social positions as best they were able to.

Marketing techniques of advertisement placement, strategic polling and market research, and presenting the populace with a product thought to suit their needs was firmly in place by the late 1960s. The evolution of political campaigns based on the individual as much as the ideological position of the parties was an undercurrent which has continued into the contemporary era. In reviewing the changes wrought on the presidency during the tumult of the 1960s George E. Reedy, in his largely pessimistic work the *Twilight of the Presidency*, captured the tone of the changes brought about by the personalisation of the office and the concentration on the individual as the enshrinement of the political product. Writing in 1970, Reedy argued that the occurrence of change in the American political system was in some ways responsive to popular needs, 'The personal campaign is not to be despised, despite its carnival air and the mindless character of the slogans and political speeches.... Even more important, however, it represented a form of communion between a leader and his people, a communion that was a two-way street. Voters who could see a man in person, perhaps even, with a little luck get to touch him, somehow felt that they shared in the processes that governed them. Candidates, on the other hand, received a sense of drawing strength from the great mass.'[49] The interchange of information, whereby elements in the electoral process fed of the position of the other was important for the nature of democratic politics, and underpinned the political marketing ethos.

Rather than persuading the electorate to move to a political position desired by the candidate, candidates would now across time attempt to understand the electorate, and move, as much as was ideologically possible, to the position thought to be the most politically advantageous to gaining an electoral victory. Part of this was policy based, but part too was to replicate the social and emotional understanding possessed by the voting body. By the turn of the millennium this was considered to be a position in the centre-ground of politics. In terms of policy the challenges of a fundamental move were difficult to overcome, particularly in the midst of the Cold War and concerns over the volatility of specific groups within America. It proved easier and more profitable to cast the candidate in a specific light and to convey images of political figures who seemed to emotionally understand the electorate and who were perceived, through the manufacturing of an image, to socially, in terms of political marketing and the individual, be at one with America. While the experiences of Nixon and Kennedy were largely unrefined in comparison with contemporary candidates they provided a backdrop to future enhancements and changes in the presentation of candidates to the American people. Their experiences proved instructive in giving guidance, in both the United States and in Great Britain about how individual political identity might be used to persuade voters to a particular cause. Even in the short term Wilson, in 1963 and 1964, considered the strategies used by Kennedy in his 1960 presidential campaign and thereafter Edward Heath examined Nixon's election strategies of 1968 to inform his own election campaign.[50] The structure and contrasts between the US and UK political systems has meant that there has been something of a lag in the replication of marketing strategies in the United Kingdom. Writing in the 1970s Lord Longford claimed that the 'use of money and the cult of the family cannot be easily paralleled in England'.[51]

Nixon attempted to use his autobiography as an asset to convey bonds of association with the electorate. This worked in part, but he modified his approach in the late 1960s, when maintaining any form of stark pretence that he still was part and parcel of mainstream society was difficult to convey. Sold as the 'New Nixon' his marketed position relied as much on creating a perception of a refreshed individual, as it did on claiming that Nixon was a new person. Although Humphrey made a number of claims about the superficiality of Nixon's new image and the problems encountered by this type of marketing, he was unable, largely on account of the predicaments faced by his party, to convince voters that Nixon's political identity was one that had been artfully created so as to make him appear accessible and in tune with the voting block.

Kennedy ran largely on a ticket that did not shield the fact that he was from a wealthy family, but his wealth was not flaunted either. Rather he tried to advance the idea that although from an elite background this did not stop him from understanding the needs of the dispossessed and the poor, a feature carried forth with greater meaning by his brother in the 1968 campaign. He had also served his country with dignity. Kennedy's wealth and social position would be mirrored by a number of the candidates who would contest the presidential office in later years. However, they would approach the issue of wealth and its presentation in a fundamentally different way. Kennedy did deflect attention from the issue of wealth partly because at the time other issues were perceived to be potentially more divisive. At an early stage in the evolution of political marketing Kennedy did not try to pretend to be poor or accentuate aspects of his childhood to exploit public sympathies. He did accentuate his military career to highlight that his social class was not an impediment to his serving his country, and utilised his family to provide a backdrop to his campaign. In later years candidates would be more pronounced in selecting autobiographical characteristics which would mask any notions of privilege or wealth, indeed the marketing of impoverishment would become the uniform position from which to create a political identity. There were efforts to mirror Kennedy's political identity in later years and be the 'next JFK', most notably in the campaign waged by Gary Hart in 1984, however they failed to recreate the Kennedy 'charisma' and the outcome was one which appeared to be artificial in its construct.[52]

3
Thatcher and Major: Marketing a Conservative Identity

Political marketing with respect to the portrayal of class and wealth was present in British politics in advance of the rise to power of Margaret Thatcher in 1979. It was only brought to the fore however as an essential aspect of political presentation with a popular appreciation of the use of advertising agencies by the Conservative party in 1979.[1] Thatcher's ascendancy through the ranks of the Conservative party and final rise to the position of prime minister marked a clear breakthrough in the realm of political marketing. Not only were advertising agencies used to advance the Conservative cause in the 1979 general election, but Thatcher carefully portrayed herself as a product of lower-middle class Britain, as a woman in tune with the needs of those who were adversely affected by industrial disputes and the winter of discontent which had afflicted Britain at that time. This image was slowly deconstructed during Thatcher's time in office, culminating in her being ousted by her party in 1990 in anticipation that she was an electoral liability in any forthcoming general election, and that she had become aloof and disconnected from the voting mass. Her successor, John Major, followed a familiar furrow to that ploughed by Thatcher in the creation of a political persona designed to appeal to popular sentiments. He accentuated his working-class roots, played heavily upon his social connections with the British people and had both the skill and good fortune to lead his party to a narrow victory in the 1992 general election. Although not always greeted enthusiastically by the candidate himself, Major's election campaign commercials unashamedly pushed his social and emotional attributes as centre points in his political identity. By the time the Conservatives left office in 1997 the party had transformed political marketing and had, in many respects, changed the nature of the presentation of British politics. This was not merely an issue to do with the passage of time, but had its roots in research, the utilisation of factors in the marketing realm previously outside the remit of British politics, and in the resultant success enjoyed by the Conservative party. This success ensured that both Labour and the Conservative party would see presentation and political identity as central to the successful capture of power in future election and campaign challenges. This was understood by those associated with New Labour, and Tony Blair in particular, in the run-up to the British general election of 1997, and his political identity was largely based on learning from the successes and failures of his predecessors. The issue in British politics was one of both the manufacturing of the candidates, as well as the marketing of them. This challenge was not consigned neatly to an election cycle or a short-term campaign, but had to be advanced persuasively and frequently across a long period of time to assist in conveying the type of candidate thought to appeal to the British public.

This chapter considers how political marketing engrained itself into British politics. It firstly examines the dilemma that faced the Conservative party, a party on the centre-right of the British political spectrum. The party faced, and continues to face, challenges in dispelling impressions that it favours elite and moneyed interests and is divorced from the interests of the ordinary person. Thatcher had to create a party image and personal identity which would allow her to entertain a broad demographic support among the populace, and show an appeal to persons on a diverse range of income levels. She marketed her character to this end, reinventing her personal background when becoming party leader and then prime minister. Also under consideration in this chapter are issues such as the strategic use of her gender, her portrayal of wealth and her effort to socially and emotionally connect with the voter. It briefly addresses how the efforts to maintain Thatcher's connections with the voter in these areas disintegrated as the 1980s progressed. Thereafter consideration is given to how John Major created a political and public identity which exploited his background, and how he utilised and exploited specific aspects of his past once in power. However, he was unable, across the long term, to create sufficient ties with the voting public so as to ensure that the Conservative party was perceived to identify with ordinary people. The underlying problems it faced in identifying, both subjectively and objectively, with ordinary people when Thatcher took office remained in place when Major left office 18 years later.

Elite or ordinary: A Conservative dilemma

In the 1970s British politics had clear water between left and right, and bore the traditional overtones of a left leaning Labour party, supportive of industry and the unions, and a Conservative party supportive of business, opposed to union strength and comfortable with the principles of free market capitalism. Initially the Conservatives were thought to have a strong role to play in siding with middle-class interests and opposing working-class interests, however perceptions of the Labour party as representatives of the working-class interests were damaged by the onset of strained industrial relations, culminating in the winter of discontent in 1979. The class-based foundations of British politics appeared, at least temporarily, to have been set aside, albeit during a period of unconventional and bitter industrial relations. At a superficial level at least the Conservative party were perceived to have transformed their relationship with at least part of the British political community, although the change was essentially superficial in nature. The brief association with working-class voters, and especially skilled manual workers, who essentially voted against their own rational economic issues, often titled Basildon or Mondeo man, was transient. Nevertheless, Thatcher had been at the forefront in making the party appear more inclusive and giving it a more universal appeal, taking swing voters from the centre-left of the political spectrum and creating across the short term a new political coalition.

Through the 1980s poll statistics suggested that the 1979 election, and the presence of Margaret Thatcher as a political leader, had little bearing on the underlying long-term interpretation of the Conservative party. Although Margaret Thatcher argued vehemently, as detailed later in this chapter, about her class origins she was perceived to have little credibility when contending that she was in touch with the populace, and the party was not thought to have much to bond it to the ill-defined concept of 'ordinary people'. As Green argued in the work *Thatcher*, the distinctive role of class and political affiliation was largely entrenched in the period in advance of Thatcher's assumption of national leadership: 'The period from when Thatcher first became politically active to her election as Conservative leader was the time in British political history which saw the closest correlation between class and voting allegiance.'[2] With respect to the period of office for Thatcher, commencing with questions first asked in 1983, MORI polls asked about statements which were considered appropriate to the identity of the Conservative party. In 1983, 48 per cent of respondents thought the party to be out of touch with ordinary people, the figure rising to the mid-fifties during the later part of Thatcher's time as party leader. Similarly, only 23 per cent thought that the party looked after 'people like us' in the early 1980s, falling to 9 per cent in 1989 and a meagre 8 per cent in 1990.[3]

It is evident that the Conservative party, during Thatcher's era of leadership, struggled to have resonance with any broad demographic group which might express or categorise themselves as having their interests advanced to a positive end. This was in stark contrast to the impression entertained by Thatcher herself. Shortly after her acquisition of the prime ministerial office she argued 'the Conservative Party has demonstrated that it is the party of all the people'.[4] Thereafter, it is clear that a similarly bleak position existed, across the decade, with respect to those who might consider themselves to be both ordinary and Conservative party supporters. Additionally ordinariness is not a feature or attribute that is specifically class based. As Chapter 1 indicated, it is largely dictated by self-reference. As Thatcher's tenure progressed a decreasing number considered her party to be in touch with their own subjective interests and increasing numbers considered the Conservatives to be a party that was out of touch with mainstream society. The party stereotype of it being one which represented narrow interests appears to have been largely unaltered by either environmental events or by the evolution of new policies, leadership or revised marketing strategies.

With specific reference to Margaret Thatcher, the marketing of her personal political identity did not succeed when advancing inclusiveness and her political marketing did not, it appears, succeed across time in making her appear to be genuinely at one with the British people. In keeping with the problems encountered by the party in socially associating itself with the populace, poll samples made for similarly grim reading with respect to Thatcher's association as an individual. In 1981 poll statistics showed that 43 per cent thought her to be 'out of touch with ordinary people'. Across the 1980s this figure, although prone to marginal alterations, slowly deteriorated. By 1990, 62 per cent considered her to be out of touch.

The marked deterioration in the perception of Thatcher as a leader who could be identified with ordinary people was pronounced by the end of the 1980s. By the time of her departure from office she appeared to be a leader to whom few could relate personally, and led the Conservative party as an individual who seemed detached socially and emotionally from the public. In short, both her socio-economic class-based associations and social and emotional connections with the voter were a political liability by the time her party decided to remove her as leader.

The explanations for the deterioration appear to be grounded upon factors which are central to the marketing of an individual and their wealth. Ordinariness appears to be a factor considered significant in earmarking a candidate's suitability for election to office. However, once the candidate has occupied political office, the opportunities and ability of the candidate to convey a sense of ordinariness appears substantially reduced. In turn, attempts to play an autobiographical card appears to become more difficult the longer the leader has been removed from the rigours of mainstream society.

By way of contrast, and to emphasise the party gulf between the Conservative and Labour party in the realm of voter association, there were pronounced differences between the parties in terms of their popular associations. Through the 1980s the highest figures for those who thought the Labour party out of touch with ordinary people was a mere 17 per cent. Similarly, Neil Kinnock, the Labour leader through much of the 1980s, was thought to be more in touch with the experiences of British people. For most of the 1980s he entertained single figures when poll samples asked if he were out of touch. This is largely unsurprising given the social background and make-up of the Labour party at that time. However, on their own, social origins and emotional connections were insufficient to allow Kinnock, or his predecessor Michael Foot, to seriously challenge Thatcher across the decade. Part of this was rooted in the problems that had faced Labour with respect to policy in the late 1970s, and part was an acceptance, in the short term, that although Thatcher did frequently come across as aloof and managerial, these were admirable character attributes to possess when holding a political office. When seeking office she was the Grocer's Daughter, when in office she was the Iron Lady. In getting to the office ordinariness was an important factor to convey; when in office decisive leadership was a similarly desirable feature.

At first sight the Labour party might be thought to have held the winning hand with respect to political marketing. However, Thatcher was also thought to be a decisive leader, and revolutionised British politics with the reform of a number of institutions. She addressed industrial relations and waged effective general election campaigns which presented her with three general election victories. In keeping with the general thesis advanced in this study she used social and emotional issues to elevate her to a position of Conservative party leader and then, when in office, accentuated the decisive and authoritative qualities that, it could be argued, she was elected specifically to display. That her image during her time in office was one that gave her a political identity that was aloof from the mainstream voter was partly a product of her time in office, with a natural outgrowth being that she would not be in a position to partake in an ordinary life or existence. As a consequence both she and the Conservative party as a whole were never able to cast off the perception of the party as an elitist institution. That is not to say that the political marketing undertaken by Margaret Thatcher was wholly unsuccessful, or was markedly inferior to that advanced by her political opponents. Rather it is to argue that the aspects of political marketing which helped elevate Thatcher to power in the first place were effective in enhancing her appeal, but across the long term the erosion of the Thatcher image was one that could not be forestalled meaningfully by marketing strategies relating to her individually or counteract the stereotypical image of her party.

The remainder of this chapter considers how Thatcher created a political identity that sought to portray her as one with the British people in her pursuit of the party leadership. It then considers how she marketed herself as a potential prime minister and how she diminished perceptions of her wealth and social standing so as to enhance her electability. Thereafter the position of John Major is considered. His position contrasts with that of Thatcher as he could genuinely contend that he had humble origins. He assumed aspects of Thatcher's initial marketing strategies to portray him as a leader who could associate with a cross-section of the British people and presented himself as a product of a working-class environment, with campaign commercials which unashamedly accentuated this facet.

Margaret Thatcher

The political context

In evaluating Margaret Thatcher's position as a political candidate who entertained market-based concepts it is evident that she tried, as with the other candidates and leaders in this book, to accentuate a number of core features central to her political character and to stress, for public consumption, personal criteria which might be entertained positively by the public. This was particularly evident in two areas, her background and her gender, areas which were cultivated, modified and manipulated so as to give Thatcher an association with the British public, and also to give her a distinctive edge over her opponents.

Thatcher's political career has been extensively researched and chronicled, with an array of associated discussions on the regional and national ramifications of her policies. She was born in 1925 in

Lincolnshire, went to Oxford University and then worked as a research chemist, later studying law and qualifying as a barrister. She was interested in political issues from an early age, and was attracted by the ideology of Conservative party. She was elected to represent Finchley, a suburb of London, in 1959 and had time in both government and opposition holding several important posts. Following the Conservative election victory in 1970, she became Secretary of State for Education and Science. She courted controversy by being accused of ending the provision of free school milk for children over 7, leading to negative publicity, 'Mrs Thatcher Milk Snatcher', and a perception that she remained largely immune to public opinion and cared little on issues perceived to have strong social and emotional content.[5]

Following the loss of power in 1974 by Heath and the Conservative party Thatcher saw her opportunity to challenge for power and to take her brand of leadership to the heart of British politics. She campaigned with vigour, albeit merely within her own party, as the leadership post was one decided internally within Conservative ranks. She defeated Edward Heath by 130 votes to 119, and then in a second ballot received 146 votes to William Whitelaw's 79, becoming the first woman to lead a major political party in British political history.[6] Thatcher campaigned against Labour under its two prime ministers of this period Harold Wilson and James Callaghan. At the forefront of her leadership were the values of the free market, questions about the role of the state and a deeply ingrained dislike of socialism and its inherent values.

Thatcher's opportunity to practice her values in government came with the disintegration of Labour's political authority in 1978–79. Denis Healy, Chancellor of the Exchequer, implemented a number of economic reforms which included cuts in spending in key areas of public provision, most notably in the areas of health and education. Union discontent was manifested with the onset of the 'winter of discontent', a term employed by the editor of the British tabloid newspaper the *Sun* to describe a wave of popular dissatisfaction with the path taken by a number of generally unionised interests in the nation at that time. High unemployment, strikes and wage freezes alongside a press sympathetic to the idea of ideological chance presented Thatcher with the opportunity to present an alternative vision for Britain if she were able to sell both her own character and policies to a national audience.[7] Poll statistics suggested that much of the opportunity presented to Thatcher arose from ineptitude on the part of Labour rather than a determined swing behind the Conservative party. As environmental conditions worsened so did the fortunes of Labour.

Marketing a political identity

Thatcher had two distinct challenges in presenting her character and identity as attributes which mirrored those possessed by the mainstream population. Two issues were of importance. Firstly, she needed to appeal to the political and social identity of the Conservative party membership and be perceived to reflect its make-up and identity. Secondly however, she also needed to have a broader appeal to entice swing voters and those alienated by the political environment and other political parties to her cause. Her political character and identity were marketed primarily as products of her own impressions of her childhood and background. These were pivotal in placing her in a position where she advanced and understood moral values, felt herself to be part of 'Middle England' and allowed her to contend that she was the product, politically and personally, of hard work and endeavour. She recalled in her memoirs, *The Path to Power*, 'Nothing in our house was wasted, and we always lived within our means'.[8] Placed neatly alongside the cultivation of an identity shaped by a personal history was her perception that she was a woman who had entered a previously male bastion, namely that of politics. Her gender became significant in shaping her identity, but not entirely in a fashion which allowed her to contend that she was a woman who could attract, on its sole account, other women to her political cause. Her strategy involved pointing out the hardships faced on the grounds of her gender and, in accentuating the will and determination needed to advance her position, she addressed one of the core remits of political marketing outlined with respect to leadership. Being a woman was an asset to Thatcher as it was a tool she could utilise politically. Coming from an ordinary background she demonstrated that she had socially and emotionally experienced the same lifestyle as the voter. In rising as a woman, to the head of her chosen political party, she had shown that she had an exceptional talent in politics. These issues had to be sold to the populace to create a political image which would prove attractive to the voter, and marketed in such a way so that it looked as though Thatcher could appeal to a broad range of socio-economic groups. The combination of the political and social, her gender and determination, alongside her ability to address the class-based structure of British society made for a complex make-up of a candidate who was multidimensional in her construct, but appeared simple in her message and identity. Wendy Webster, in *Not a Man to Match Her* observed of Thatcher, 'The individual mobility that Mrs Thatcher presents as a matter of talent, energy and ability was much more than this, it was to do with manners, style, money, marriage, ballroom dancing classes, accent, clothes and an acceptance which she was never given by much of the establishment, particularly by the intellectual establishment'.[9]

Emerging from an ordinary background

Interpretations of Margaret Thatcher's life rest upon a number of romanticised ideas, impressions central to an understanding of a desired image rather than a real and stark impression of how she entered into politics. John Campbell, in a key work on Thatcher, *The Grocer's Daughter*, argued that from the outset Thatcher's background was consumed by idealism and spin.[10] Thatcher's interpretation of her own political identity was formed by her social environment and her interaction with it. She perceived herself as the product of the corner shop, and as a person immersed in the dynamics of market economics. Playing to the areas which would naturally be expected in political marketing on socio-economic issues she stated, 'I had the most marvellous upbringing. It stayed with me the rest of my life. ... My goodness it was hard as a young person, it was hard, but it was right.'[11] As with each candidate mentioned in this text she entertained a collection of social and moral concepts she believed would enhance her political position and used her autobiography as a tool through which to describe the evolution and maturity of her political character.

Central to political marketing is the use of the past to justify the present and provide a political narrative to which the audience can relate. Thatcher used her personal history both when competing for office and when in office, to shape her political identity and popular appeal. In a keynote speech to the Conservative Party conference in 1981 she alluded to the impact of her personal life upon the political philosophy she advocated to the nation. 'First among these is the deep and heartfelt concern for the personal hardship and waste reflected in every factory closure and redundancy. I learnt from childhood the dignity which comes from work and, by contrast, the affront to self-esteem which comes from enforced idleness. For us, work was the only way of life we knew, and we were brought up to believe that it was not only a necessity but a virtue.'[12] Several core themes emerged with respect to Thatcher's memories of her past. They cast her as an ordinary person accustomed to hardship and commonplace experiences, far removed from wealth or elite society. She accentuated her childhood interaction with the corner shop environment, enhancing her awareness of public service, financial management and the workings of the housewife's purse. Furthermore she adulated her father in particular, and stressed the importance of family stability to her perceptions of her ethics and morality.

On its own the concept of an industrious and engaged childhood would not have much resonance. However it was mentioned frequently in media opportunities by Thatcher and raised in interviews by those intent on uncovering her political motivations and political ethos. For example, in an interview conducted on Channel 4 television, the interviewer cast Thatcher's childhood in the following form, 'you mentioned just now Grantham and your childhood in a relatively modest home in Grantham'.[13] This played, at least theoretically, to a realm where she could present herself as ordinary and inclusive within mainstream British society. The concept of ordinariness on account of social and geographical origin were also present in advance of Thatcher's elevation to a position of national office. In 1975 she was asked about how her geographical origins might impact upon her support across the nation, a radio interviewer arguing, 'but you always had the *image* of a lady of the south'. Thatcher responded, 'Well, I was born and brought up for the most telling years of my life in Grantham, Lincolnshire. ... all my ideas about life, about individual responsibility, about looking after your neighbour, about patriotism, about self-discipline, about law and order, were all formed right in a small town in the Midlands, and I've always been very thankful that I was brought up in a smaller community so that you really felt what a community could be.'[14] Overall Thatcher's upbringing and the impact of her Lincolnshire past was advanced by her as a topic with some frequency. As leader of the opposition she brought Grantham and its impact upon her character into discussion 11 times, and when prime minister 28 times.[15]

Thatcher's identity was also shaped by media profiles which conveyed her as a woman who, in keeping with an increasing number of women in the country at the time, shared the demanding task of juggling work and domestic life. She had two children to raise in the early part of her political career, and both in the media and through her own efforts to shape an image, her role as a mother was an integral part of an identity marketed to appeal to women, and professional women in particular. She did however employ a 'nanny-housekeeper' to assist her in her domestic duties immediately after their birth, and this allowed her to return to full-time study and later full-time work.[16] By the time of her position as leader of the opposition in the mid-1970s her children were in their twenties and were not part of the daily challenges of motherhood for Thatcher. Her media profiles however played upon her position as a mother and accentuated her position as an instrumental figure in her household, one constructed around conventional and ordinary routines. Thatcher sold different images of her as political circumstances demanded. In 1970 she declared in a television interview, 'When the children were young I always had an English nanny'. Yet in a newspaper article in 1979 she painted a different portrait of her domestic arrangements, 'Bringing up a family gives you a lot of experience of coping with instant crises...because in most cases, it's your job because Dad has gone to work and Mum is left to cope. So you do cope.'[17] At a later stage of her career, in 1975 the *Times* reported: 'She is up at half-past-six every morning to get her husband Denis his breakfast before he leaves for his job. ...Thatcher gets to her hairdresser for a set once a week about half-past-eight.'[18] On its own this type of reporting might not have had much resonance, but it served as a prelude to a more cohesive image where Thatcher was portrayed as organised and authoritative while retaining a number of homely features which created social bonds. It was later used to embellish her political as well as her personal identity with discussions on 'handbag diplomacy'. The long-term opportunities presented by social marketing are clear. They allow a permanent campaign of image and identity building which can be maintained to press home to the voter a set of attributes which make the candidate appealing, largely in a non-political capacity. In the absence of policy declarations, or the pressing glare of a general election campaign, they offer the opportunity to connect to the voter on issues which can form meaningful bonds, and inform later decisions involving party affiliation and political identification. Additionally they offer a political component that is tangential to policy, and an issue that allows the voter to relate to the candidate when possessing only marginal political knowledge.

Thatcher also made light of conditions of impoverishment and an awareness of the need to be thrifty and considerate of the prevailing economic climate. Again in the prelude to holding a national office she aimed to be perceived as a person who had experienced normality and could mount a campaign for office based upon an appreciation of the pressures facing those on a budget. In the midst of a winter of discontent and widespread social disrepair this type of message was important. When asked about whether she adhered to the stereotype of a 'lady of suburbia' she responded that 'I learned to have a jolly good store cupboard, again by virtue...of being the daughter of a very prudent [Beatrice Roberts] housewife. And we did then, I mean we used to bottle things when they were cheap and put them in your store cupboard and you could in fact that way see yourself through the winter, frequently with your bottled fruit.'[19] The association with the workings of the home naturally portrayed her as a person who was in touch with the politics of ordinariness and the mundane aspects of day-to-day life, particularly with respect to issues affecting women. The use of a housewife image as an electoral tool was advocated in advance of her leadership contest for the Conservative party by Gordon Reece, a media advisor. Thatcher assumed the role with enthusiasm and some aplomb. She told the *Daily Mirror* 'What people don't realise about me is that I am a very ordinary person who leads a very normal life. I enjoy it – seeing that the family have a good breakfast. And shopping keeps me in touch.'[20] Indeed it was women who formed the 'backbone' of support for Thatcher and were significant in her accession and retention of power.[21] Thereafter, Thatcher could play to men on the grounds of her resolute character, strength and association with class groups who thought she advanced their interests. The presentation of an austere and thrifty background was conditioned however by the underlying nature of Thatcher's rise to a position of power and influence. Although she emphasised issues of personal economics, as Webster highlights, 'Few of the tickets for Mrs Thatcher's journey away from Grantham were bought with money from her own earnings. The state funded her first step, her grammar school education, and her father paid for her Oxford education. ... It was Denis Thatcher's money which financed her move to the bar.'[22] The marketed image and the financial reality were somewhat removed from one another.

The duality of Thatcher's presentation, as a person grounded initially in the traditions of Lincolnshire, aware of the strengths of family and relationships, strategically placed alongside her reputation of being a conviction politician was not lost on the media, or on Thatcher herself. Her image altered radically across her time as a political figure and reflected in large part her efforts to convey the impression that she was emotionally at one with the British people. Webster observed, 'In the 1980s images of Mrs Thatcher proliferated, and she was understood in many guises – as nanny, warrior, queen, Iron Lady, housewife, Boadicea – but in the early 1970s her image was much more unitary. The words most commonly used to describe her were "smug", "self-righteous", "condescending", "snobbish". ... it was the idea that she was remote from the concerns of ordinary people, that she had no understanding at all of their everyday lives that was continually reproduced.'[23] In keeping with the argument advanced in this text that there are two marketing strategies, one which accentuates hardship as a grounding for office, and a second which advocates exceptionalism as a justification for office an interviewer, Gill Nevill, asked, 'that talking to people about you in preparation for this interview that I have come across two Mrs. Thatchers. One of them very firm, very resolute, the strong leader with the economic principles – and I think probably that is how a lot of the nation, friend and foe, sees you. But then, talking to your close advisers, the image was completely different: warm, thoughtful, approachable, immensely considerate.'[24] The multidimensional approach evidently allowed Thatcher to seek to market the elements of her personality deemed suitable to attract voters to her cause. However, there were problems for Thatcher across time as her authoritative command of her party and its agenda seeped into public perceptions of her as a leader. She was increasingly considered to be uncaring and disassociated from the interests, experiences and position of ordinary people. Memories of Thatcher's advocacy of the hardships she faced faded. The changes in perceptions of her across time were notable and reflected changing successes and failures in her marketing strategy. In 1987, during the general election campaign, she was asked about how perceptions of her had changed across time. Robin Oakley, interviewing her for the *Times* asked about whether Thatcher was worried about being thought of as 'uncaring' or being talked of as 'that bloody woman'. Thatcher responded by claiming that she was concerned about conveying this type of impression but again used her childhood to underline her general approach and philosophy in politics. 'I sometimes feel it would be better if I talked more and did less – but of course it wouldn't. We do a lot more and talk a lot less and that's the way I was taught from childhood.'[25]

Thatcher's failure to fully convince the electorate across the long term of her ordinariness rested largely upon variation in the marketing of her as a party leader and her associations with a party that was identified as a vehicle for middle-class and elite interests. Indeed, Thatcher did not shy away from appealing directly to that body, identifying her own background as part and parcel of Middle England. However, she did appeal to sections of the populace who were enticed by both her status as a conviction politician, her portrayal of herself as a woman who had faced commonplace challenges when juggling a career and domestic life, and opposed the political interests advanced by the Labour party. Although she addressed how she was perceived as a person and how this might be sold in the political realm, her image as a person who could sympathise with the populace on emotional issues was overshadowed by images of her authoritarian presence within politics. In large part this emerged on account of changes in political marketing and in the manner in which she portrayed herself to the electorate, 'in the 1980s the idea that Mrs Thatcher was an ordinary woman just like any other became noticeable mainly by its absence in her publicity, and increasingly gave way to a quite different emphasis on her extraordinary qualities and abilities'.[26] Thatcher failed to expose her private life, particularly when in office, to the full glare of the media and this created an impediment to the marketing of her in a social and emotional context. All of the prime ministers, however reluctant to do so, who followed Thatcher in British politics were much more dynamic in seeking to create profiles of themselves which incorporated overt social and emotional dimensions, both in advance of their assuming office and during it. While Thatcher struggled to make indents in the polls in this area her legacy and the problems faced by a leader on the right of the political spectrum informed British political marketing and the interweaving of personal and political components.

John Major

A product of Brixton

John Major assumed the office of prime minister following the decision of Margaret Thatcher to resign her position in 1990. He had previously been Chancellor of the Exchequer and had risen through the ranks of the Conservative party in a quiet and unassuming way, influencing the elite party membership and avoiding open and direct controversy. Major appeared to be largely unknown by large sections of the British public upon his appearance at number 11, and later number 10, Downing Street. In this sense his ability to present himself as an ordinary person, unaffected by the trappings of office was a realistic objective. This was enhanced by the fact that, having operated under the shadow of Thatcher he could try to distance himself from her on character grounds, if not policy issues, and create meaningful comparisons between their political and autobiographical identities. As Ivor Crewe identified, 'Major was never the "son of Thatcher", as his opponents initially claimed and his Thatcherite supporters hoped. His social background was very different – insecure, déclassé, metropolitan, and secular; hers was secure, petit bourgeois, provincial, and Methodist. He shared her passion for sound money, but for little else.'[27] This difference would be marketed to provide ideological distinction, while giving the voter a fresh start with respect to the identity of the leader and the party. In an international context Major was presented as a man of the people. For example, three months after becoming prime minister the *New York Times* said of him: 'Though he lacks the upper-class private school or university education most recent Conservative Prime Ministers have had, his working-class roots and manner of speaking have endeared him to many voters who hated Mrs. Thatcher.'[28] In the transference of power, social and emotional connections were important facets of a sea-change in British politics.

Major was born into a family which had a background that he could later use to demonstrate his associations with those who faced hardship under his government. He was born in 1943 to parents who were involved in the entertainment profession, his father being a showman. His parents moved accommodation when he was young, but settled in Brixton, a working -lass area of London, in 1955. A principal reason for this move was the failure of the family garden gnome business. The Brixton location was to have an impact upon Major, and more importantly in the context of this text, on how he could portray himself to the public.

Having acquired a moderate but unexceptional education Major applied to take a number of jobs which did not suggest that he was from an elite stock. He was turned down for the position of bus conductor, worked with his family in the garden ornaments business and spent a period as a clerk; however he personally chose to terminate his employment in the position. He spent time unemployed and worked at the London Electricity Board. Thereafter, following a correspondence course in banking he worked at the Standard Chartered Bank. As is clear from this material the background and underpinning of Major's political career was unglamorous and indeed almost adverse to the commonplace routes to the position of prime minister undertaken by others who rose to the key governmental position. Major clearly had the background, experiences and, although ill-defined, the 'ordinariness' to contend that he had indeed risen to national prominence through a route that might be taken by a majority in mainstream society. In this context he found himself in a position which could be marketed with some ease – that he had risen from obscurity and from a normal background and then through hard work, aptitude and successful decision making, had found himself in a position where he could display his natural political talent.

Major's rise to the position of prime minister was quiet and unassuming, yet rapid. He was elected to parliament in 1979, after having failed to get a seat in London twice in 1974. He entered the cabinet in 1987 and was unexpectedly made Foreign Secretary in 1989, moving to the position of Chancellor later the same year. He became Prime Minister in

1990 and replaced Thatcher who resigned following pressure from her party. He played on his origins from the outset, appreciating it seems both the unconventional background he entertained given British prime ministers of the past, and clearly being aware of the strength his background afforded him politically. Gary Taylor in *Contemporary Review* wrote of Major's acquisition of power, 'On his first day as Prime Minister, on the way back from his audience with the Queen, Major claims he considered his rise to power and his humble beginnings'.[29] Although Major faced widespread scepticism from both the public and the Conservative party he competed against Labour in the 1992 election and marketed himself, as outlined later in this chapter, as a leader who had the common touch and could reach out to the interests of the nation in a way that neither his predecessor nor his opponent could match. Throughout the campaign Kinnock was judged to have appealed more frequently on the grounds of his ordinariness, however Major went on to win the election, albeit with a very narrow and precarious majority. After a turbulent term in office, facing internal party dissent, criticism of his economic strategy and attempts to resolve many of the issues facing Northern Ireland, Major took the step of resigning as party leader, putting himself up for re-election as leader of the Conservatives. He won the contest, but the message sent to the nation was of a leader facing internal party division and lacking the authority to maintain a credible government.

The demise of the Major government marked the end of an era for the Conservative party and the loss of power which demanded serious reconsideration of what the party stood for and who it represented. The Conservative party endured one of the worst defeats in its history in 1997, losing by such a degree that the recapture of power was generally deemed unrealistic in the short term. Additionally the party's reputation was in ruins as it was deemed to have failed to maintain control over areas of traditional strength, most notably the economy. As discussed in Chapter 5 the movement of New Labour to the central ground of British politics made it increasingly difficult for the Conservatives to advance themselves as representing or encapsulating the views of the ordinary person, and for at least a decade they were cast as a party which required a reworking of its political identity.

John Major left office having held his parliamentary seat of Huntingdon and with a reservoir of genuine respect from a wide array of politicians and public. He was considered to be a likeable individual, but had inherited a party that was ridden with internal tension, and subject to implosion at key moments, whether it be in the area of policy on Europe or with regard to the plethora of sexual scandals that afflicted the party elite. His legacy since leaving office has been mixed, with revelations that he had an affair with Conservative MP Edwina Currie, which retrospectively suggested that his morality-based campaign Back to Basics was lacking in both credibility and substance.

Selling the person

In advancing himself as a person who could associate with the British electorate Major was in a prime position to reshape the identity of Conservative party after the demise of Margaret Thatcher. His marketability rested firmly upon his background, his life experiences and his reputation within the political environment. His nickname was 'honest John' which suggested, at the least, that he was out of kilter with the traditional reputation of politicians and leaders, and might thereafter be considered in a different light.

Major's experiences as a child and adult who frequently faced hardship and difficulty translated well to his ability to market himself as a person in the political realm. In large part he faced difficulty in pushing himself to the fore on the grounds that the reputation of his party conflicted with his personal experiences. This had ramifications in shaping the perception of the Conservative party, and slowly ensured that there was an appreciation that ordinariness, or the perception of it, had a role to play in shaping the future potential success for the party. When Mrs Thatcher was ousted from office by her own party, partly for being perceived to be out of touch with the electorate, a clear choice had to be made about the type of candidate that was desired, alongside the nature of the policies he or she would pursue. In the first instance the prime candidate was Douglas Hurd, a prominent member of the Thatcher government and an individual with strong leadership credentials. He had been to Eton, and was both the son and the grandson of an MP. The emergence of Major as a candidate was partly based on his social position alongside his policy preferences. Watkins identified the core problem for the Conservatives when considering the candidacy for leadership by Hurd, 'Before 1965, when his party moved to a system of election, he would have been the obvious, perhaps the inevitable choice to emerge from the customary processes of consultation. ... But Mr Major (as he was then) was billed as the boy from Brixton, in this capacity winning the support of Old Etonians such as the late Alan Clark. In desperation, Mr Hurd was forced into playing the game of Lowlier Than Thou, in which he claimed to have been a scholarship-winner whose father was a tenant farmer.'[30] This type of leadership contest, where social class and origin were considered to be factors which might influence the outcome was beneficial for John Major and has come to earmark the issue of leadership and ability in modern politics. Philip Norton observed, 'There was also a social dimension: Heseltine was a self-made millionaire, Hurd the scion of a landed family. Major was neither.'[31] Major profited from the obvious comparisons that could be drawn between himself and Hurd during the leadership election and between himself and Thatcher, and his social identity and considerations of his origins on wealth grounds was important.

There was a marked change in how the public perceived the Conservative leader when Major took the position from Thatcher, one which appeared to vindicate the choice, as least on perceptions of the leader being in touch with society. The poll figures cited in earlier in this chapter testified to problems in this realm for the Conservative party under the leadership of Thatcher. In the final poll statistics taken by MORI in September 1990 before she left office 63 per cent of those questioned thought her out-of-touch with ordinary people. As further explained by Philip Norton when looking at the transition, 'In September 1990, substantial majorities agreed with the statement that the government had failed to stop Britain's most important problems ... 76 per cent that they looked after the interests of the rich [and] not ordinary people'.[32] Major was thought to be out of touch with ordinary people by only 13 per cent in February 1991. At the time of the 1992 general election, in the spring of 1992, Major was considered to be out of touch by about a third of the electorate, a feature which suggested that he was in a beneficial position, in a party context, compared to that entertained by Thatcher. His victory in the election was attributed to some media dissatisfaction with Kinnock, the Labour leader, alongside several widely criticised appearances by Kinnock, particularly a disastrous one at Sheffield in the run-up to the election where he engaged in a chorus of adulation with the audience. The General Secretary of the Labour party at the time, Tom Sawyer, stated of that performance, that Kinnock was, 'a very ordinary guy with very ordinary instincts that hadn't really been tamed even by all the political advisers; so on occasions like that there was always the chance that he would do something that the average football supporter would do. And he did it.'[33] Although Kinnock was considered to be more 'ordinary' than Major, he was also considered to lack the qualities and policies needed to lead the United Kingdom. When presenting himself to the populace Major had the combination of attributes, an ordinary background combined with desirable leadership qualities, which assisted in tipping the 1992 general election in his favour. Thereafter poll statistics suggested a familiar deterioration with respect to ordinariness. Major was considered to be out of touch with ordinary people by 50 per cent of poll respondents in 1993, rising to 55 per cent in 1995, and ending with 47 per cent in the prelude to his leaving prime ministerial office.[34]

Several allegations were made about Major as he undertook the role of prime minister when Thatcher stood down. Major, generally unencumbered by the evolution of new communication strategies, argued throughout his time in office that he wanted to be himself and not become entwined in an array of manufactured politics which might spin his character and identity. However, upon taking office accusations were levelled at Major. Andrew Rawnsley, writing in the *Guardian*, alleged that Major had updated his image by taking elocution lessons, and in seeking to resonate with the British voter talked with 'a huskier, deeper, gravelly sound'. When asked in a radio interview whether this was a legitimate allegation Major shunned the notion of personal image as a tool of political marketing, 'I am what I am and people will have to take me as I am. Image makers will not find me under their tutelage. I shall be the same plug ugly.' This in large part goes against the strategies employed by the other political figures considered in this text, with a determination by Major to present an authentic and unadulterated political image. However, unlike the vast majority of the other political figures discussed in this text he could genuinely advance the argument that he was legitimately from working-class origins and use the social connection created to his advantage. His position did not demand an artificial creation of an autobiographical portrait of impoverishment.

During the 1992 general election campaign Major reluctantly agreed to accentuate his origins and background as part of the campaign strategy. His most marked effort to portray himself as the product of a humble background emerged in a party political broadcast which highlighted, in keeping with this thesis underpinning the conveyance of personality politics, both his exceptionalism as a national leader alongside the downtrodden origins of his original home life. Naturally, given the diversity and colour of Major's life, there was selectivity in pinpointing the areas of Major's previous domicile. Great play was made of Brixton, as an area widely known in the United Kingdom as one of impoverishment, unemployment and urban discontent in the early years of the Thatcher government. Major, it was contended, was part and parcel of this environment, and was shaped by his memories of his time there. This was underscored by the presentation of a political party broadcast which concentrated upon Major's origins. Major himself was reluctant to press home any political manifesto which concentrated upon his past. Following discussion and persuasion Major eventually acceded to the creation of a broadcast.[35] It was produced by John Schlesinger and was entitled 'Journey Home'. It concentrated upon the character and social origins of Major and had an unashamedly autobiographical imprint. In many respects it mirrored an attempt by Kinnock to present a personalised party political broadcast in 1987, which had appeared to have boosted Kinnock's opinion poll statistics, but was disliked by Major.[36] Nevertheless the prime minister was pictured arriving at his childhood Brixton home, expressing his surprise that it still stood and reminiscing about the times he had spent there. In addition he ventured out to buy tomatoes and kippers. Shaun Woodward argued that the presentation was important in that it implied a classless society and, central to the policy implication, accentuated 'Major's own character and achievement'.[37] However, for all the efforts to present an image of a poor individual who had transcended class barriers the message was not greeted particularly enthusiastically. Research highlighted that 'Major was seen as a bit of a wet. They [the public] don't deny that he is a nice bloke, but he came across as too soft.'[38] Similarly Reese argued, 'The film's only error was to concentrate on shots of John Major talking about his early life from the back of a comfortable car – the visual image projected was hardly that of an accessible man of the people'.[39] Popular concern also focussed on the fact that Major toured the impoverished area in a Daimler, and that he was not wearing a safety belt when in the back of the car.[40] There were evidently problems in ridding the stereotypical image of the Conservative party as elitist, and thereafter accentuating the social attributes of John Major as its leader. This was largely because Major was one of the few candidates on the centre-right who could attest to a genuine background in keeping with mass interpretations of, and identification with, ordinariness.

The 1992 election was about more than rhetoric and party broadcasts. It was also about conveying an image that would be readily conveyed on national news, a realm where swing voters and those uninterested in politics might be more likely to come across political information of note. Major's approach to the election was to make himself look to be a product of ordinary society, comfortable with the mundane aspects of life, and in touch with the everyday person on the street. He declared that he enjoyed eating in *Little Chef* restaurants, as though to underscore his image as a person not attracted to sophistication and in tune with the experiences of mainstream society.[41] He undertook his campaign strategy, with attendant security and personal risk, by speaking to audiences atop a wooden crate. Nicholas Jones considered this to be a feature designed to give a distinctive appeal to the campaign. It was a gesture to the recent political past, and generated a sense of positive feeling for the future. He observed how Major linked Socialist Workers' Party protesters to the mob-rule of the winter of discontent, and when a child joined Major on his crate, he proclaimed 'This is the boy the future's about. This is what the election's about...this boy's future.'[42] He conveyed his understanding of the strategy in his memoirs, 'The soapbox became one of the icons of the election, much mocked, but whenever it appeared a sure crowd puller'.[43] Moreover Major portrayed himself as a political warrior whose appeal transcended traditional class barriers. During the campaign he alluded to an incident where he was campaigning directly to a crowd: 'a tattooed skinhead pushed his way into my path. I tensed inwardly as I felt my protection officer thrust himself between us. The skinhead reached out to clutch my arm. "Ere, John," he cried out. "Don't let Labour get away with it" – and he shouted more encouragement as the crowd bore him away. The opinion polls never caught the views of people like him.'[44] Major battled during the election to counter perceptions of his own social status and standing, and party stereotypes concerning who the Conservative party stood for and how this manifested itself in the electoral theatre. Although not necessarily decisive in 1992, the role of the party leaders, alongside how much they were perceived to be in touch with ordinary people and the mainstream of British public opinion, was an issue which was considered to be important by the campaign advisors.

Major appeared to be irked by the evolution of spin, marketing and the conception of politics as a marketable product at different times of his tenure as leader. True, he did have a genuine and legitimate advantage over many of the politicians on the centre-right of British politics, but as public relations developed through the 1990s, eventually to peak with the emergence of spin as a central component of the New Labour political product, Major looked to be alienated by the overall process. He attempted to delineate himself from the processes involved and argued, 'The glib phrases, the sound bites, the ritual conflicts – all these may be the daily stuff of life for the upper one thousand of politics. But to the fifty million other people in this country, they are utterly irrelevant. My interest is with them.'[45] This type of populist rhetoric was meaningful to Major as he led the nation, but it appeared old fashioned. Increasingly candidates, whether from elite or ordinary stock had little choice but to engage with public relations. However, the emergence of skilled and adept spin machines created an environment where differentiating between the genuine presentation of ordinariness and its manufacture became increasingly difficult for the voter.

Major also associated his political policies to his social origins, attempting to portray them as a source of motivation and justification for his political platform. This was advanced through a policy mandate through the catchphrase 'Back to Basics' endeavouring to address the fundamental aspects of the causes of ineffective social policy in the United Kingdom. Major perceived the rational for this in a way in keeping with the core argument of this text. He argued 'I wanted to bring back politics on a human scale'.[46] In legitimising his perception of societal disrepair he considered, in his memoirs, that the Conservative party might be perceived to be neglectful of sections of the community affected by central aspects of social policy. However, Major perceived his own social position and understanding, combined with his political power to be an important mix in the creation of a responsive outcome. He argued, 'I never overlooked them. How could anyone with a Brixton boyhood like me do so? I knew very well the temptations which crowd the path of anyone whose life or prospects seem hopeless. I have seen how bad environments breed mischief, and mischief breeds bad environments; and how an upbringing can curse – or bless – a child for ever.'[47] Imbued served with more legitimacy than that offered by a number of the other political leaders and figures in this text Major's integration of his social and emotional credibility, placed alongside his political standing shaped his political character and allowed him, particularly during the 1992 election, to cast himself as a genuine product of the people.

Conclusion

In the 1980s and 1990s the Conservative party struggled to convey the impression that it, as an institution, was in touch with ordinary people. As identified in Chapter 1 the idea of self or subjective reference allowed significant leeway for individuals to consider themselves as ordinary, irrespective of their income bracket. Both Thatcher and Major, as leaders across a significant time period in modern politics faced challenges in presenting themselves as leaders who were consistently in touch with mainstream opinion. This entailed not only presenting policies which were considered salient to the public, but also in the creation of personal political identities which would demonstrate that leaders were akin and familiar with the plight of key socio-demographic sections of society.

It is evident that both Major and Thatcher sought to counter charges of aloofness by attesting to backgrounds and experiences encountered by virtually all the potential voting block. Both accentuated their regional backgrounds and aspects of childhood and youth impoverishment. The message was political in its orientation, but with a largely non-political content. In essence this was easier for Major to advance as he, it can be argued, could make greater political capital from his Brixton origins. Thatcher however embellished her background into a romanticised vision of England, founded on a vision of a community spirit. Both used family and family ties to demonstrate an understanding of social issues, economic conditions and to advance themselves as emotional and caring individuals. Discussion of pastimes and the mundane suggested that both had endured across their pre-political careers lives that were entirely in keeping with that of the general populace. That it made for media and political discussion suggests that, even in an era where British appreciation of spin control was largely in its infancy, there was an understanding of what was desired, as much personally as politically, of the contemporary political candidate.

The challenges presented to both Thatcher and Major were pronounced in this area. Throughout the period in question the opposition leaders of the Labour party were consistently thought to be more ordinary and able to understand the issues affecting ordinary people. This is not to say that Thatcher and Major were at a critical electoral disadvantage in this realm, as other issues and factors were, and are, needed to accommodate the overall choices of the voters. However, that both attempted to push themselves to the fore as individuals of a common stock is testament to the perceived need to associate with the electorate, whatever the true class and social standing of the leaders and candidates in question. This was, as outlined, particularly important for a party on the right, one which promoted leaders who were perceived to come from elite sections within the British class structure. Thatcher and Major both needed to attract political support outside the realm of the middle class and Thatcher's enticement of Basildon man to her electoral fold, the epitome of the ordinary voter, was key to her electoral success.[48]

The core tools in advancing perceptions of ordinariness to the public appear, in the leadership profiles under consideration in this chapter, to be grounded in areas that are initially beyond the control of the individual candidate. Place of birth, the wealth owned by the family, parental occupation and educational background; all were utilised by

Thatcher and Major to justify and explain their political understandings and ordinariness, but all were largely, in the early stages of their
careers issues beyond their individual control. Both advanced themselves as the products of their own chosen backgrounds, with chosen
periods of residency and occupation selected to stress parts of candidate
background that might create resonance with the public. This strategic
selection is now commonplace in the marketing of the personalities
and characters of candidates.

The social standing and position of the political leadership in the
United Kingdom presents challenges with respect to political marketing. In the era when marketing has come to the fore, and has been
identified as a meaningful element in the creation of the identity of a
political leader virtually every leader still comes from a social position
whereby political marketing has to be used to alter popular perceptions
of where they stand. In Chapter 7 it is evident that even for Labour,
a party once traditionally working class in its orientation, with Prime
Minister Blair and thereafter Brown, political manipulation of the social
and emotional connections of the leadership were essential in persuading the voter that they were associated with the politics of being ordinary. Voters appear, at least as far as the topic can be measured, to desire
a political leadership that is close to both an individual and subjective
understanding of ordinariness.

4
Confronting an Elite Identity

During the 1970s and 1980s there existed, within the United States, a number of elections where candidates could advance themselves with a range of social and political identities, from those of a populist disposition to those considered part and parcel of elite culture. As highlighted in Chapter 2, particularly with respect to John F. Kennedy, although elite standing was not always actively advanced as a political asset, it was not always thought to be necessary to extensively remake the identity of a candidate so as to give them electoral credibility. By the time Reagan entered office it was clear that the political environment had changed. Although not as pronounced as the manufacturing and marketing of political identity discussed in later chapters of this text there was nevertheless a change to a series of positions which embraced the remaking and shaping of a candidate's autobiographical past combined with the advocacy of populist identities and rhetoric, if not always populist policies.

This chapter considers how Reagan and Clinton marketed themselves to the American people as political candidates with identities rooted in mainstream culture. Both had claims, in many respects legitimate ones, that they could advance themselves as ordinary Americans who had discovered talents in politics and public life. Reagan advanced himself as a man who had experienced a change of political identity when young and as a person who had, in a classless context, experienced the American dream. While this may indeed have been the case, to a large extent, the image of normality and ordinariness still had to be marketed to the public. In a period of pronounced international tension and significant social and economic reform Reagan was required to provide authoritative leadership while not appearing to be aloof from his core Republican constituency or pivotal swing voters. Additionally Reagan faced many challenges and entertained many contradictions. On the one hand his economic reforms appeared to give significant advantages to the interests of corporate and moneyed America. On the other he was able to attract a number of voters to the Republican fold who appeared to vote against their own economic interests, the Reagan Democrats. Part of this was achieved on the foundation of protest against the pitfalls encountered by President Carter and the Democrats, but part was also created by the attraction of Reagan as a person and his social and emotional appeals to this group. He entertained largely positive approval ratings, as opposed to job approval ratings, throughout his time in the presidential office.

With respect to the leaders discussed in this text, Reagan's successor was faced with perhaps the most trying of circumstances. George Bush Sr found himself challenged for a second term in office by Bill Clinton, who played heavily on an autobiographical ticket. He also faced a third party candidate who had extensive personal wealth, Ross Perot. Bush therefore found himself in the middle of a difficult quandary, as to attack wealth as a socially divisive issue was problematic given his own moneyed position and that of one of his opponents. To defend wealth and elite moneyed interests and to embrace essence of Reagan's economic boom and its subsequent fallout was to also neglect those affected by the pronounced economic recession of the early 1990s. As a consequence Bush faced challenges in creating a political identity which associated him with voters afflicted by economic hardship. For Clinton and Perot the personal associations with wealth were easier to accommodate and to market. Perot dispensed with convention and simply presented himself as an individual, albeit a plain speaking and folksy one, who was unashamed of his wealth and would represent the national interest of America in the economic realm. Debate on his character did come to the fore, as did discussion about his personal wealth, however as an independent it remained unclear as to whether he was on the threshold of the emergence of a political movement of note, or whether he was simply the embodiment of a potential protest vote against Bush. Bill Clinton presented himself as a man who assumed a number of political identities and could adopt roles to suit the needs of the prevailing audience. Indeed, in keeping with the overall concept of political marketing, Clinton adopted different personas to suit the political environment, reinventing his identity to appeal to specific demographic groups. At times this entailed trying to present distinctive personal characteristics to mass audiences, on other occasions it entailed tailoring his past to convey images of inclusiveness or accentuating periods of trial and hardship.

The period during which the presidency passed from Reagan to Bush and then to Clinton marked an important benchmark for political marketing and individual candidate identity with respect to wealth. All three presidents grappled with the creation of identities during periods of economic prosperity and recession. Furthermore, all had to face the impact of the creation of the Reagan Democrats, suggesting that economic policy was not all that dictated the rational voting choice of the electorate. All faced challenges and pursued strategies that were quite distinct from one another, yet entertained the same end goal, namely to show both ordinariness in general life and in their past, and exceptionalism in the contemporaneous political realm. The lessons of the Reagan–Clinton period are many. In advance of the 2004 election, all the major candidates had, by that time, adopted quite similar strategies in trying to run on an autobiographical ticket to the public in order to demonstrate these qualities.

Ronald Reagan

A political populist?

Reagan was a president who campaigned on his image as much as his policy record and policy outcomes. His image was that of a political leader who understood the populace, attracted unconventional and non-traditional voting groups to the Republican fold and created a renewed feeling of energy and optimism in the Oval Office. This followed a period of malaise following the Vietnam conflict and uncertainty about the domestic policy path to be followed after turbulent problems with the economy and energy provision. In many contexts Reagan's popularity was attributable to the period during which he occupied the office, looking positive and outgoing in comparison to the more austere images presented by both his predecessor Carter and successor Bush. Additionally, although plagued by economic recessions, political scandals and the tensions of the closing stages of the Cold War, Reagan won two elections, and was one of the few modern presidents who actually left office with a higher approval rating than when he arrived. For all the positive and negative aspects of his presidency it appeared, superficially at least, that the American public had affection for Reagan and the way in which he marketed himself and his office.

Although a considerable amount has been written about the communications style undertaken by the Reagan White House and the communications revolution it created in presidential politics, Reagan's identity and the image he created are important to this particular work as he conveyed a manufactured image which cast him as a populist, sympathetic to an extent to the plight of the powerless and ordinary person in America. On a surface level this goes counter to some of the criticisms of Reagan as a wealthy individual who favoured the elite groupings of American society. It is of course common that American presidents are subject to a variety of impressions and interpretations across time about their personal identity and who they represented in the elite framework of politics and economics. However, Reagan appeared to reach out as no previous modern president had done before him to groups whose interests were not necessarily rooted in the traditional ideology of Republican economic policy.

Reagan's manufactured and marketed image appeared relatively easy to pinpoint even a short time into his tenure as President. That he had created an image, and one suited to public needs and consumption preferences, was not lost on elite journalists or those who had observed Reagan's career across time. Reagan was described by columnists at the *New York Times* in 1980 in the following manner, 'Ronald Reagan is by profession a performer, and it is the single most important fact about him'.[1]

Reagan embraced his childhood and the route through which he attained political office in shaping his political image. In an early autobiography, written largely to reflect upon his time as a Hollywood actor, *Where's the Rest of Me?* Reagan mulled over his childhood, spent in a family which occasionally struggled to make ends meet. He recalled, 'My existence turned into one of those rare Huck Finn-Tom Sawyer idylls'.[2] A romanticised and nostalgic reflection upon an impoverished childhood and youth is a common feature of the marketing of an individual identity within politics. Reagan made play of how his father received a redundancy notice instead of a Christmas bonus in 1931, and he shortly thereafter became a supporter of Franklin D. Roosevelt. Lou Cannon considered the publication of this first autobiography to have a purpose in legitimising Reagan's credibility in running for office. Cannon thought that 'His [Reagan's] autobiography ... published the following year when Reagan was preparing to run for governor of California, was his attempt to demonstrate the continuity of life he believed had prepared him for public service'.[3] This was related to the idea that ordinariness was a stock feature of preparation for political office. In his second autobiography which reflected upon both his non-political and political careers, '*An American Life*' Reagan identified the issues which he felt had shaped his early years and how his values as an individual had emerged: 'I'll never forget those Christmases when we didn't have much money but our home radiated with a love and warmth that meant a lot more to me than packages wrapped in colored paper.'[4] Reagan used his childhood and past to convey impressions of ordinariness and an association with the American people. The broad array of images allowed the American voter to consider Reagan, as a person, subjectively, and this assisted in broadening his appeal. There is debate about the extent to which Reagan's personality was greeted positively by the American people. Part of the problem in this instance is the number of favourability ratings that were undertaken on each post-war president, as they vary in number and average ratings are therefore difficult to attain. The evidence does however point towards Reagan as a President who was in the mid-range of the favourability ratings, suggesting that the popular perception of a President who was much-loved by the American people on account of his personality is perhaps exaggerated.[5] For example, Fairness and Accuracy in Reporting critically reviewed the adulation received by Reagan from mainstream media outlets, 'The *Washington Post*'s lead article on June 6 began by declaring him "one of the most popular president[s] of the 20th Century," while ABC's Sam Donaldson announced, "Through travesty, triumph and tragedy, the president enjoyed unprecedented popularity." The *Chicago Tribune* (6/6/04) wrote that "his popularity with the electorate was deep and personal ... rarely did his popularity dip below 50 percent; it often exceeded 70 percent, an extraordinarily high mark"'.[6] This type of reporting, alongside efforts to market Reagan as a popular individual on account of his personality and his character, created a potent backdrop to impressions of his presidency.

Reagan's background and the formation of his political identity and social and emotional associations was pinpointed by several experts on his presidency as important to his political evolution and his emotional appeal. On PBS Robert Dallek discussed Reagan's childhood and youth and how it impacted upon his political identity, 'Reagan imbibes those values. He romanticizes his childhood, remembering the quality of life there as something so appealing, so comfortable, so attractive, it couldn't possibly have been as attractive and comfortable as he depicted it, but it was part of the romantic notion that not only he had but millions of Americans share you see. And I think this was part of Reagan's effectiveness, his political genius ... his capacity to share with the mass of society so many of the romantic notions'.[7] Similarly, veteran *Washington Post* columnist and critical observer of the Reagan presidency, Lou Cannon identified the classic position of the political candidate who could reach out to the populace and use his past for positive political ends. He observed of Reagan, 'He was of humble origins. His parents were poor and his nomadic boyhood darkly shadowed by his father's alcoholism and frequent unemployment'. Further, 'Ordinary people remarked upon his simplicity and good manners and liked being around him, for he had a knack of making them feel good'.[8]

Through his time in politics Reagan tried to reach out to a number of groups and to convey his emotional and social attachment to them. Edmund Morris identified this when analysing Reagan's fist inaugural speech in 1980, 'recurring themes were apparent as his speech ran its plainsong course. One was a populism that addressed itself equally to "Shopkeepers, clerks, cabbies and truck drivers"'.[9] Reagan embraced populist messages, designed both to convey an impression that he associated with the average American, and also to further his political agenda where he was sceptical about the nature, size and role of government in the United States. Terri Bimes considered Reagan's populist rhetoric to be largely located to minor speeches and presentations and rooted historically in his time as a spokesperson for General Electric. When considering how Reagan, an experienced politician by the time he reached the White House, managed to distance himself from government itself Bimes argues, 'Big government, Congress, the Democrats, and intellectual elites were the preferred targets of Reagan's populist appeals. These targets were linked by the broader argument that wasteful intrusive government is sustained by the combination of pork minded Democratic members of the Congress, demanding liberal interest groups and their associated clienteles, and out-of-touch elitist intellectuals. The victims of this combination were the American people, who were generally depicted in their role as taxpayers, as small businessmen and workers, or as the American family.'[10] Again the appeal to ordinary American and ordinariness is pronounced. Similarly Reagan made play of moral issues and his faith in the American people. He largely cast himself as an outsider within government, able to use his past and the manufactured images of his career to sustain an impression that suited the expectations of the American people, particularly in the aftermath of the disaffected politics of the 1970s. Reagan played a populist card that led to both an ideological movement, and also responded to the political marketplace of the time. Populism, as practiced by Reagan, unified social groups around a political message which presented the candidate as part and parcel of the voting block. It also offered a degree of control for the ordinary person who felt alienated by the interests of business and politics. As Bresler commented 'Populists speak to the unarticulated frustrations of ordinary citizens beset by economic and cultural changes beyond their control or comprehension'. In addition, 'Reagan understood that working-class Democrats no longer equated their economic interests with the growth of the state.'[11] The marketing of Reagan's economic policy created a new political coalition which the Democrats found hard to reabsorb into their fold in the short term. Reagan Democrats, attracted by morals, anti- government and anti-communist rhetoric, alongside a candidate who seemed to mirror their emotional and social thinking, were perceived as an important force in American politics in the 1980s. Reagan's targets were often ill-defined, but his main grievances revolved around big government and the liberal elite.[12] He advanced the interests of families, underpinned by strong moral values, and entertained the idea of 'diligent toil, moral piety, and self governing communities'.[13] A core feature of Reagan's political thought and action however was that the impressions he conveyed were not necessarily carried through into active policies. His appeal to ordinary Americans was based as much on balancing out the interests of corporate America as it was in serving the needs of blue-collar America. Reagan cast himself as an ordinary person who, particularly in the fledgling era of his political career was the product of an ordinary background. In a historical context, Bimes identified that this was in keeping with Truman's portrayal of himself as a citizen politician, Truman having stated that he was an 'ordinary citizen of this great Republic of ours who has the greatest responsibility in the world'.[14] Bimes believed that Reagan 'retained the same basic populist sense that politics was largely a struggle between ordinary Americans and a self serving elite'.[15] This largely allowed Reagan to play to both an elite and ordinary constituency at the same time, advocating expansive tax cuts for those on high incomes on the one hand, with a promise and expectation that the same cuts would bring about abundance for the many through trickle down, or supply side, economics on the other. This was considered to be a form of conservative populism that would appeal to all social groups, although it appeared to have greater credibility as a theoretical concept and lost much of its legitimacy when it failed to live up to its initial promise.[16]

Reagan's attempts to associate himself with a number of social and economic groups appears to have had a complex impact upon the electorate. While he associated himself culturally with the electorate, and played to an array of disparate constituencies there nevertheless remained an underlying perception that while Reagan might be portrayed as an ordinary America, and cast himself as such, Reagan's policies clearly advantaged the wealthy in America. As the 1980s progressed Reagan's policies were increasingly perceived to have disproportionately favoured the wealthy. Although he retained his folksy image, and was considered to be a person who cared, the practicalities of his Republican ideology appeared to present the voter with a person whose manufactured identity did not always sit squarely with his policies. In a Conference Board/National Family Opinion National Poll taken in 1988 a sample was asked, 'Compared to eight years ago, how do you feel the circumstances of each of the following groups are today?'[17] The reply included these statistics:

	Better (%)	Same(%)	Worse(%)
High-income families	82	15	3
Middle Class	20	40	39
Poor People	11	23	67

Note: Statistics are as in original.

This is not to say that Reagan was thought to have wholly neglected or had alienated those in the lower income brackets. In 1980 and in 1984 he acquired the vote of one in four Democrats, testament to his appeal to those in class positions which did not sit squarely with his Republican free market ideology.[18] Across time however the limitations in the concept of trickle down economics were pronounced, and Reagan's associations with the poorest in America became increasingly strained.

Reagan's legacy with respect to political marketing was to suggest that an array of images and rhetoric could be persuasive in forming personal support and a voting coalition that transcended class boundaries. Subtle populist rhetoric and the presentation of an individual who had come from humble origins gave Reagan an ability to reach out, personally as well as politically, to social groups on account of his political identity. Reagan embraced a mythical concept of the West, cultivated a reputation as a great communicator, yet still celebrated the accumulation of wealth and the splendour of his Hollywood past. In passing the baton to George Bush; Reagan left a political office that was conscious of image, identity and the power of selling a president on the grounds of character and optimism as much as policies and political ideology. Following Reagan's death in 2004 the *San Francisco Chronicle* offered its own observation of the former Governor and President, 'But even as the politically powerful recall Reagan's impact on their lives and careers, it is the "regular guy" who found it easy to connect with a governor and president who seemed like such a regular guy himself'.[19]

George Bush Sr

The experience of George Bush Sr is instructive when considering the interplay between wealth, elitism and presentation of political figures as ordinary. Having served as vice president for eight years under Reagan, and having also sought to contest the presidency by running in the Republican primaries in 1980, Bush was well placed to observe and thereafter create an identity which might appeal to both the Republican voter of the Reagan era, and the pivotal Reagan Democrats discussed previously in this chapter. However, his political experience and party affiliation aside, he faced problems because of his socio-economic position and how it was perceived. One Bush aide believed that for all success enjoyed by Reagan in terms of the celebration of his character there still existed an opportunity for Bush to craft his own distinctive, and 'regular' identity. He stated, 'The office of the President tends to stiffen you and Ronald Reagan knew how to deal with that almost incomparably. Bush may not have the movie-star finesse of President Reagan, but he comes across as a genuine guy. He just has to work to get that earthiness across.'[20] Other issues which impacted on Bush's tenure included the nature of his opponents and the environmental conditions present in America in the early 1990s. Recession, a resurgent Democrat party with a credible presidential candidate and a third party protest in the form of a maverick billionaire made the 1992 election and the period preceding it one where political positions relating to wealth, identity and the electorate, were important.

In the 2004 American presidential race reflections were made about how George Bush Jr was orchestrating his campaign strategy and how this contrasted with the strategy entertained by his father. The *Christian Science Monitor* argued that Bush Jr had to be, and was being, careful not to replicate history. It contended that 'Bush is also making sure that he doesn't repeat the mistake of his father, the first President Bush, who in 1992 appeared out-of-touch with the concerns of average people and failed to convince the public that the nation had pulled out of recession'.[21] It also argued that in 1992 Bush's opponent, Bill Clinton, had pioneered aspects of a populist marketing strategy designed to encourage voters to feel that he was on the ground and was in touch with their concerns, the 'technique of touring by bus'. Clinton argued that this was a strategy designed to 'bring us into small towns and rural areas never visited in modern presidential campaigns'.[22]

George Bush Sr faced several difficulties when trying to create a political identity that would resonate with the interests of voters. Firstly, he could not advance himself as an outsider, as a person who was removed from the policy process and political character of the Washington establishment. He was tied integrally to the policies and identity of the Reagan administration and as such, advancing political ideas that were critical of Washington institutions, in the way that other candidates were able to do, was largely beyond his remit. Secondly, it was difficult to advance his own personal political identity as one rooted in the ordinary or mundane. Although he had served his country bravely in the Second World War, and had been shot down twice over the Pacific, he was perceived to be an individual from a wealthy background, and a beneficiary of business interests in oil. His dual identity of having a Texan background but a family base in Maine also lent some weight behind the impression that he was a man of wealth, somewhat removed from mainstream society. As detailed with respect to the Reagan presidency, the policies pursued by that administration were thought, by small majorities in opinion polls, to have favoured the wealthy. Reagan attempted to counter this with a muted populist message. If Bush was going to retain a broad cross-section of voters he had to dispel with the perception of favouring the elites without creating rifts within his party about the ideological direction he was pursuing. This was pronounced when Pat Buchanan launched an irksome, but ultimately futile, run for the Republican nomination in early 1992. On top of Bush's problems, and taking account of the environmental background that was present during the era of his candidacy and presidency, there also existed the contrast with Reagan on character. Affection for Reagan was, as previously discussed, perceived to be prominent as he vacated the presidential office. Although there was dispute about the impact and nature of his policies, on a personal level he was admired and perceived as a warm and caring individual. Naturally part of this was down to the impression that was desired by his White House; however, it set a difficult benchmark for Bush to emulate.

Bush succeeded in seeing off the challenge of Michael Dukakis in the 1988 presidential election. Bush appeared to suffer in the first instance from his social position and was perceived to be part of America's elite, the same elite thought to have benefited from Reagan's economic policy. There were fears that this would create a gulf with the electorate.

As observed in the *Sunday Times* 'Reagan is western boots and chopping wood to Bush's Lacoste shorts and tennis shoes. ... Reagan makes all those in the lumpen electorate who also went to a mediocre college feel better. Then along comes George Bush, who is everything they're not – Greenwich, Andover, Yale, captain of the Yale baseball team, elitist clubman – and because he cannot be identified with any issues, people focus on the manners of his class.'[23] In order to try and create a distinct difference between himself and Dukakis, Bush tried to concentrate on presenting himself as a more compassionate individual than some of his Republican predecessors. Part of the reason for this was to create emotional bonds and 'to emphasise shared values, with their emotive charge, as distinct from the managerial emphasis of Dukakis'.[24]

By way of a marker for Bush's successes and failures in advancing himself as a person who could identify with the electorate, discussion largely involved a consideration of how he was presented by the media, and how opposition forces failed to capitalise on his position in 1988, but capitalised on it in 1992. Kevin Phillips contends that in 1988 the Democrats, and their candidate Michael Dukakis, shied away from accusing the Republicans of elitism, and were reluctant to wage a campaign based on class or socio-economic based politics. As Phillips said of the Republicans, 'All too aware of George Bush's own upper-class background and presumed vulnerability to populist themes, Republican strategists could hardly believe their luck'.[25] Dukakis failed to create any momentum which criticised Bush as an individual, nor did he make the issue of wealth one which could be utilised so as to provide him with a populist mandate. Newspapers cast the candidates as being from the upper middle class, and in this context there was little to be gained from trying to criticise individuals or opponents from the same social stock. Bush did try to reach out to the ordinary voter – with phrases and ideas reminiscent of Nixon's appeals to a great silent majority in 1968. At the Republican convention of 1988 Bush stated, 'I may sometimes be a little awkward but there's nothing self-conscious in my love of country. I am a quiet man, but I hear the quiet people others don't – the ones who raise the family, pay the taxes, meet the mortgage. I hear them and I am moved, and their concerns are mine.' While this had resonance, it only worked against a backdrop of the Reagan era, and against a weak opposition candidate who struggled to shrug off doubts about his policies, particularly on the environment and crime, and his personal attributes. Iain Duncan Smith tried the same approach in the United Kingdom with little success. Nonetheless the appeal to emotions and to values over policy detail was a feature of the campaign. It rebounded badly against

Dukakis, who was negatively branded the ice-man on the grounds of his unemotional demeanour. Bush's aides sought to exploit this issue through stark contrasts, 'Bush strategists had known they had to spruce up the Vice President's image. George Bush was seen as awkward, wimpish, maladroit. So Bush's handlers engineered a makeover. They had him utter self-deprecating cracks about his lack of charisma. They arranged for him to be photographed amid his photogenic grandchildren. ... His aides later christened the contest the Nice Man vs. the Ice Man. The idea was to portray Bush's occasional goofiness as engaging, and Dukakis' competence as soulless.'[26] Pollster Richard Wirthlin argued, 'You move people's votes through emotion, and the best way to give an emotional cut to your message is through talking about values. Bush has to do that. He has to touch the values of family, self-esteem, hope, opportunity, security!'[27] This appeared to work in 1988. Yet, by 1992 Bush appeared to have become disconnected from the electorate and the issue of his wealth, and the connections he was able to make with the voter emotionally were limited and increasingly strained.

The 1992 election

A pivotal shift in the emergence of a political identity that was marketed on the ground of wealth came with Bush's contesting of the 1992 presidential election. This came against a background where he had entertained both high and low points in the opinion polls. His waging of a war in the Middle East to liberate Kuwait from an invasion by Iraq led to historically high job approval figures. These however proved to be short-term and somewhat superficial in nature. The onset of a pronounced recession within the United States, and the perception of outside interference in the American economy from the Tiger economies of South East Asia created both a material and psychological concern for many Americans. This created a peculiar backdrop to the election. Bush was experienced, had successfully won an election in 1988, had workable coalitions and could point to a successful stewardship in foreign policy. However, when it came to issues that were considered important to the American voter, the domestic economy was considered the most salient. When many Americans, including on this occasion segments of the middle class, suffered from unemployment and downsizing, Bush appeared to be immune and removed from the plight of ordinary Americans.

This was interpreted in several different ways and was a prominent feature of the campaign. The battle lines were clear. Bush was thought not to care about the plight faced by those burdened by the recession, and had to try to sell himself as a person who could identify with those Americans suffering economic problems. The opposition candidates aimed to show that they cared, that as individuals they had not only the policies that were needed to alleviate the recession and inflate the economy, but also that they understood and could socially and emotionally associate with the American people. Bush was cast in a simplistic light by the media, as a person who, as much as he protested, was unable to forge a new political relationship or bridge the gulf with the American electorate. Goldman et al. observed in the *Quest for the Presidency 1992* that by the time of the presidential election, 'His seeming diffidence till then had only reinforced the deadly impression that he was out of touch with the people and that he was unconcerned with their problems'.[28] By way of example, Bush himself recited this type of problem as a meaningful one when discussing his presidency and its legacy with the Academy of Achievement. He mentioned reporting of his activity by the media, specifically pinpointing a comment that 'Bush is a President that's out of touch. He came from a privileged background, [and] doesn't understand the hurt around this country.' Thereafter he discussed how he had been shown a scanner in a grocery store and had commented on its innovative technology. Although he was aware of the widespread use of supermarket scanners, this particular type utilised new methods and Bush's enthusiastic response was, he claimed, as a consequence of this particular innovation in the product, not as a consequence of his being unaware of the nature of contemporary supermarkets. In the Academy interview Bush stated:

> A lazy little journalist with a famous name working for The *New York Times*, the son of a decent and honorable father, but a lazy little journalist, was sitting in another room. He didn't see this. He wrote that, 'Here is Bush, he's out of touch. He saw a scanner. He didn't even know that at supermarkets you can scan something.' It played right into the hands of the press that wanted to show I was out of touch and it was picked up.
>
> We pointed out to the press afterwards that, one, the guy wasn't there; two, this was brand new technology. CBS, not my favorite, came and defended me. Another one of the wire service reporters said that I got a bum rap, but the people don't remember that. What they remember is that I was out of touch, that I didn't even know what a grocery scanner was. You can't fight back against that kind of thing.[29]

In political marketing Bush was clearly, in this instance, unable to convey to the populace that he was genuinely aware of, and sympathetic to, the plight of those affected by recession, or that he was in tune with contemporaneous developments. While he may have claimed that the miscommunication in this instance was down to ineptitude on the part of elements of the press corps there was evidently an inability, even when Bush argued that he did care, to convey it as a genuine and well-meant emotion. At face value it was a minor issue. However, it was a theme to which every American voter could relate.

One of the reasons for the problem was communication, and the perception of Bush's personal wealth and its political ramifications were hard to dispel. Bush's methods of politics and political campaigning, while evidently credible, were largely rooted in old school politics, and when challenged by Clinton in 1992 there appeared a gulf, of both method and understanding, between the candidates. By way of highlighting the division between the candidates and the more efficient marketing of a personal political identity by Clinton the 1992 presidential debates serve as a marker. Although all the debates were considered to be interesting and informative, particularly with the presence of third party candidate Ross Perot, whose good showing made for extensive news commentary, the debate at Richmond, Virginia was particularly important in highlighting the main premise of this text, that a political identity in the modern era must increasingly revolve around the impression that the candidate shares the life experiences and understandings of the electorate, and that personal wealth does not, if marketed effectively, create a gulf of feeling or understanding between the elected and the electorate.

The three candidates in the election debate, Bush, Clinton and Perot were all asked the same question by an audience member and then were given an opportunity, in turn, to respond. There was room therefore to endorse the answer given by others in the debate or to forge an individual political identity by assuming a distinctive or unique answer to any set question. A woman, Marina Hall, asked a double barrelled question of the candidates. Firstly, 'How has the national debt personally affected each of your lives?' and secondly, 'How can you honestly find a cure for the economic problems of the common people, if you have no experience in what's ailing them?' In this instance each of the candidates adopted slightly different responses to one another, and each received distinctly different interpretations of the merits of their answer.[30] Once again however, as the questions used by Hall indicate, the common person was deemed to be an important player in the election cycle, as ill-defined and broad as the term 'common people' was.

Perot argued that he, although only marginally affected by the deficit, cared enough to serve a public calling and sacrifice his private and business life for the common good. He was not in a position to argue any degree of impoverishment, his billionaire status being a prominent feature of campaign discussion. He did stress a modest background, his wealth having been self-made, but, in keeping with the overall thrust of his campaign, he presented himself as an economic reformer who could advance wealth for all through a revived American economy. Perot's overall approach to the campaign did not rest exclusively on trying to present himself as a poor person who had come to wealth through personal effort. That aspect was known, but Perot concentrated on trying to give the impression that his economic expertise would give him electoral credibility rather than play heavily on his life story. In some respects Perot was trying to buck the trend in 1992, with an unorthodox and innovative campaign. Ultimately with his 30 minute infomercials, his stepping down and then re-entering of the race, and problems with his campaign staff Perot had little chance of making an impact. Although in the debates he was thought to have been a credible and worthy candidate and the perceived victor in several of the discussions, he did not win a single state in November and therefore received no electoral college votes.

Clinton's approach to the deficit question was to try to associate himself with the questioner by expressing a personal interest in the question. Although he could not personally testify to having been affected by the deficit in an untoward manner, he tried to associate with the questioner and the issue on an emotional level, trying to subjectively address the problem. This was in contrast to Perot's objective consideration of the issue. Clinton could advance a strategy on two fronts in this instance. He related his understanding of impoverishment on the basis of his prior experience as Governor of Arkansas and as a consequence of his having assisted in the economic development in one of the poorer states of the Union. He stated, 'Well, I've been governor of a small state for 12 years. I'll tell you how it's affected me. Every year Congress and the president sign laws that make us do more things and gives us less money to do it with. I see people in my state, middle class people – their taxes have gone up in Washington and their services have gone down while the wealthy have gotten tax cuts.'[31] Clinton tried to empathise with the questioner. Anne Wortham considered Clinton to be in a position in this regard that was advantageous when compared to the other candidates. His personal background combined with his political experience placed him in a position where he could testify, with some legitimacy, that he actually did understand the problems faced by the questioner. She stated about Clinton's general communication strategy, 'His remarks were well received, and both the press and the public defined him as someone who could "relate" to people's troubles'.[32] Wortham considered Clinton to be a 'victimist populist' who used problems, both his own and those experienced by others, to facilitate in building a political relationship with voters. Maggs considered that Clinton was provided with a platform for debate that allowed him to communicate with the populace in a form that allowed him to 'feel their pain'.[33] The emotional content of Clinton's response sold him as a political figure who identified with those beset by problems, and as a person able to forge emotional bonds with the electorate. *Time*, in identifying Clinton as its 'Person of the Year 1992', alluded to Clinton's responses in the Richmond debate as part of its reasons for its selection. It commented, 'Bill Clinton has a side of his character that is a mellow talk-show host. The nation saw this Donahue–Oprah style at work during the second presidential debate in the campaign'.[34]

President Bush faced difficulties in addressing the deficit question, and in an era of recession and alienation about the economy, the mix of the political and the personal presented him with a number of problems. He could not disassociate himself from the economic plight of the nation having been integrally tied to economic management across a number of years. Although the issue was a shared one with other institutions in the American political process it fell to Bush to try to alleviate concern, assert that the problems could be dealt with and demonstrate that he cared about the economic fallout the recession had created. Bush struggled to address the question as he was pressed to give an answer that emphasised his personal association with the deficit, rather than any objective considerations about the national impact of the deficit. At one point in his response he stated, 'I'm not sure I get it. Help me with the question here and I'll try to answer it.' This was interpreted as a sign that Bush was distanced and aloof from the conditions experienced by ordinary people.[35] The questioner in the audience repeated the question to enhance its personal impact on Bush, stating, 'I know people who cannot afford to pay the mortgage on their homes, their car payment. I have personal problems with the national debt. But how has it affected you and if you have no experience in it, how can you help us, if you don't know what we're feeling?'[36] The emotional content of the question alongside its subjective nature made it difficult for Bush to disassociate himself from his wealth. He declared that he did care about those suffering from economic distress, but his most important comment was deemed to show a logical understanding of the issues, but not an emotional one. He stated, 'But I don't think it's fair to say, you haven't had cancer. Therefore, you don't know what's it like. I don't think it's fair to say, you know, whatever it is, that if you haven't been hit by it personally. But everybody's affected by the debt because of the tremendous interest that goes into paying on that debt everything's more expensive. Everything comes out of your pocket and my pocket. So it's that.'[37] Bush's response was greeted critically by the media. However, it had a logic that appeared to give credence to his political experience and his awareness of problems. The assumption that he actually needed to be affected by economic misfortune in order to understand it was evidently erroneous. Anne Wortham considered that the question was presented in such a fashion that it created a scenario where, on the grounds of their personal wealth and positions within politics, all the candidates lied to try to create an impression that they were part of mainstream society. 'Each candidate must have grasped that his credibility rested on telling a lie in order to give symbolic substance to Hall's fallacious assumption that only a leader who had himself experienced the economic problems of "the common people" could find a solution to those problems.'[38]

Bush's concerns were pronounced in the aftermath of the debate, with no upturn in the national economy, a persistent perception that he did not care and an impression that his wealth created a divide between himself and the rest of the nation. That both Clinton and Perot were wealthy individuals did not seem to have a significant popular impact on their campaigns as both adopted different strategies in trying to associate with the American people, Perot adopting an objective and business oriented approach which largely did away with social and emotional connections, and Clinton fully embracing personal issues as a central part of his campaign. With many problems in his personal life, he worked to create a connection with voting blocks regardless of their socio-economic standing or background.

Clinton emerged into the 1992 presidential election race as something of a surprise candidate. He had prepared the groundwork to allow him to run, but also had reservations on the grounds of there potentially being candidates who might be better suited to the Democratic nomination, such as Mario Cuomo. His legacy from the Democratic convention of 1988, where he had badly overrun when giving a speech, was considered to be detrimental to his prospects. These potential problems dissipated as the race unfolded and Clinton was able to bring a candidacy to an election where he exploited both his personal strengths and weaknesses, autobiographical elements and a troubled private life. On the face of it Clinton emerged from a typical and familiar background, having been the Governor of Arkansas. Yet a strategic exploitation of personal failings allowed him to claim a personal association with many voters, and in contrast to his opponents his social standing and personal wealth was surpassed and overshadowed by his emotional relationship with voters.

Bill Clinton

Bonding with 'regular' Americans

Clinton was in a very beneficial position when it came to marketing himself to America's voters. His wealth and elite social position were not a campaign issue, and indeed were marginal considerations through his time in office. Even with the evolution of the Whitewater scandal and widespread dissemination of details on the Clintons' wealth and investments, accusations of social elitism were not levelled at the Clintons as an issue of controversy or contention. Bill Clinton was able to advance himself, partly through personal skill and partly through marketing strategy, in a number of guises. As Martin Walker outlined in *Clinton: The President They Deserve* there were many dimensions to Clinton the man, and these could be used as necessary to sell particular messages to specific audiences. Walker identified two dimensions as follows. On the one hand Clinton could market himself as

> born poor in a poor and backward state.... His daddy died in a car wreck before he was born. His mother married five times, twice to the same man, and buried three husbands. He was raised by an alcoholic stepfather, who beat his mother, fired the occasional drunken pistol shot into the house wall to get her attention, and was only deterred when young Bill challenged him.

By way of contrast, there existed another Clinton

> the classic scholarship boy, from a modestly comfortable home. He was a perfect symbol of the great American meritocracy that exploded after 1945 into the creation of that profound social revolution, a mass middle class...his mother applied herself to improve her skills and become a nurse anaesthetist, and resolved that her elder son should

rise even further and faster. He was spoiled by his mother, given the master bedroom in the ranch-style suburban home, and drove to high school in his own car[39]

As Clinton's political career progressed he could choose which of the images he wished to convey and sell himself to the appropriate audience. It was a similar case with his marriage to Hillary. On the one hand he could present their partnership as one founded on intellect, affection and a drive to serve the American public. On the other the relationship appeared to be beset by difficulties. It was subject to press scrutiny, which at times appeared to be excessively intrusive and destabilising to Clinton's campaign. Numerous claims were made that Clinton had strayed from his marriage when Governor of Arkansas. One individual, Gennifer Flowers, claimed to have had a 12-year affair with Clinton and timed her revelations to coincide with the pivotal New Hampshire primary at the start of the election year.[40] However, instead of avoiding the issue the Clintons appeared on 60 minutes, in a primetime slot following the Super Bowl, and argued their case about Clinton's alleged extra-marital affairs. Ordinarily, as was the case with Gary Hart in 1984, this would have been enough to sap the credibility from Clinton's candidacy, but through subtle and strategic presentation, and marketing themselves to couples and interested observers across America, the Clintons presented the allegations as commonplace and similar to those experienced in many marriages across the nation. Clinton argued against a standard of perfection that should be applied to candidates, while his wife contested that if people were upset by the accusations then they simply should not vote for candidate Clinton. The core of Clinton's argument was that of a shared emotion. As reported by the *New York Times*, he stated, ' "You know, I have acknowledged wrongdoing," Mr. Clinton said. "I have acknowledged causing pain in my marriage. I think most Americans who are watching this tonight, they'll know what we're saying, they'll get it, and they'll feel that we have been more than candid." '[41] Although allegations of infidelity were not dissipated, they appeared to increasingly seem irrelevant to the campaign, particularly when the initial accusations appeared to have a limited impact upon Clinton's credibility.

Clinton, although a front-runner in the Democrat primary race in 1992, had to adjust his election strategy as poll information suggested that he lagged behind the other key contenders in the presidential race, namely Perot and Bush. In April of 1992 Clinton's campaign team redesigned their strategy to address issues raised by market research and consideration of information provided by focus groups. One of the areas pinpointed, among several, was 'Clinton is privileged, like the Kennedys'. The historical change in the perception of wealth and political credibility is evident here. As a consequence one of Clinton's aides, Greenberg, tried to modify Clinton's profile by ensuring that his biography was repeatedly mentioned, including his impoverished background and social and emotional hardships. In poll samples this elevated Clinton from third in the race to first. Including social background and autobiographical information was thereafter deemed essential to enhance Clinton's campaign and profile. Polling and the use of samples became pivotal to the Clinton campaign, led by Greenberg and later Dick Morris. Greenberg claimed to have spent $125 million on polls in 1992 in pursuit of a Clinton presidency.[42] A 'Manhattan Project' report detailed the campaign strategy thereafter, 'We must begin immediately and aggressively scheduling the popular talk shows to introduce the real Bill Clinton. That includes the national popular culture shows and the regional radio interview and call-in shows. We should start with Johnny Carson, and move to Barbara Walters, Oprah and Donahue, Larry King and Rush Limbaugh. These shows must introduce these elements of biography, our principal "change" message and the human side of Bill Clinton (e.g., humor, sax and inhaling). Our goal is to break the political mold [sic].'[43]

Clinton exploited the new media format to get his message over to voters, both in terms of advocating policy, and in selling himself as a political candidate who could relate to the American voter in 1992. Chat shows and more informal occasions proved pivotal in getting a branded message over to voters. This had a multidimensional impact upon Clinton, the nature of political marketing, and the outcome of the 1992 campaign. Firstly, it introduced a dynamic to Clinton's campaign which was hard for his opponents to reproduce. Clinton exploited an issue rooted in political identity and style and utilised political scenarios where both Perot and Bush appeared to struggle to forge emotional connections with the voter. Secondly, it exposed Clinton to audiences that were not commonplace targets in politics at that time. The daytime television audience and the chat show viewer were presented with a political candidate who appeared to share the same issues and concerns of the viewership. Thirdly, Clinton appeared to be of the masses. Going on talk shows and discussing his background made him appear to be of the people, and not above discussing issues about his life, his experiences and his failings. Clinton was at ease with the forums in which he participated, and this contrasted him with President Bush, in particular, who did not avail himself, to the same extent, of the more informal talk shows, the Larry King talk show on *CNN* being one of the more favoured discussion forums. On shows like Donahue, Clinton pushed forward the idea of victimhood, and played the part of a confessional individual in keeping with the most frequent and stereotypical participants on daytime television. This was a new passage in politics, where the bridge between public and private was transcended, and character was marketed as a core element in advancing a campaign. One of the key issues which earmarked Clinton's ability to connect to the ordinary person was the extent to which his private life was exposed to public view. Part of this was by design, but in large part media hunger for salacious detail about Clinton's life, interweaved with the life experiences of Clinton himself gave great strength to the marketing of Clinton as a person who, irrespective of his personal wealth, shared experiences that could be understood by many Americans.

Conclusion

The presidential office during the Reagan–Clinton era was one where elements of populism and appeals against vested institutional and financial interests went hand-in-hand with public relations messages designed to cast the presidential candidates in a preferential light. It is clear that both Reagan and Clinton could legitimately argue that they came from blue-collar backgrounds and that they pursued the presidential office having demonstrated that they had a particular skill in the realm of politics. Both argued that they understood ordinary people, mixed in expansive social circles and were aware of the plight of individuals affected by adversarial circumstances. While they appeared to sing from the same hymn sheet, there emerged a number of features that earmarked the era and provided some differences between the two with respect to the marketing of the individual as ordinary in nature.

Reagan adopted a populist card, and advanced it in a subtle manner. While he protested about the problem posed by government itself and argued against special interests, he did so from a particularly distinctive position. Rarely did he assail the special interests in a concerted or specific way. Rather, he addressed the position of government to select audiences and thereafter used symbolism, public relations and imagery to convey an impression that, despite having been involved in political life for a considerable time, he was from an alternative stock, removed from the trappings of traditional politics. An impoverished youth, family hardships, and problems faced en route to several distinctive and successful careers, were heralded as testament to his endeavour, personal motivation and credibility for office. That he changed his political affiliation from Democrat to Republican was portrayed as an astute political decision rather than the consequences of indecision. Throughout his political career, when both campaigning for office and when serving in office Reagan, alongside his advisors, was aware of his strengths and weaknesses while selling his political identity to the American people. As such, his appearances were controlled, limited in informal and spontaneous forums, and exploited when Reagan's control of set scripts before the camera could be utilised. Being known as the great communicator was no accident, but the method and skill of delivery was about more than the simple choreographing of events, stage lighting, or the nature of Reagan's opponents. It was about the long-term marketing of a president as an ordinary person, who, in spite of political failings and the rollercoaster nature of the American economy tried to convey the impression that he was at one with the American people. To simply ascribe the defection of Democrats to Republican interests in 1980 is to bestow Reagan's policies with the power to win arguments about economic policy without taking into consideration his image as a person. He was actively sold as an ordinary person, and played a role in shaping popular perception of character and individual leadership. His statistics in terms of personal approval, in contrast to job approval, were testament not only to the nature of his individual communication but also to the way in which his past was selectively sold to the American public. His divorce was given little play, his activities during the Second World War were rarely raised for scrutiny, and the nature of his policy decision, internal infighting and the political role of Nancy Reagan were given little prominence until after he left office. The creation of Reagan Democrats as a distinctive electoral grouping who appeared to buck the trend of traditional party voting was down in part to the portrayal of social and emotional appeals to groups who saw Reagan as a person who could understand ordinariness.

Those who followed Reagan were aware of the importance of marketing and individual political identity when campaigning for political office. This was important not only in the United States, but was thereafter imported and copied in the United Kingdom.[44] Initially Bush appeared to have control of the electoral mandate in 1988 and managed issues of personal political identity and marketing well, but he was outflanked by Clinton in 1992, who strategically used both successes and personal failings as instruments to show that political issues and political figures were multidimensional in nature and need not simply be sold in the form of an asset. The transition from Reagan to Bush, and then to Clinton, was small in terms of the years involved, but marked a fundamental change in the way that impoverishment and its portrayal, regarding its impact on the character of leadership, were sold to the American people. In part this evolved because of the arrival of a recession in the early 1990s, but there were core features which suggested that an active marketing of problems, poverty and an accentuation of an autobiographical feature were beneficial in shaping voter perceptions of the candidate. The nature of the marketing was however quite complex in nature. On the one hand credibility for office had to be maintained, and on the other the candidate needed to appear both vulnerable and open to the problems posed by wider society. Clinton appeared able to master both, suggesting problems in his marriage yet solidity, trust and authenticity with the voter at the same time. Similarly, while he invested heavily in a number of economic projects and areas in the early 1990s, he was able to convey to potential voters that he was at one with their understanding of the economic ills that afflicted the nation at that time. In contrast President Bush, who had played on the trustworthy nature of his character in 1988, was unable to disassociate himself from wealth and thereafter persuade the American people that he could understand the issues that faced the nation.

This was attributable to several factors. Bush was associated with the Reagan era and its emphasis on the accumulation of wealth, alongside the impression that elite groups had benefited to the greatest extent because of the economic policies pursued. They were acceptable in 1988 but had less resonance in 1992. Secondly, Bush failed to engage meaningfully in the presentation of himself as a political victim. In 1992 in particular he failed to empathise with those affected by recession, the deficit or other forms of hardship. That none of the other candidates in 1992 had been affected either was besides the point. They attempted to convey an impression that they had sacrificed themselves to a cause. Bush cast himself as a person elected to cure problems, not necessarily experience them. As shown in Chapter 6, this had pronounced consequences for future elections, with the travails of Bush in 1992 having a marked impact on the extent to which individual candidates would present themselves as emerging from common stock. No longer was it possible to advocate political competency as a solution to national ills, or use it to persuade social groups that individuals from beyond their social class could be trusted to deal with issues affecting different socio-economic groups in differing ways. There was a pressing need to be perceived to have had experienced a number of life trials and to be able, at the least, to appreciate how national problems imprinted themselves at an individual level.

The Reagan–Clinton era left several distinct marks on the nature of political marketing. Leadership became a feature which was derived from the perception that when moulding a political identity and political career, social roots should ideally be part and parcel of mainstream society, or if they are not, they should be constructed so as to appear as such. In part, for both Reagan and Clinton this was quite easy to accommodate into their political make-up. Reagan could identify himself with the disaffected groups of the 1930s, and suitably, advance a tale of hardship combined with a change of heart from a Democrat identity to that of the Republican party. Although he followed a meteoric route through a variety of careers, he could nevertheless indicate that an autobiographical past was instrumental in underpinning his successful career route. Similarly, Clinton could cultivate an impoverished past, with social, economic and personal problems. However, as with Reagan these were not considered a handicap. Rather they could be contrasted with later successes to highlight exceptionalism and endeavours above and beyond the abilities of the ordinary person. This allowed a portrayal of a political candidate who was both of the mainstream and aware of the routines and emotions of mainstream society, and who thereafter was disposed with exceptional political ability. The presentation of political character in this form allowed them to be of the mass and above it at the same time.

This was not simply about the persona of the individual, their material background or the way in which they addressed career and environmental problems to advance their political opportunities. It was about the way in which they presented their cause to the public and sought to market themselves as individuals to a mass audience. In part this was about identifying niche audiences and catering to narrow socio-economic interests and groups thought to be pivotal as swing voters. From the Reagan era onwards the concept of the mass audience was limited and thought to be applicable to presidential debates and a select number of media opportunities. Narrowcasting was the norm and the selecting of core groups who could appreciate specific messages was considered important. This allowed variation in the presentation of political identity and the marketing of the candidate in ways considered appropriate to make specific links with audience concerns and beliefs.

The year 1992 was an important benchmark in the evolution of presidential marketing and the appeal to different socio-economic classes. Elections thereafter would take on board the lessons of that particular election with respect to autobiographic campaigns and references, and the stressing of hardship as a qualification for office. With Perot understandably unapologetic about his personal wealth, Bush seeking to associate himself with those affected by recession and Clinton assuming the role of a chat show host, conducting an empathetic investigation of individual circumstances, there was an abundance of examples from which lessons could be drawn. Clinton's success in the 1992 presidential election, despite an abundance of well publicised personal problems, indicated that issues which had previously been considered the death knell of electoral campaigns could be reshaped to advance the interests of the candidates. Candidate problems, including allegations of impropriety and controversial pasts could thereafter be considered to be political assets, with hardships and personal travails now being marketed to advance a perception that political credibility was in tune with ordinariness and the plight of the individual. Affairs, alcohol-related problems and issues related to the absence of military service were no longer matters that might end a political career. They could all be advanced, marketed or spun to give a positive impression of how an individual was in touch with the issues that affected voters, across a number of class spectrums. As Chapter 6 demonstrates, the impact of the 1980s and 1990s was pronounced and gave an indication that an autobiographical past, warts and all, was a beneficial commodity that could be sold as an electoral asset to the public.

5
New Labour and Tony Blair

The emergence of Tony Blair and New Labour was an event in British politics which would shape the bedrock of the political establishment for more than a decade. Blair's control of the political agenda, decisive election victories and, overtly at least, control of his party and political apparatus was important in conditioning the evolution not only of his own party but also that of his opponents, the Liberal Democrats and the Conservative party. There were several areas of note regarding wealth, identity and marketing in British politics which are relevant to the issues addressed by this text. Blair was from a wealthy background and enjoyed a lifestyle and education removed from that of the mainstream populace. As already discussed in Chapter 3 he faced an opponent in 1997, in the shape of John Major, who could realistically claim to come from a background with which many in the electorate could associate. However, Blair could rely upon widespread dissatisfaction with the Conservative party as a whole. There were a number of unpopular aspects of the party with respect to its economic profile and perceptions that it was immoral and sleaze ridden. On the face of it, the strength of Blair as a leading political candidate in the run-up to the 1997 election was not based on a direct comparison between the two leaders or a mere personality contest. It was largely an election where the prevalent impression was that a discredited political agenda and a faltering party could and should be removed in favour of a leader and party which had undergone a modern reinvention to cater to voter needs in the 1990s.

Needless to say the position of the party leader and how he conveyed himself was a fundamental aspect of how Blair's New Labour would be received, and how he, as an individual, would be considered across time by the voter. Blair was untypical of the traditional Labour party leadership and tried to change the ideological position of Labour, so as to reposition it more in the centre-ground of British politics. He distanced himself from a number of traditional Labour policies, particularly regarding union links and public ownership and, partly in conjunction with President Clinton, advocated the uptake of a new and innovative third way in politics. Blair's advocacy of a politics which sought to entertain elements from both left and right, and unify society was naturally subject to criticism and open to debate, but appeared, for some considerable time to pose problems for opposition parties in deciding where to stake a claim on the political spectrum.

The context

The evolution of party and personal marketing was pronounced by the time Blair assumed the leadership of his party and there was a significant embrace of technology and strategies to refine how party leaders might associate with and appeal to the voting block. Marketing strategies adapted lessons learned from the American political system which was more receptive to the selling of political leaders to the populace, partly as a consequence of marketing having been embraced there at an earlier stage. In 1987 Republican consultant Richard Wirthlin introduced the Conservatives to the use of computer technology to classify voter preferences, and the use of power phrases to elicit specific voter responses. In parallel the Labour party looked to the United States to try to enhance its electoral position in the contemporary era. Part of this entailed a simple observation of the Clinton presidency and the remaking of the party and its identity, from the Democrats to the New Democrats under Bill Clinton. Technology also had a part to play as observed by Gerry Sussman: 'Labour too did not shrink from the opportunity to garner foreign advice and use foreign consultants hiring the U.S. Democratic Party firm of Mellman and Lazarus to teach them the art of "people metering" (also known as perception analyzers) – the use of electronic handsets to test focus group members' "visceral reaction to phrases slogans, advertisements, styles and other political symbols and behaviour".'[1] A second feature of note is that even though there were claims, addressed later in this chapter, of the emergence of greater class mobility in Britain the perception of leadership by the elite being problematic still remained through the tenure of Blair's leadership from 1997–2007. The presentation of party leaders as ordinary and unaffected by the trapping of office was commonplace, with pronounced efforts to show that candidates mirrored the core voting blocks. Indeed the

Independent in 2005 offered its own summary of the convergence of elite political office and ordinary individuals. It commented on the prominent emergence of the ordinary tag and how it did not seem to sit comfortably with the political realm in the United Kingdom: 'Most of what we learn about our leaders contains a grain of truth, and probably much more. But it still gives a false picture. If you reach the top in politics, you aren't like other people. Your overriding preoccupation is with power – for that, you will sacrifice friends, family and principle – and the more of it you have, the less ordinary you become.'[2] Even with the advent of increased class mobility, political figures were still considered to have an inherent inability to blend with mainstream society, and the ambition to become a leading political figure meant that any trappings of elitism had to be either cast aside or manufactured so as to give a perception of social integration with the ordinary person.

By way of example of the nature and tone of the coverage of the divergence between the perceived social position of the elected member of parliament and the general public, in 2003 the *Mail on Sunday* ran a piece on the wealth held by members of parliament. It should be recognised that the *Mail* was not a publication that was, or is, particularly sympathetic to the position and ideology of the Labour movement, whether old or new. It sought to publicise the divergence between the wealth held by politicians and the wealth held by those in mainstream society. It claimed that Labour had largely abandoned its association with the poor, with a stark headline 'Labour, the party of the rich'. It ascertained that the Conservative party still had the largest number of wealthy individuals but that 'party politics is becoming less based on class – Tony Blair's Labour Party has demonstrated that having a great wealth is no longer a bar to being a socialist. Together, the 100 richest MPs are worth an incredible £352 million; they own 249 houses worth a staggering £179 million and last year earned a total of £10.6 million.'[3] As an individual Blair was profiled by the newspaper as some way from being the wealthiest member of parliament. He was ranked as the eighty-first most wealthy, with an estimated wealth of just over one million pounds. However, the inference of the piece was that a discernable gap existed in wealth and privilege between ordinary people and members of parliament. What the gulf signified was not made clear, but the ongoing concern about the difference between elected and electors was maintained.

Additional evidence from the period of Blair's tenure adds to the perception that ordinariness was a desirable feature in politics. Reviewing the 2005 general election which pitted Tony Blair against Michael

Howard, Stephen Coleman evaluated election preferences in comparison to the type of choices made by those who actively voted on the popular television game show Big Brother. Evaluation of those who watched the show, and thereafter expressed their preferences through voting suggested an audience who were as interested in politics as other segments of society, and had issues of salience, such as global warming and the election outcome, as concerns when considering voting intentions. Coleman asserts, 'Big Brother viewers and voters were neither inattentive nor inactive citizens during the 2005 campaign'.[4] The political leaders who presented themselves for election in 2005 were thought to be trying to present themselves as contestants who, like those involved in the game show, could appeal to the watching public and appear to have the personal credibility to sway the voter to their cause. Coleman observed, 'From Major's humble soapbox to Blair and Cameron's abandonment of their once-obligatory neckties, cultural democratisation requires would-be representatives to manifest ordinariness by appearing on the public stage as if they were off stage and being themselves. It is precisely this offstage lifeworld that the *Big Brother* format illuminates, providing its viewers with new ways to see and judge those who claim to speak for or as the public.'[5] Coleman confirms the trends which underscore the case studies and examples recited in this text, that 'the role of being a representatives entails appearing to be someone who is extraordinary enough to represent others, but ordinary enough to be representative of others'.[6] The samples used by Coleman to highlight what the viewers of Big Brother wanted of their ideal political candidate throws up pertinent material. The characteristic most preferred by the sample in their choice of political candidate was that they were an 'ordinary person' (53 per cent) and that they were a 'good listener' (52 per cent). Conversely only 10 per cent wanted their candidates to be an 'extraordinary person'. Coleman then asked how the sample group perceived the 2005 election. 'When asked how, in reality, they would characterize the candidates standing in their constituency, only 17% of panel members selected "ordinary" and 9% "straight talking", while 29% chose "slimey", 35% "arrogant" and 53% "false".'[7]

Although the Big Brother audience is commonly thought to be interested solely in a television show which has accumulated a number of prominent critics across the years of its broadcast, it offers some understanding of what a segment of the viewing public desire in public figures. It assists in explaining why political figures market themselves as ordinary even if they are, generally, in different income brackets and of a different social standing than mainstream society. As the previous two topic areas highlight there still exists in modern British politics doubt about the influence of wealth on the conduct and value of public office. Hand-in-hand with this there appears to be an appreciation of the merit for office for those considered to be ordinary. That this scenario exists goes some way to explaining why there has been an ever more pronounced effort by the political elite to market themselves as ordinary. It also underscores the issue of political marketing as a core feature of modern political life, with perceptions of public needs and wants having a role to play in determining elite political behaviour. Although the mainstay of writings on marketing centre on policy and party positioning, and political science is concerned primarily with measurable outcomes of voter preference, the available evidence suggests that political expectation and thereafter political action hinges on the impression of there being a cultural norm which political figures, and leaders, in particular can aspire to.

Tony Blair

The problem for Blair as a person and a political figure on the national stage was to appear to be in touch with ordinary people in a way that the Conservative party and its leadership had appeared not to be. As discussed earlier in this text with reference to party leadership and ordinariness, traditionally Labour party leaders were thought to be more attuned to the emotions and social identity of ordinary people. A major difference however was that Blair appeared, through his biographical profile, to be more suited to possessing the background of a Conservative leader as opposed to a Labour one, and this potentially proved a stumbling block in creating the impression that he was at one with the British people. An asset to Blair was that he could observe the practices and issues entertained by prior British leaders, and also accommodate the activities undertaken in the United States to try to manufacture a personal image which would both appeal to traditional Labour voters and those who had deserted the Conservative party in 1997. In the main Blair accommodated the lessons learned from the Clinton experience, and cultivated a persona that was frequently disassociated from the political arena. The intent was to convey an impression that he shared common pastimes and interests with the general populace. Although he received criticism for this type of activity it gave him a national profile which allowed a narrative to be created about him, his family life and his lifestyle.

This chapter considers how Blair constructed and manufactured a political identity which downplayed his background and accentuated his integration with mainstream society. This was done purposefully and, although on paper Blair emerged from the elite of British society his aim was to minimise this interpretation. Thereafter consideration is given to the methods and activities used to create this impression, enhanced by the use of spin, polling, and the creation of negative images of other party leaders, most notably those of the Conservative party leadership during Blair's tenure. Blair forced other leaders to try to occupy the ground he held and thereafter, accused them of replicating his position, or mirroring their leadership and personal style on his. This suggests that Blair perceived that he had achieved a position where he was in kilter with the feelings of the British people and was determined, through a mix of principle, and pragmatic moves when necessary, to hold to a position where he captured the emotional mood of a bulk of the British people. This was done via strategic polling and through research about policy and political standing, the objective being to occupy a political position which would squeeze the voting interests of competing parties. Part of this was socio-economic in its nature and was based on perceptions of where the bulk of the British voting block stood in the voting spectrum. Jennifer Lees-Marshment observed, 'The party focused on gaining the support of voters in what Blair himself called "middle income, middle Britain." The party thus devised a plan using target marketing, aimed at seeking the support of these voters. This was done through changes in policy and organisation which would find favour with such voters as evident from the post-1992 market intelligence.'[8]

Blair, alongside the policy and party changes had to present himself as a person with tangible electoral credibility. As is discussed later in this chapter he portrayed himself as a father facing problems and concerns, as with many families across the nation, as his teenage children grew up. He had personally faced concerns when young and had, according to his wife, slept rough for a night, and had aspired to be a rock star rather than a politician. He also created romantic notions of his childhood and embellished stories about his growing up. Nevertheless, even though both the facts and the fabrications were presented to the public and greeted with some cynicism Blair managed to entertain approval figures, on a personal level at least, that suggested that his leadership of his party and thereafter of the nation was credible.

The BBC reported, in the prelude to Blair's relinquishing of power in 2007, that Blair was not the product of mainstream society or an enigma in British politics. 'The story of his rise to power is certainly not a rags to riches tale – he was born with every advantage in life – but it is no less remarkable for that.'[9] Moreover Blair came through a route normally enjoyed by a small minority in society, one more atypical of the path entertained by a Conservative leader. Wheeler argued of Blair, 'It is the story of how a middle class, privately-educated barrister – the son of a would-be Tory MP – went on to become the most successful leader in the history of the Labour Party, profoundly changing it and the country in the process.' That Blair was from a middle class family was not in doubt, but what mattered was how this was managed and how Blair's ascendancy into power was perceived. As has already been outlined in this text several tasks faced Blair. The first was to convey the impression to the electorate that his elite status had not automatically conferred political office upon him. Secondly, he had to be seen to appreciate the concerns of the nation, and to be considered to be appreciative of the pressures of the mundane lifestyle, and not aloof from mainstream society. Thirdly, he had to assuage those in his party who considered his social background to be of such a nature as to distance him from traditional Labour policy and identity. He had also, on a national stage, to be seen to share the concern of the nation over the politics employed by the Conservative party, and to be perceived as a person who was affected socially and emotionally by them. Impressions were important, and with a media team oriented towards the creation of an image that dominated reality, Blair was in a position to identify a target audience, the end goals he desired, and be armed with the apparatus to bring about change.

Blair's central concern in the first instance of his stewardship, following the untimely death of John Smith, was to create a party brand. There is considerable literature available on the methods and means through which the New Labour organisation structured itself so as to utilise several commercial elements when advancing itself to the British public. Jennifer Lees-Marshment identified several of these features, already employed in a personal and institutional sense by many of the candidates discussed in this text. She identified the use of market intelligence and the use of focus groups, an adaptation of behaviour to suit prevailing environmental conditions, and the efficient transition between policy formulation to policy execution.[10] One of the key instruments in the re-branding of the party and its repositioning in the party spectrum was leadership, and with Blair at the helm there were demands that he demonstrate authority and credibility in key areas of leadership. He assumed tight control of the party and its policy agenda.

The approach Blair took, assisted by close and loyal aides, was draconian in nature and ensured that internal divisions within the party were minimised. This made him appear tough and although change was difficult for some party members, it suggested that Blair had the exceptionalism to lead both his party and, at a later stage, the nation. This resonated with the voters, especially with internal divisions within the Conservative party which were perceived as detrimental to its fortunes.[11]

Assessments of Blair as a person who was equipped to lead his party were mixed upon his ascension to power. Esteemed commentator on British politics Anthony King considered Blair to be a product of a form of identikit politics, '[Blair] might almost have been a product of computer-aided design. He was young, He was classless. He was squeaky clean.'[12] While King considered Blair to be classless, he clearly was from an established elite within British society, and it might be more appropriate to consider that Blair was manufactured to appear to be classless. His background, wealth, social associations and marriage to a woman who was engaged in her own successful and wealth creating career was not typical of the mainstream of British society. Of course Blair was derived from a social position where he might be expected to provide leadership and have access to compete for power. In Britain however the surprising aspect was that he pushed forward to lead and then reform the Labour party, a party which in its old form would have been dismissive of Blair and his background. As cited by Lees-Marshment, Ken Coates, a Labour member of the European parliament, thought Blair to be 'quite simply a Liberal. ... This young man has not the faintest idea of how socialists think, and does not begin to understand the mentality to which he has been elected to lead.'[13] In essence Blair was pushed to the fore to lead a party which did not appear to be at one with his thinking. The internal party reforms and ideological changes wrought upon the party by Blair are well known and earmarked him, much in the Thatcher mould, as a conviction politician who aimed to achieve his objectives through single minded determination.

While Blair clearly had policies which resonated with the British people across his tenure as leader there were other issues which made him popular, or at least appealed to the British people on personal grounds. He was in a strong position in many areas when he assumed the party leadership. As David Denver asserts, 'On becoming Labour leader in 1994, Tony Blair immediately became the electorate's choice for Prime Minister by a wide margin and he maintained his lead over John Major into the election. More detailed Gallup data show that larger proportions of the electorate believed that Blair was caring (82 per cent) and effective (64 per cent) than was the case for Major (62 per cent and 37 per cent respectively).'[14] The strength of the impression that Blair cared is significant for this study, suggesting that the emotional strength of Blair was a feature where he stood to gain considerable benefit at the hands of the Conservative government. That he was in opposition at the time and it was relatively easy to forge bonds against an increasingly unpopular government is acknowledged; however Blair made purposeful efforts to be seen to be in touch with the electorate.

Discussions of who Blair was and what he stood for were prominent both before and when he took office. Part of this was structural, with an increasing perception that he transformed the office of the prime minister into a presidential forum, with popular and media attention directed at him as a power hungry individual rather than as servant to the supremacy of Parliament. This concentrated media attention on the individual at the expense of the party. Blair was the personal embodiment of the New Labour movement and the focal point of the party's visions and intentions. Andy McSmith, a political columnist for the *Observer* newspaper, in *Faces of Labour: The Inside Story* discussed the social origins of Blair and how he cast himself as a person. He cited Blair's personal understanding of wealth, economic disparity and how he perceived societal problems. 'In my own mind, I have complete confidence in the beliefs I hold dear. I know why I am in the Labour Party I know why I have joined this Party and worked for it for the last twenty years. It is because when you look around your society you see the injustice, you see the opportunity denied, you see the unfairness, you see all that elitism at the top, you see that establishment.'[15] On the face of it, this type of rhetoric was standard populist fare, presented to enhance Blair's standing to a trade union audience and boost his credibility that, as a leader of the opposition, he could and intended to bring about change. However McSmith also discussed how Blair, the product of a middle-class upbringing, could also link his social past to times of hardship. He stated, 'Blair himself does not encourage the idea that there is an early formative experience which made him a man of the left, which can be uncovered by rooting around in his early life. His father's illness caused a sharp drop in his social status and in the family income, but this seems to have had less effect on Blair than a similar blip in the family income had on an adolescent John Major.'[16] As discussed in Chapter 3, John Major accentuated, somewhat reluctantly, the impoverishment of his youth to highlight his awareness of socio-economic and demographic issues in the United Kingdom. McSmith advances a somewhat romanticised interpretation of Blair's social background and how it might have informed him in his efforts to create a political movement which transcended class issues. Giving attention to Blair's origins he argued 'However, since much has been made of Blair's middle-class background, it is perhaps worth pointing out that, like Vladimir Lenin, he was only a generation away from humble beginnings.'[17] Blair did endure trials of his own, with family illnesses to address and a temporary move to Australia; however, his winning a scholarship to Fettes and his later move to train as a barrister set him apart, in both his wealth and his experiences, from mainstream society. However, it is evident that in a personal capacity Blair was aware of the need to stay connected to those he wished to serve in his constituency. McSmith quoted Blair as stating that he liked to go to Trimdon Labour Club in the Sedgefield constituency to 'keep himself in touch with what the average Labour voter is saying and thinking'.[18] A Labour secretary within the Sedgefield constituency identified the type of voter Blair was going to have to appeal to with his brand of Labour political identity: 'They are not the intellectual side of the Labour Party that like to spout on about their socialism but are not really in touch with the reality of what people want. These are ordinary people who know what they want.'[19] The relationship which would help Blair to capture a seat in North East England was established, partly of course on policy and ideological standing, but also it appears that part of the association was one where the electorate were identified as ordinary, and Blair actively sought out their views to allow him to appreciate and enhance the bonds between the elector and the elected.

In an informative article on Blair's media approach to the 1997 election, Michael Pearce identified the enhancement of the autobiographical profile to give identity to political candidates. This was particularly the case with one specific party political broadcast with Blair as its centre point, but in a wider context it has been used by Blair, his successor Brown and by those in opposition, particularly David Cameron. Several themes are evident in the presentation of Blair at this time which draw upon historical material, and have since been further exploited by candidates on both sides of the Atlantic. Blair adopted a language which could readily be understood and employed communication strategies such as hesitation to give the impression of him as a 'normal person'.[20] He associated himself with the middle class and appealed strongly to the centre-ground of politics. In analysing Blair's autobiographical strategy Pearce argues 'The Blair film seeks to exploit the audience's sense of intimacy with its subject for political purposes. In particular, it does this by assuming that viewers' experiences of other examples of the genre might lead them to expect a degree of candidness and honesty from the film, therefore making them less inclined to be suspicious of the broadcast's political motives.'[21] This is reminiscent of Nixon's approach to the Checkers speech where he deflected attention from charges of corruption by approaching materials in an open and candid fashion. Thereafter Pearce addressed the issue of ordinariness, the core feature in the presentation of the individual candidate in modern politics. 'We first meet him in the back of a car at night when he talks about his youth. This is followed by a sequence illustrating the public Blair and then, after he has reminisced about his childhood footballing dreams in the back of the car, we find ourselves in his kitchen. He is dressed casually: we see him make tea and chat with his children. The domestic setting is strategically significant. The unremarkable middle-class kitchen reinforces the nation that Blair is an ordinary family man.'[22] Parts of the overall format were drawn from past experiences, particularly 'The Journey', a party political broadcast used by John Major where he too reminisced about his past from the back of a car. Similarly Blair's use of family illness to convey an emotional attribute, a caring dimension and a universal experience allowed him to advance himself as a person who could readily be identified with subjectively by individuals across the electorate. The issue of family health has become a core feature of the marketing of politicians on both sides of the Atlantic. It was used widely by candidates in the 2004 presidential election to convey an awareness of health care issues and policy and to forge emotional connections. As Chapter 7 makes clear, both Brown and Cameron have continued the practice into contemporary British politics with narratives of both their own, and their families', medical needs.

By the time Blair was in command of the Labour party there were fundamental differences in the political environment that he had faced in the past and had been a mainstay of British politics. The class identification in Britain which had been perceived to underpin traditional voting patters had diminished significantly. In a thorough examination of the evolution of party support in the period between 1964 and 2001 Harold D. Clarke et al., taking into consideration socio-economic and geographic issues concluded that, 'At the end of the twentieth century class had come to play a very limited role in determining the voting preferences of the British electorate'.[23] As the propensity of class voting diminished across this period there was a need for the candidates in the political spectrum to both give their parties an identity, and to address their own image to allow consideration of their personal and leadership abilities. Relying on party associations with class demographics increasingly had its shortcomings. Arguments were advanced by Jenny Lloyd, among others, that the voter struggled to identify the clear blue water between the parties. She argued, 'when considering the relative merits of the brands ... judgements tended to be based upon the characteristics of the party leaders rather than the party as a whole because, as leaders, not only did they tend to receive the most media coverage, but also their position inferred that they were the best example of what the brand had to offer.'[24]

Shortly before he won the 1997 election Blair cast himself as a person who was not elevated above the populace on account of either his wealth, his background or his occupancy of a political office. Writing in the *Independent* newspaper in 2005 Cahal Milmo examined how private interests of public figures were presented to the public, with the familiar intent of promoting ordinariness as a feature which endears them to the voter. Of Tony Blair he asserted 'Mr Blair, however, had mostly got his image right. Enthusiasm for football and pop music and a touch of youthful rebellion go down well with the post-1945 baby boomers who form the backbone of his vote. Even the freebie holidays don't do much damage, because getting holiday bargains is a national preoccupation.'[25] In 1997 Blair was invited to appear on a popular radio show, Desert Island Discs, where individuals are invited to identify several records they would wish to have in their possession if they were isolated from society. Blair's first choice was a song about a jobless man pleading to his lover. It was made by an obscure band, Ezio, and appeared to send the message about associations with the plight of the unfortunate. It also gave the impression that Blair was not of elite stock, and availed himself of an array of popular music. Questions were immediately raised that the song choice was more political than personal and that Blair had approached the show with a discreet political agenda. This forced a statement which sought to offset political allegations and separate Blair, the trendy and fashionable individual, from Blair the political statesman. It read, 'Every record was chosen by him. He knows more about music than anybody who works with or for him. He has been working on the choice for several weeks.'[26] There is credence to this claim given Blair's interest in rock music when young and his playing of the guitar; however that the question was asked about the genuine nature of his choice suggested a level of cynicism about the marketing of Blair as an individual. When speaking to the *Sun* newspaper in advance of his election in 1997 Blair claimed that he liked the Beatles, REM, Simply Red,

Bruce Springsteen, and also was a fan of Debussy and Samuel Barber. In other words Blair, in a musical context, wished to appeal to as broad an audience as was possible.[27]

In another effort to convey a social association with the electorate Blair posed, in 1995 at the Labour party conference, with football legend Kevin Keegan. At the time Keegan was manager of Newcastle United, was a well-known figure in popular culture and could capture popular attention. When meeting Blair, they engaged in a game of football head tennis which received considerable media coverage and suggested that Blair was faithful to his claims of having linkages with the North East of England, could play the most popular team sport in the United Kingdom and entertained an earthiness that would not be replicated by Conservative Prime Minister John Major. Major's passion was cricket, a game which at that time was largely considered to be a game played by people who were not working class and was the preserve largely of those who had enjoyed private education. The contrast was clear. Blair was adept at the game enjoyed by the masses, Major was adept at a game played by elite stock. That said, Major had visited Newcastle United's home stadium St James' Park in 1995 and had received a Newcastle United shirt from Keegan. He was also an occasional visitor at Stamford Bridge to see Chelsea. There were concerns about Blair meeting Keegan behind the scenes, as Alastair Campbell's diaries indicate, 'Everyone was horrified at the prospect of TB [Tony Blair] playing football and being made to look silly but I insisted we get a ball. Keegan was a nice, warm man, and I sensed he was basically onside. There was a huge media turnout. It was a fantastic success and provided the best pictures of the week.'[28] Appearing to be associated with the popular sports stars was evidently deemed to be advantageous to political standing, and Keegan was happy to oblige.[29] Media coverage of the opportunities afforded politicians was greeted critically in some quarters. Football fans and the sports media were less impressed by the photo opportunities created by prime ministers and aspiring politicians. The football magazine *When Saturday Comes* highlighted football as an opportune issue through which an artificial interest in the game might bring electoral credibility. It observed, 'It's only recently that football was an electoral pariah, the campaign equivalent of telling constituents you spend your Friday night drinking and stealing traffic cones. These days, however, a display of awkwardly staged soccer-fandom has become required shorthand for candidates interested in projecting an ersatz common touch.'[30] At the European football championships Blair made use of the fact that the tournament was held in England. 'Blair had been pictured in the stands at Euro 96. He cultivated a mannered ordinariness, of which football became just attention after the travails of previous decades, but it was to be a brief affair.'[31] Blair did periodically display an interest in football when in office, including an appearance on a BBC football discussion show, but his utilisation of photo opportunities in advance of the 1997 election was testament to his awareness of a social identification with a mainstream pastime. Much of this was in keeping, as expressed in Chapter 6, with the use of sport as an election tool. While Blair used football to convey social bonds, George Bush Jr and other presidential candidates took an increasing interest in NASCAR, a sport popular in the states where acquisition of the vote was key.

Although excellent play was made of Blair's associations with popular culture, particularly in the realm of sport and music, he was not infallible and a number of occasions demonstrate that the practice of personal embellishment was not watertight. When making a TV appearance in December 1996 Blair discussed his past with popular chat show host Des O'Connor. He claimed that when 14 he ran away from home, made his way to Newcastle airport and boarded a plane destined for the Bahamas, 'I snuck onto the plane, and we were literally about to take off when the stewardess came up to me'.[32] The story was recited to other parties to clarify its precise nature. Queries arose as to how Blair was able to get onto an international flight without a passport or a boarding card. Blair's father could not recall the event and research showed that there were no flights from Newcastle to the Bahamas when Blair claimed that the episode took place. Blair's intent was to assure the watching public that when young he faced social and emotional challenges; however the evidence showed that it was simply not a true event. In 1997 Blair told an interviewer that he had watched Jackie Milburn, a Newcastle United football player, from the seats behind the goal at St. James' Park. Blair claimed that this had been when he was a teenager. However, research showed that Blair was only four years old when Milburn played his final game for Newcastle and there were no seats behind the goal at that time. Again, Blair's embellishment of his biographical past stretched credibility.

In evaluating Blair's social and emotional connection with the British electorate it was important that he was considered to be in touch with the British people, and as was highlighted in Chapter 2, the Conservative party struggled, under both Thatcher and Major, to appear to be in touch with the British electorate. Poll questions tried to identify whether Blair was seen to be in touch with the populace, and questions were also asked about whether he was considered to be down to earth. In October 1997, shortly after coming to office only 6 per cent of those polled thought him to be 'out of touch with ordinary people'. This figure slowly increased in the period during Blair's first term, reaching 54 per cent in September 2000, before falling back to 36 per cent at the time of the 2001 general election.[33]

As experienced by Major and Thatcher, Blair found that as time progressed it was challenging to maintain impressions of ordinariness. The impression of his being down to earth halved across the tenure of the parliament, and those who considered him to be out of touch increased significantly. By way of party and individual contrast, the Conservative leader of the time, William Hague, had figures which still advanced the impression that it was challenging for a Conservative to market oneself as ordinary, or overcome long-held stereotypes about the social origins of the Conservative leadership. In October 1997, 29 per cent of a MORI poll sample thought him to be out of touch with 'ordinary people'. This figure remained relatively consistent in the period before the 2001 election, never dropping below 28 per cent.[34] Throughout his tenure as leader Hague struggled to appear to be a person derived from ordinary stock. He frequently lagged behind Blair when poll statistics were considered and although he tried to engage in strategies to make him appear more in touch with the populace they evidently failed to eradicate stereotype or remould the Conservative leadership brand. Consequently the stereotype of Hague came to the fore and outweighed the more populist image he tried to convey. Some of his attempts to make him appear to be a man of the people actually worked significantly towards making him look out-of-touch and disconnected, as a later section of this chapter makes clear. Policy issues aside, the impressions of the party leaders demonstrated that there were identifiable and long-standing differences in the perception of leadership, even when the middle ground of politics was becoming increasingly saturated.

Maintaining a manufactured image

Blair's efforts to maintain an image of ordinariness faltered as his stewardship of his office continued. This is largely unsurprising and mirrors the experiences of other leaders, who were perceived to be more detached from a social norm as the length of their tenure progressed. When Blair entered office, following public relations measures designed to make him look like an ordinary person, only 6 per cent though him to be out of touch. Following the 2001 election, where a comfortable victory was achieved over Hague, Blair appeared to be further and further distanced from the voting block. While he was considered to be out of touch by a minority in 2001, his figures deteriorated to 44 per cent in 2004, and 51 per cent in 2006.[35] The changes in the figures testifies to an ongoing difficulty of seeming to be at one with the voting block, the social isolation imposed by political office across time playing a role in enhancing the problem.

The reasons for the decline in perceptions of ordinariness are rooted partly in the familiarity with Blair, a rising level of cynicism about spin and presentation in politics, and assaults upon the character of Blair and his chosen pastimes. Several episodes undermined Blair's position across the long term and slowly stripped the impression that he was derived from the masses. Additionally it was not merely Blair as an individual that came under scrutiny, but the activities of his wife, and how he selectively used his family on specific occasions to portray an image of a family man, yet on other occasions when issues might have proven detrimental to his case, advanced an argument for a respect of his privacy.

Two examples serve to highlight some of the areas where Blair was accused of being out of touch with mainstream experiences and portrayed as elitist. In 2003 Michael Howard, leader of the Conservative party challenged Blair on education. In the midst of a heated period of debate about the introduction of tuition fees for students attending universities Blair was challenged about his background and his association with those affected by any financial charge to be levied in this area. Blair claimed that the objective of fee raising was to increase the number of students going to university, particularly those from working class and non-traditional backgrounds. Labour had at the same time launched a public relations exercise designed to demonstrate that it was listening to the country and was in touch with ordinary viewpoints, the program entitled the 'Big Conversation'. In Prime Minister's Questions, Michael Howard engaged in a heated debate about the nature of education in the United Kingdom and of the intent to widen university access for the working class. Howard used Blair's background to undermine his claims for enhanced access to education. He argued, 'This grammar school boy is not going to take any lessons from a public school boy on the importance of children from less privileged backgrounds gaining access to university'.[36] Howard's exploitation of Blair's past gained him the advantage in this particular debate and highlighted that Blair and Howard were not necessarily representative of the commonplace assumptions about their parties' stereotypical identities. Nevertheless, the Labour party were successful in getting the legislation passed which initiated fees for university education.

Perceptions of elitism also surfaced when Blair's cabinet selections were discussed in 2006. New Labour appeared to be top heavy with individuals from the traditional elite stock of political leadership. A report produced by the Sutton Trust (discussed further in Chapter 7) identified that Blair's cabinet had a far from ordinary education. The report was discussed in the *Times*, which claimed, 'When it comes to picking his top team, the Fettes-educated Mr Blair still prefers the products of top public and grammar schools'. Furthermore, 'Sir Peter Lampl, chairman of The Sutton Trust, said that the make-up of the Cabinet showed how difficult it was for ordinary pupils from ordinary homes to make it to the top.'[37] Again the concept of how much the political elite should reflect, socially and emotionally, the experiences of mainstream society had come to the fore. That the issue was raised throughout Blair's time in office and was largely unresolved by the time he left office in 2007 highlights the nature of a criticism that occurs with frequency, but the rationale for which was rarely brought to the fore or considered with any depth or resonance.

Blair's contribution to political marketing in British politics was pronounced. He re-branded the Labour party, pulled it into the centre-ground of British politics and worked to reform the impression of the party as one rooted in the traditions of the British working class. In conveying a sense of political ordinariness to brand his own political identity he was largely successful. Poll statistics on the nature, tone and interpretation of the Conservative party granted Blair an immediate avenue of opportunity in this area. He was further assisted by political associates, Mandelson and Campbell among them, who understood the need to present political figures not only as leaders, but also as individuals who had the capability to be familiar with the experiences of ordinary society.

Blair's mandate and message were clear from the outset, and observable from the period before he became prominent as a leading political figure. His appreciation of sport, music and the nature and role of the family provided an abundance of resources for effective political marketing. His personal past also provided a level of authenticity which helped to mask and cloud any perceptions of elitism that might have been held against him. His understanding of music worked in conjunction with pictures of him aspiring to be a rock star and aided in conveying an image of a young man aspiring to ambitions shared by many during their teenage lives. That he could play football to a competent level also lent credence to the idea that Blair shared in the pursuits of the masses. When prime minister he sought to cultivate his associations with the game further. His family gave further legitimacy to the idea that the presentation of him as an ordinary man was one that was both legitimate and authentic. He could relate, above and beyond the realm of policy and politics, to the electorate. They, in a classless capacity could relate to him. In family life, in marriage, in pastimes and in social habits Blair could create the social and emotional associations that gave the impression that he was in touch.

However, two key legacies stand out from the Blair era as significant, yet they do not make for easy bedfellows. Firstly, popular appreciation of the nature of the Blair spin machine led to popular cynicism about the true standing of Blair, his wife and how he presented his past and his social habits. The appearance of Blair as an individual with an elite education, as a man with a wealthy and highly accomplished wife and as an individual who embellished aspects of his past for political convenience gave the impression that it was hard to separate fiction from reality in the realm of political identity. Ironically Blair, and the modelling of his character as one rooted in the normality of ordinary British culture, has provided the template against which other British political figures have tried to model themselves. Secondly, both Conservative party leader Cameron and Blair's successor Brown have used the success enjoyed by Blair as an indicator of how ordinariness in politics can be used to transcend class divisions and present an array of characteristics to both broad and niche media interests.

William Hague

An exercise in ordinariness

William Hague was leader of the Conservative party following its defeat in 1997 and led it until after its defeat in the 2001 general election. He was from a Yorkshire background and was considered an intelligent individual with a quick wit and a long-standing passion for politics. He tried to cast Blair as a person from an elitist background, criticising his holidays in Italy where he was loaned a house and enjoyed a private beach. He also advanced a concept that New Labour represented a liberal elite which had lost touch with voters. In 2000, writing in the *Guardian*, Madeleine Bunting argued, 'What Mr Blair has to worry about is that the Tories had more than a decade of government before they faced accusations of elitism while it has taken New Labour only three years. There is a crucial issue here for Mr Blair to ponder: the secret of Conservative electoral success in the 20th century lay in the ability of an elite to mask itself with a powerful populism.'[38] While Hague could make play on the social habits, associations and background of the Blair family, he too had to come across as a populist by nature and as an individual who was more in tune with the public than Blair. This however proved to be an uphill task.

Of all the episodes which mark a misplaced and badly calculated effort to portray a sense of ordinariness, action by Conservative party leader William Hague, in 2000, demonstrates that a poorly executed strategy can misfire and create perceptions of an even greater social gulf than previously existed. Hague, as opinion poll statistics indicate, was considered albeit narrowly to be less in touch with the electorate across time than Tony Blair. He had tried to modify the image of a Conservative party leader when first taking the position, being photographed in a baseball cap and attending the Notting Hill Carnival. As the *Guardian* reported, Hague was, 'A young, happening-kind-of Tory leader, one who cared, had taken over, was the not-so-subliminal message'.[39]

In the autumn of 2001 he gave an interview to *GQ* magazine, a publication aimed primarily at young men with disposable incomes, and an outlet where he could gain credibility with that element of the voting body. Hague argued that the stereotype of him as a zealous young Conservative, obsessed with politics and unlike others of his generation was misplaced. He had been shown on television, on many occasions, giving an address to a Conservative party conference when a teenager, and seemed to have lacked the same interests as other teenagers. As party leader he appeared to be a career politician, a person who had only one objective in life and who did not share the common life experiences and concerns of the electorate.

In the magazine interview Hague made a number of claims regarding his youth. He stated, 'Anyone who thinks I used to spend my holidays reading political tracts should have come with me for a week'.[40] Hague had previously, for a period of six years, worked for his father's business delivering soft drinks to clubs. In the first instance this seemed to be opportune to allow Hague to show that he understood the issues and the lifestyle of those, largely Labour supporters, whom he encountered in Yorkshire. In keeping with the idea of social association he claimed 'It was a great education, actually – knowing what Labour voters feel like as well as Conservatives. I think I learned more going round the clubs of Barnsley than I learned at Oxford [university] about the human race in general.' On a superficial level Hague appeared to portray an understanding of the type of community that he ordinarily would appear divorced from and his comments and experiences might have been advantageous in softening the impression that he was out of touch with northern England, traditionally an area difficult for the Conservative party to persuade to its cause. However, additional comments by Hague stretched credibility and created adverse perceptions of his social position.

He claimed, 'We used to have a pint at every stop – well the driver's mate did, not the driver, thankfully – and we used to have about 10 stops a day. ... You worked so hard you didn't feel you'd drunk 10 pints by four o'clock, you used to sweat so much. ... It's probably horrifying but we used to do that then go home for tea and then go out in the evening to the pub.'[41] He agreed that by the end of a day's work he could have consumed 14 pints. His remarks were greeted with humour and deep scepticism that he had made exaggerated and excessive claims in an attempt to be seen to be in touch with the electorate. The media jumped at the chance to highlight Hague's claims which seemed to undermine his credibility. Hague's former work colleagues on the delivery round were interviewed to ascertain the legitimacy the story. One of those who was assistant manager in a club where Hague delivered said that he was known as 'Billy the Pop' and 'Billy Fizz' and that 'The idea of him sinking 14 pints is laughable – nobody has seen him around here for years.'[42] A delivery driver who worked with Hague argued that 'I worked for his Dad's soft drinks firm for 20 years and I have to say he's not the boozer he'd have us believe', and 'Six pints and he was sozzled'.[43] The story without the claims of excessive alcohol consumption would not have made any headlines. With those comments it became a prominent news story that made Hague seem more out of touch than ever. The British tabloid media exploited the plight of a national party leader. The *Daily Mirror* ran a headline, 'I was Britain's biggest boozer' while the *Sun* had a simple and stark headline, 'Billy Liar'.[44]

Hague was invited by pub owners to drink 14 pints at no charge, as long as he promised to consume them all. One of the bar owners thought that 'this could be a case where a politician is trying to be one of the lads, so we're hoping he'll come down here and prove he can still do it'. The Deputy Prime Minister, John Prescott commented on the hollow nature of Hague's claims, and the prominent and media savvy public relations agent Max Clifford commented that 'you don't look at him [Hague] and see a 14-pint man'.[45] To add insult to injury charity groups advocating moderate alcohol consumption condemned Hague as being irresponsible.

The remarks clearly created the impression that Hague was more out-of-touch than had previously been thought. While trying to advance the impression of openness and being personable Hague advanced information about his personal life and his choices in fashion. In some respects this was unsurprising given the nature of *GQ* magazine. This was an effort to demonstrate that he was just like the ordinary voter. However although he claimed to support a football team he was unable to name the captain of England at the time, a fact that again appeared to show his disconnection from the issues that might draw a typical *GQ* reader to his cause. Conservative advisors claimed that statistics taken on phone-in polls had shown that people were more likely to vote for Hague after the alcohol revelations. However, in terms of political marketing and social connection they clearly had not gone according to plan and the matter was one that was not going to lure undecided voters to the Conservative cause or give the impression that Hague, as a person, could be trusted.

Following the loss at the 2001 election the *Observer* considered Hague's personal attributes and how these had fared in the political environment. It was not enthusiastic about his fate, 'he could never escape the public's perception of him as a bit of a drip. He was remorselessly pilloried in the media for his baldness, his looks, his accent, and his laboured "14-pints-a-day" attempts to prove he was just one of the lads. Apart from Neil Kinnock, no other British figure has received such a media drubbing.'[46]

Some time after he stepped down as leader of the party, having been defeated in a general election of 2001 by Tony Blair and New Labour, Hague reflected upon the way he was marketed to the public and how the image he conveyed was unnatural and failed to resonate with the voter. The *Independent* identified problems during Hague's leadership: 'There are other examples of bad calls that Hague made during his leadership – the much mocked Princess Di-style water ride at a theme park, an ill-judged appearance at the Notting Hill Carnival, the claim that he used to drink "14 pints of beer a day" as a teenager, the wearing of baseball caps – all of which were clearly intended to try to extend the party's appeal to a more youthful audience.'[47] Without the pressure of leadership Hague reconsidered the nature of the marketing of the individual. The *Independent* reported that Hague had shrugged off the mantle of personal marketing, ' "Well, stuff it, I'm not normal" he has said. One of the things he found most uncomfortable about being leader of the Conservative party was that he had to pretend to be normal.'[48] He was a politician who made significant money from his interests and speaking engagements outside parliament, and his political writings. He could advance himself as a person who was exceptional and for whom the impression of being normal would happily be cast aside. Evidently the case of Hague shows that political marketing and the selling of the individual can be problematic in the modern era. Although Hague had been involved in politics from a young age, had grown up in the era of marketing and presentation, and had advisors well versed in the art of presentation, clearly trying to be marketed as normal was a significant challenge and one that sat uncomfortably upon Hague's shoulders.

Ordinary women and ordinary children

A further issue of relevance to an understanding of the presentation of ordinariness in politics is that it is not enough for an individual leader to portray themselves as ordinary – the image must be consistent with the family group, family past and presented in such a way that it remains plausible to the watching public.

In both the United States and United Kingdom the position of the spouse and their influence upon key political positions has received ever greater prominence across time. Although some First Ladies and some of the wives of prime ministers have shied away from publicity in the contemporary era, in the shape of Cherie Blair and Hillary Clinton the media found themselves with abundant news materials through which they could portray the domestic settings and social context enjoyed by the leaders of the respective nations. This assisted in creating a public forum for the presentation of the private sphere. It was not enough to be seen to be a supportive individual however. In an assessment of how Tony Blair mirrored the political style employed by Bill Clinton, the American Enterprise Institute considered the similarities in how the leaders' wives portrayed themselves. 'Tory Prime minister John Major took to having his more traditionally domestic wife, Norma, accompany him on the campaign trail to tell how she grates and freezes stale bits of cheese and uses a tea bag more than once. The point was to contrast loyal homebody Norma with Cherie. Hillary-like Mrs. Blair responded by reporting herself a devoted knitter. "The quest for ordinariness among politicians' wives is the sine qua non of modern electioneering, so terrified have we become of their bewitching powers and hidden agendas," wrote Leslie White. ... "One might have hoped that the late twentieth century would demand charisma, brains, and deep political convictions of these women, but no, we seem to want bread-makers and quilt-makers."[49] Both Cherie, who was a successful barrister and a Queen's Counsel and Hillary Clinton, again a successful lawyer in her own right, had to appear to be women with domestic concerns and individuals not aloof from the issues and concerns of many ordinary women.

Cherie's image as a woman who had to face the trappings of ordinary life was severely tested following a scandal involving a property deal in 2002. Prior to the episode Cherie had portrayed herself as a modern working woman. She had a law career, a husband in a high-profile demanding job and a family to look after. Tony Blair argued that his wife was a woman with 'her own career and three kids to worry about'.[50] Writing in the *Independent* Helen Wilkinson said about the Blairs and their symbolic reflection of British mainstream society: 'As a dual earner couple inhabiting No. 10, the Blairs certainly have a strong symbolic appeal. They act as a reference point, mirror to our own lives. We see them juggling work and life, pioneering new roles, wrestling for that elusive balance between work and life.'[51] The problems encountered by Cherie came about as the consequence of a property deal and the exposure of her associations with individuals who appeared to have credibility problems and upon whom she seemed to be very dependent for advice. All the core elements for a political scandal and allegations of corruption were present and the Prime Minister's wife was subject to a rigorous investigation of her personal life. A large part of the media coverage was highly critical of her on account of her judgement, her associations with a lifestyle guru and on the grounds that the financial dealing she had been involved in suggested that she was not a person who experienced the trials of modern life. In the *Sunday Mirror* Carole Malone contrasted the image of Cherie Blair pre and post the revelations about her private associations. She stated, 'The fact is, yes, we used to like her. We liked her ordinariness, the fact she was brought up in a council house, that she was grounded and clever and raised a family while holding down a high-pressure job. And then she got fame and celebrity and, just as it corrupts pop stars and TV presenters, so it corrupted her. Cherie Blair is no longer ordinary. She has a retinue of slaves to execute every mundane task, yet she still says to working mothers "I'm just like you"'.[52] The consequences of Cherie Blair's action was to deepen the cynicism about the extraordinary/ordinary debate. She personally claimed that 'The reality of my daily life is that I'm juggling a lot of balls in the air ... some of you must experience that'.[53] The reaction of Malone in the Mirror, a paper predominantly bought by those on the left of the political spectrum and from a working-class background was severe. 'This is the Prime Minister's wife, a 250,000 pounds-a-year-barrister who never has to set foot inside a supermarket, who no doubt has help with the washing and ironing, who never has to clean the house, find a plumber, cook the dinner, travel on public transport, cook the kids' breakfast.'[54]

The attacks on Cherie Blair in the aftermath of her public revelations were pronounced and concerted. In part they rested upon an opportunity to attack her, and exploited the unforeseen manner in which she had opened herself up to the attacks. Her associations with gurus and individuals of little credibility appeared to show a pronounced lack of judgement and, with intimate links to the Prime Minister offered a chance to indirectly impact upon his position. However, as the quotations cited here demonstrate, there were concerns also that she had portrayed herself as an ordinary person and then in the full glare of publicity had come over as a wealthy individual unencumbered by the pressure of ordinary life. Two key issues were at stake. One was judgement, and a second was social credibility. Cherie Blair was heavily impacted upon by both.

A minor issue, but one worthy of brief mention is that of the family as a tool through which to emphasise a position of social ordinariness. In 2000 Tony Blair's son was arrested for being 'drunk and incapable'. This came a short time after Blair had called for fines, which could be issued by the police, for drunken behaviour. Naturally this gave fuel to the media and presented an opportunity to criticise the Prime Minister for failing to provide sufficient guidance to his son on a matter of political salience. Moreover, when detained by police, Blair's son gave an old family address and stated that he was 18, when he was actually 16 at the time of the incident. Blair made light of the incident, not as a failing or an episode which might undermine the principles he hoped to advance, but rather of his position as a father and the trials of trying to raise children. He stated, 'Being a prime minister can be a tough job, being a parent is probably tougher, and sometimes you don't succeed. But the family to me is more important than anything else.'[55] The emphasis on a household which faced problems similar to others in the nation with independent teenagers partly defused the situation for the Blairs. It emphasised the ordinary, suggested a leeway for Euan Blair that was similar to that experienced by other 16-year-olds in the nation and underscored that Tony Blair was in touch, and tried to keep his children in touch with reality. There existed a difference of opinion about how the Blair family was associated with politics. Conservative party leader Iain Duncan Smith contended that 'Tony Blair uses his children ruthlessly. Once you open the doors to your children it just gives the press an excuse for intrusion.' However, no.10 responded and dismissed Duncan Smith's allegations, 'As the media well knows, the prime minister jealously guards the privacy of his family and does everything he can to keep them out of the public eye.'[56]

Conclusion

The Blair era in British politics witnessed the extension of political marketing, from the political to the personal, in ways that had not previously been explored. The use of the past as an instrument of persuasion in politics was raised to new levels to convey the ascension of Blair to a position of leadership as the weaving of the ordinary with the exceptional. In part this was assisted through the available comparisons with the Conservative party which had problems in dispelling impression of incompetence, elitism and sleaze. A further reason for the use of personal considerations in the marketing of Blair as a political leader was that the changes he brought about in the political foundations of the Labour party threatened to create divisions and intra-party hostility within ranks, on account of Blair's determination to reposition the party. In policy terms Blair acted, largely as Thatcher had done for the Conservative party previously, as a political figure determined to master the helm of party ideology and take with him as many traditional Labour voters who could be persuaded to move from familiar positions. Lilleker and Lees-Marshment considered that this, while politically advantageous to Blair as a reformer, created other political problems in the longer term. 'Such concern may be the result of adapting an MOP (Market Oriented Product) approach, for such a strategy can result in a hollowing out of the internal core of a party, which, while yielding short-term electoral success, generates long-term problems.'[57] The stretching of party identity and Blair's determination to press on with reform threatened to dilute what the party stood for, bar that it was not replicating the model or practices of the Conservative party that it had replaced in power.

In part, the selling of Blair as a person assisted in papering over any cracks, cynicism or misperceptions that may have arisen as a consequence of the repeated reforms of party policy and identity. The electorate need not know, nor have cause to have historical understandings of party tradition. Rather Blair could be sold to the electorate as a person who manifested the typical traits of mainstream British culture. His personal profile, and the marketing of him as the embodiment of New Labour, therefore became an important facet in persuading broad elements of political coalitions that he could be trusted on political issues and that he was authentic in his portrayal. Additionally, the party structure was altered so as to allow Blair, personally and politically, to dominate the party apparatus. He was the embodiment of New Labour and this message, as unadulterated as it was, was important to the position of the candidate and the party. Labour strategist Philip Gould had aimed to alter the party infrastructure in advance of Blair's occupancy of no.10: 'Labour must replace competing existing structures with a single chain of command, leading directly to the leader of the party.'[58] Blair thereafter faced charges that he lacked a coherent ideology to lead his party to a new political position, based on principle as opposed to pragmatism. Blair became the central focus of the party, its direction and mandate shaped by him as a politician and a person. As defined primarily by media concerns, when events occurred which demanded an exceptional political response, they came from an ordinary person in touch with national feelings. Simon Jenkins captured the spirit of Blair and his associations with the British people with regard to how the environment offered Blair the chance to demonstrate his personal qualities. 'With no particular destination, events were to spur his action, his friend and ally, his call on stage. The death of Princess Diana, 9/11, foot-and-mouth, the tsunami, the Olympic bid, the London bombs were like scripts delivered to his door by the casting director of history. How would the people's Tony turn them to account? Each offered a chance to master ceremony, to express pain, joy, action or repose.'[59] Emotional expression allowed Blair opportunity to form bonds that accommodated ordinariness. Furthermore there was an appearance of authenticity. Blair could accommodate the exceptional qualities demanded by leadership alongside the habits, passions, social positions and emotions that identified him as an ordinary person. His personal wealth and position within government could largely be downplayed as a result.

The predicament faced by those who struggled to accommodate the concept of ordinariness is clear. In seeking to represent the populace and to convey ordinariness as a political facet two key themes come to the fore. One is that the political figure appears authentic, or that the presentation of their political character is sufficiently seamless as to convey this aspect as fact. A second consideration is that the issues that are raised to give credence to authenticity are in themselves persuasive. In the Blair era the Conservative opponents he faced proved unable to present themselves as authentic, in touch with the emotions of the nation and unable to create events or scenarios suited to a credible presentation of social associations. In part the problem lay in the continued presentation of the Conservative party, by both media interests and the New Labour organisation, as still being entwined in the politics and principles of the Thatcher era. Stereotypes and superficial impressions of Conservative leadership candidates prevailed. Thereafter, as the examples advanced in this chapter make clear the miscalculation as to how ordinariness could be marketed undermined the standing and status of the party. Only with the election of David Cameron to the party leadership did the Conservatives have an individual who could balance the aspects of exceptionalism demanded of the leader; an Eton education, social contacts and personal wealth, with the attributes of ordinariness that appealed to the voter in a period of relative party uniformity; family life, social habits and displays of overt compassion and emotion.

6
Bush, Nascar Dads and Wal-Mart Moms

In 2000 the outcome of the presidential election rested upon perceptions of a fight on the grounds of morality, economic success during the Clinton years and a battle to shape the global position of America, in advance of the unforeseen terror issues which would later impact upon the nation. Gore's prominent position as vice president granted him partial credit for the marked upturn in the American economy, balanced by the liability of occupying the same White House as a president largely discredited on personal terms. His campaign for the presidency appeared to be a logical and natural progression into an office he might have inherited even though Clinton had endured impeachment and survived a trial in the Senate. Bush by contrast emerged from a successful period as Governor of Texas, with a political track record that was generally admired, particularly in conservative circles. However his past was chequered, particularly in the realm of his personal finances, with questions being asked of his position during the savings and loans scandal, and how his assets had been managed during periods when he appeared to elude financial disaster through unconventional means. Neither candidate had a pristine past, but the election was not merely about their individual political or personal merits, it rested as much on the legacy and record of the Clinton years and how the new millennium would be perceived by the American people. In addition Bush tried to present himself with a folksy image, against a candidate already tainted by the trappings of eight years of association with Washington politics. The *New Yorker* pointed out the irony of the election race and the nature of populist politics: 'American populism operates more by a logic of culture and background than by a logic of present day circumstances. In the 2000 campaign, in which two sons of prominent officeholders, educated at prep schools and Ivy League colleges, were pitted against each other, Bush succeeded in putting himself across as the populist and Gore as the elitist.'[1]

The contest of 2004 however was grounded upon different foundations. September 2001 and its aftermath shaped the remainder of the first term of Bush's tenure, and ensured that foreign policy would have a decisive role to play in both the promises made during the 2004 election about the future, alongside reflections on past conduct. However policy issues and party considerations aside, 2004 was notable in the presentation of candidates and how they were portrayed to the American public. Bush's credentials and his folksy image were of course relatively well known following the 2000 race, but the Democratic candidates had to advance themselves to the American people and try to contest firstly for the party nomination and then to oust an incumbent president who had enjoyed respectable approval figures for much of his first term.

What was notable about 2004 was that all the candidates ran on similar personal platforms, accentuating personal failures, impoverishment, and presenting themselves as part and parcel of mainstream American society. The election was one where ordinariness was central to the personal characteristics of each candidate. Of interest too was the fact that Bush embraced the 'regular guy' characteristic and pushed himself to the fore on a similar personal platform to those Democrats who wished to contest the presidency. By 2004 campaigns grounded upon autobiographical aspects of a candidate's past had become the norm. Wealth was downplayed, ordinariness was accentuated, and the effort required to scale the ladder of politics was used as a justification of merit for office. This was far removed from the politics of the 1950s and 1960s. In the midst of the Democratic primary contest, when several candidates struggled to gather delegates to gain the nomination as the presidential candidate, the *Washington Post* reported on Michelle Goldberg's interpretations of the contest (in *Salon.com*), 'In poll after poll, voters say that what really makes them vote for a candidate is "that they are a regular person just like me." '[2] Again, a core piece of the jigsaw when marketing a presidential candidate was that they were ordinary rather than exceptional, and this built upon the lessons of previous elections.

This chapter firstly examines who the candidates were thought to want to appeal to in the election of 2004, and then looks at how firstly Bush and thereafter the Democratic contenders followed a similar strategy in trying to advance themselves with a broad demographic appeal.

Target audiences

The 2004 race was notable in that there was a social uniformity among the candidates who wished to run for office. While there were some familiar and distinct differences of interpretation between the candidates concerning policy, there was little to choose between them with respect to their backgrounds or their wealth. In contrast to past elections the concept of wealth as a factor in conditioning and shaping candidate image was one that, as shown with the experiences of George Bush Sr in Chapter 4, had to be taken seriously. By 2004 television shows such as *The Simple Life* were taking rich socialites and trying to integrate them, via comic and challenging tasks, into mainstream society. There was no effort to hide the underlying concept of two detached and divorced societies, one rich and one poor. However in the political realm the issues were altogether different. Entertainment provided individuals eager to offer themselves for public ridicule and happy to expose themselves to the glare of publicity with little in the way of a substantive outcome, bar perhaps when Paris Hilton was sentenced to a 45-day period in prison which was considered an authentic 'real life' experience, albeit one she seemed unhappy to embrace. In the political realm the stakes are higher, as is the glare of publicity. As identified in Chapter 1 of this work, in the early to mid-twentieth century the political wealth and the autobiographical details of a candidate, although of note, were not marketed so as to try to persuade voters of associations between the elected and electorate on social and emotional grounds. With respect to the changes that occurred in politics Rich commented further, 'When this kind of posturing comes from politicians vying for our vote in an election year, it's harder to laugh. At a minimum it makes one nostalgic for the day when the Roosevelts and Kennedys didn't pretend to be anything other than the fat cats they were.'[3] In 2004 the social profile of the candidates was one which fitted in with those of Kennedy and Roosevelt, but the image and identities that were marketed to the public were altogether different.

In advance of the 2004 election the financial disclosure of candidate wealth gave an interesting and informative profile of the assets held by those who wished to be president. Although a number of the figures that were advanced were approximations or estimates, they pointed to a collection of candidates that shared significant wealth, wealth far in excess of that enjoyed by 'regular' Americans. The Center for Public Integrity used 2002 financial disclosures to estimate income and assets. The wealthiest candidate running in 2004 was John Kerry, who would end up ultimately challenging Bush. He was deemed to have wealth of between $165 and $626 million, with Bush thought to have a personal wealth of a minimum of $9 million. Thereafter the Vice President, Richard Cheney, was worth at least $22 million. Democrat contenders of note, discussed later in this chapter, included Senator John Edwards worth $8.7 million, Senator Bob Graham, $7.3 million and Howard Dean, Governor of Vermont, worth $3.9 million. Of the main figures who featured in the 2004 election only Senator Joseph Liebermann was considered to have personal wealth of moderate standing, with means of at least $376,000.[4] Many of the candidates had ongoing financial investments with incomes above and beyond that bestowed upon them by their political careers. The wealth of the main contenders for the presidential office was clearly at odds with mainstream society, yet if the candidates were to be seen to be ordinary then the wealth they held had to be marketed so as to be a meaningless factor and one which did not create social and emotional divides with society. If Kerry had been elected to office he would have been the wealthiest president for over a century.[5]

The issue of wealth in the 2004 election had a twofold consequence and impact. Firstly, the individual wealth entertained by the candidates could be used to suggest that they were of a different social class and standing from the general American public and that, as a consequence they would or could not understand the issues which afflicted America. Secondly, there were concerns that the presidential office might be acquired simply through the ability of individuals, most particularly Kerry, who could spend their personal wealth to supplement the effectiveness of their campaigns for office. Although he could still be considered wealthy in his own right, his wealth was largely derived from his marriage to Teresa Heinz. Kerry tried to discount wealth as an issue or political tool in the campaign, and indicated that he would not immediately spend his own money. His spokesman Bob Wade argued, 'He's not ruled it out but he has said that he has never used his money to run for office before and it is not the way he would like to run for office. ... But if it is the only way to respond to a vicious attack, he may have to consider it.'[6] The wealth accumulated by the candidates during the 2004 election campaign was vast, and it was subject to careful scrutiny.[7] However, in the public realm, while there was interest in the general figures accumulated and spent on the election, the specifics of liaisons between candidates and their sources of wealth were not prominent. Part of the reason for this was the efforts made by candidates to shape this feature and market it to their political advantage.

The 2004 race appeared to be about marketing the identities of candidates who bore a striking resemblance to one another. In marketing the candidates there was a perceived need to identify the social groups and swing voters who would prove decisive in the election. Databases were set up and utilised to gather profiles of prospective voters for each party. As the *Atlantic* pointed out, 'The Democratic National Committee has acquired a database of 158 million voters it has dubbed the "DataMart". Appended to every name are as many as 306 "lifestyle variables" gleaned from voter files, consumer databases, and other sources. From these, candidates can find out a citizen's voting record, number of children, kind of car, favourite television shows and magazines, and even number of pets.' The Republican party has a similar database, the "Voter Vault" with records on the lifestyle of 165 million people.[8] This strategic research allowed the political parties to present material tailored to each individual voter, and to imprint consumer orientation into the election process. Karen White, a political director for a pro-choice group, argued, 'In the past we've always tried to bring voters to us on our issues. This time we're getting so much insight onto their personal lives that we can actually bring what they need to hear to them, on their terms'.[9] Political marketing is clearly evident here. This allowed candidates to try to identify who could be persuaded to their cause, where to allocate campaign funds and how to sort individuals into 'lifestyle clusters' which might indicate their voting preferences.

One feature of 2004 was that strict income measurement did not really assist in showing where party votes would be placed. Rather, values were considered to be important in shaping voting preference. An emphasis on values required the parties to be seen to have an appreciation of the emotional approach held by voters. This in part assists in highlighting why Bush adopted a compassionate conservatism ethos in 2000 and distanced himself from the more zealous Republicans who had previously captured the Congress in 1994 and had largely set the conservative agenda of the 1990s.

While there were opportunities and challenges in trying to capture the mood of the voter rather than simply dissecting groups based on income, there were social groups who were considered to be important in 2004 to whom the major candidates tried to market themselves. Debate exists as to the importance of specifically delineated groups who are considered to be critical in determining the outcome of elections. In advancing themselves to the populace in 2004 the leading contenders did appear to perceive that there was a pivotal group with whom they could identify and bond, both socially and emotionally. In previous presidential contests the 'soccer moms' had been considered to be pivotal to a successful strategy. In 2004, controversially, 'Nascar dads' were pinpointed as a group who held the keys to electoral success, the term being coined by a Democrat pollster, Celinda Lake.[10] The problems of trying to profile groups such as this led to a great deal of cynicism among media pundits, but suggested that there was an awareness that specific groups had to be addressed despite hesitance about their validity. As stated in the *New York Times*, 'Sadly, Nascar dad, lionised by left and right alike but understood by neither, has become in the last year another strategic abstraction, another tiny, lifeless stick figure in the dim shadowbox of American politics.'[11] The stereotype of Nascar man was not that of a wealthy, cultured and sophisticated individual. Indeed the profiles advanced during 2004 to try to define the individual voters covered a broad cross-section of society. Political scientist Larry Sabato considered them to be 'middle – to lower-middle class males who are family men, live in rural areas, used to vote heavily Democratic but now usually vote Republican'.[12] It was the task and desire of both conservative and liberal interests to appeal to this group. The cynicism directed at the establishment of swing groups who would decide each election outcome, previous candidate groups having included soccer moms, is only one aspect of the overall strategic targeting of the groups. Bush, and the array of Democrats who wished to contend the presidential office could not afford to appear detached from social groups who might strategically use their vote, feel alienated in large numbers, or were considered to be swing voters with little long-term political allegiance. Furthermore, all candidates who embraced the 'group de jour' could reasonably portray themselves in keeping with one of America's modern interests and pastimes, particularly in the southern states.

To highlight the perceived need to reach out to ordinary Americans, and Nascar dads in particular, 2004 witnessed the arrival at Nascar tracks of a number of candidates eager to demonstrate that, policies and international diplomacy aside, they too were aware of Nascar and its supporters. Clinton attended a Nascar race in 1992. He was booed loudly by fans, creating an unwelcome image during a presidential election campaign. Nevertheless in the prelude to 2004 Democrats once again sought to give themselves the desired image which might influence Southern voters in particular and create social bonds between elected and electorate. In late 2003, Governor Mark Warner, Senator George Allen, Senator Bob Graham and Senator John Edwards were all visitors to Nascar races. *The Christian Science Monitor* reported this as a 'populist campaign designed to draw mostly white country boys back to the party of their grandfathers'.[13] The general perception of Nascar dads was not, it appears, solely a strategic one to present candidates to key swing voters. In keeping with the context of this text it offered social and emotional connections with voters, and tried to anticipate cultural and lifestyle associations which transcended policy identification. Dave Saunders, a Virginia Democrat argued, 'The Democrats had done a terrible job with the culture in the South. And Nascar is one way that we can move through the culture and start talking about issues and ideology.'[14] Similarly Jim Wright, a Florida sociologist argued that 'This Nascar dad strategy is a conscious effort to regain some of that lost constituency, to reach out and connect with voters whose fathers never voted Republican in their lives, and whose grandfathers certainly never did'.[15] The importance of appealing to ordinary Americans on the one hand, and strategic target groups on the other, was not lost on the Republicans either, for all the cynicism of the media and those who had analysed previous elections. In February 2004, Bush involved himself in the race circuit. He attended the Daytona 500 in Florida to affirm his relationship with individuals who were morally, if not economically, in tune with the Republican party. Again, although the fans at the race track did not necessarily have their own interests and causes advanced via Bush's tax reforms or record on employment, it was important that he align himself with the blue-collar communities. As one fan at the race track stated, 'He's like me. ... His swagger, his confidence – I can relate to his thinking.'[16] This social and emotional bonding was designed to invoke loyalty, a feature considered significant with respect to the Nascar community. The emergence of Bush's appreciation of Nascar was slow but nevertheless significant, suggesting an understanding across time of the need to build a base of support among groups not aligned to the Republican party on socio-economic or class grounds. The *Washington Post* observed, 'In 2001, champion Jeff Gordon received no attention from the White House. But the 2002 champion, Tony Stewart, got a visit to the Oval Office. Last year, champion Matt Kenseth was heralded on the White House South Lawn, where presidential aides lined up seven stock cars to help attract cameras.'[17] This of course was mirrored in the United Kingdom by leaders keen to be associated with football and its culture.

As each election season comes around there are different perceptions of who matters. In 2004 it is clear that both Republicans, looking to a group of potential voters on grounds which did not match the economic profile of the party, and Democrats, looking to try to recapture a group who had class alignment with the party but had defected largely on moral and religious grounds, had every reason to try to reach out to a distinctive social group easily reachable in the context of a sporting event. Although the debate about the statistical significance of the group was pronounced and there were accusations that the true electoral meaning of the groups in a national context was limited, nevertheless, both parties took time to try to address it as a demographic and social entity of note.

In 2004 both President Bush and the Democrats who challenged him tried to advance to the American voter images of their identity, their interests and how they as people, as well as politicians, could relate to the interests of the American people. Policies were obviously important with the ongoing war on terror, the issue of Iraq and major debates about the American economy holding centre stage. How the candidates tried to run on an autobiographical past and market their shortcomings as well as their successes was testament to previous election experiences and the need to appeal to social groups who had diverse economic interests.

George Bush Jr: A regular guy

Bush was obviously known to the American people as a political figure and as a person long in advance of 2004. The successful campaign of 2000 and the time spent as Governor of Texas suggested that little could be done to reinvent Bush. His personality was known and the exposure he received as President appeared to suggest that he faced the same challenges as several of the leaders discussed in this text, that when in office it was particularly difficult to convey an impression of ordinariness to the electorate. Nevertheless Bush tried to argue that he was in touch with regular Americans and part and parcel of mainstream American society.

Bush faced problems in using an autobiographical ticket to advance his personal identity. He obviously emerged from the shadow of his father's esteemed position within politics, with suggestions of a dynasty emerging to explain the ongoing prevalence of the Bush family in the elite realm of the political environment. Bush faced criticism concerning his business past, and tried to paper over the cracks in a number of areas regarding his business activities in the period before his emergence into politics. The record suggested that Bush had been rather fortunate to emerge with his business credibility intact and was able, through creative accounting procedures, to create the impression of success from apparent failure. The image however was not one that could be flagged up to the American public. Rather the impression conveyed was of Bush overcoming business difficulties and emerging through skills and hard work to a period of personal prosperity. A large part of Bush's success was based on his status within the business world as a person and the financial manoeuvres used to evade financial disaster. Esteemed economist Paul Krugman argued, 'In 1986, one would have had to consider Mr. Bush a failed businessman. He had run through millions of dollars of other people's money, with nothing to show for it but a company losing money and heavily burdened with debt. But he was rescued from failure when Harken Energy bought his company at an astonishingly high price. There is no question that Harken was basically paying for Mr. Bush's connection.'[18] Bush also had a period as the owner of the Texas Rangers baseball team and his own personal wealth aside, enjoyed an upbringing which was removed from that enjoyed by mainstream America. Reflecting on Bush's economic misfortunes and his eventual economic success Krugman stated, 'The point is the contrast between image and reality. Mr. Bush portrays himself as a regular guy, someone ordinary Americans can identify with. But his personal fortune was built on privilege and insider dealings – and after his Harken sale, on large-scale corporate welfare. Some people have it easy.'[19] Clearly, as the figures discussed at the start of this chapter show, Bush was a wealthy man in his own right, with important and influential political and business connections. It was difficult for Bush to try to claim that he was self-made, had endured impoverishment or had emerged into politics from mainstream society. Other means of stressing Bush's vulnerability had to be found to justify claims that he was a regular guy.

One area where Bush could demonstrate both his vulnerability and his resolve was with respect to the consumption of alcohol. Bush was, reluctantly, forced to concede in the 2000 election campaign to having been arrested for driving under the influence of alcohol in 1976. At the time the disclosure of the arrest appeared to be largely in the interests of the Democrats, as the release of the information came in the immediate prelude to the national vote. However, Bush's aides argued that although the prospective President had erred on a particular occasion it was not newsworthy, and that he had been open about his alcohol consumption and its associated problems on previous occasions. In 2000 Bush argued that he had associated with those who had been afflicted by problems with alcohol, but did not class himself as an alcoholic. He met individuals in a charity centre that assisted people struggling with addictions, and stated, 'I was able to share with some of the men and women here that I quit drinking in 1986 and haven't had a drop since then. And it wasn't because of a government program, by the way – in my particular case, because I had a higher call.'[20] The moral tone of Bush's argument fits well into the emotional connection needed between the elected and electors. He had faced a trial during his life and had endured trying times, and yet as an indication of his resolve and personal motivation, on his fortieth birthday he had ceased to consume alcohol. The 'higher call' component also suggested that Bush embraced the type of morality central to his neo-conservative message and important to several demographic communities. The approach of Bush to the issue of alcohol also had another important component. He tried to convey a sense of unity with respect to alcohol as a social problem, and thereafter suggested association on a social front. He argued in early 2000 that he identified with those struggling with alcohol, 'Just like you, I'm on a walk, and it's a never ending walk as far as I'm concerned. I used to drink too much and I quit drinking. I want you to know that your life's walk is shared by a lot of other people. Even some who wear suits.'[21] Bush perceived alcohol abuse to be a classless problems, and portrayed himself as an individual and a leader who could associate with people across the class divide.

In 2004 Bush tried to use his past experiences to further the interests of his campaign. As mentioned, as an individual, impoverishment was hard to argue. Similarly, given the wealth and standing of his parents, a campaign based on adversarial family experiences was also difficult to entertain. There was one area however where Bush could strategically contend that he was from ordinary stock. Bush exploited the advantages afforded him by his incumbency in late 2003. Reporting on a state visit to the United Kingdom the *New York Times* observed, 'on the eve of his visit to London this week he [Bush] hit a characteristically phoney note when he told an interviewer, "I never dreamt when I was living in Midland, Texas, that I would be staying in Buckingham Palace." Mr. Bush, who was born in New Haven, lived in Midland until only the age of 15 before moving on to such hick venues as Andover, Yale and Harvard when not vacationing in family compounds in Kennebunkport, Me., or Jupiter Island, a tony neighbour of Palm Beach.'[22] Although few locations could be used to provide a contrast to Bush's upbringing, Buckingham Palace offered itself to this end.

In 2004 Bush's economic strategy, particularly in the realm of tax reform, came under scrutiny. The policies and their merit are not the central focus of this text, but their general thrust was used by his detractors to try to give an impression that Bush was not a man of the people. Through his personal wealth and tax policy, they argued that Bush had discarded the mask which had helped to create and sustain the Reagan Democrats, individuals on the lower levels of the socio-economic spectrum, and was distancing himself from the poor. An increase in the federal deficit, in alignment with greater foreign policy commitments in the Middle East and in Asia, brought tax and spend issues to the fore. *Newsweek* rounded on the President for marketing himself as an ordinary person but then lacking the substance to show that he was one, or associated with them. Jonathan Alter argued, 'President Bush is a regular guy who doesn't care a whole lot about regular people. The first is a political asset; voters like his guyness. The second is his greatest vulnerability, and he offers more evidence for it almost every day.... Last week – despite bipartisan action in the Senate – he still hadn't lifted finger in the House for a measly $100 million to keep AmeriCorps from being slashed by 40 percent, leaving kids untutored and after-school programs facing closure. Who is he for first? The question is not just if the president tells the truth but if the truth – finally – will be told about him.'[23] In a similar vein there were criticisms of the President's image and demeanour from his opponents. The individual who would ultimately challenge the President for office, John Kerry, was cited on *Meet the Press*, 'He said that his colleagues are appalled at the ... president's lack of knowledge. They've managed him the same way they've managed Ronald Reagan. They send him out to the press for one event a day. They put him in a brown jacket and jeans and get him to move some hay or move a truck, and all of a sudden he's the Marlboro Man.'[24] Bush dismissed the criticism and claimed that Kerry did not know him. Moreover, it was clear across time that Kerry and the Democrats entertained a marketing strategy similar to that advanced by Bush.

Bush's efforts to advance himself as an ordinary and regular American were pronounced during the campaign of 2004. It was not a case of individual positing of an advert or of trying to give a single impression of George Bush. Rather it involved an effort to portray, across time, the image of a man of the people, one integrated and in touch with the electorate and aware of their problems. This contained issues to do with image, pastimes, experiences and contextualising his social position. In the realm of political marketing Bush embraced a sales technique where he took his image and manufactured it to suit prevailing needs. This attuned his image to the social and emotional requirements of the nation. Additionally as the Nascar discussion highlighted, social groupings deemed necessary to the retention of power were integrated into Bush's political identity across time, giving him a mass appeal as an individual who enjoyed mass spectator sport, but also handing him the opportunity to address and play to groups, rightly or wrongly, identified as pivotal to a coalition of voters. Bush had to create this identity which was difficult, given the lack of a credible autobiographical portrait on which to run. His resolve in overcoming the challenges of excessive alcohol consumption allowed him some leeway to contend that he was socially inclusive, but in the political and economic realm Bush stood out as an individual who was neither ordinary nor shared the common subjective experiences of the American people.

Democrats: Towing the line

The 2004 race was significant in the marketing of the individual because all the serious Democratic candidates adopted a similar approach in shaping their political identity when seeking to oust Bush from office. All played autobiographical cards, played down impressions of elite standing and highlighted areas of impoverishment, personal failing and the nature and context of their upbringing. The issue of political identity was important for the Democratic party as a whole and for the individual candidates. The defection of individual voters to the Republican party who voted against their own rational economic interests posed problems for the Democrats. As cited previously in this chapter, there were perceptions that Bush's regular image was superficial and his economic interests and political ideals were more in line with traditional stereotypes relating to his party. However, in order to accentuate this as an issue of gravity the Democrats, each of them wealthy in their own right, had to try to create a party and individual identity that portrayed them as being more in tune with the populace than the President. As mentioned in Chapter 4, Clinton had been successful in appearing to be a man of the people and for the people in 1992, partly because George Bush Sr was less accomplished in pursuing this type of political marketing and identity creation. Similarly, in 1996, Clinton could replicate his folksy image, and persuade the voters that he was a man who looked to the future, contrasting himself with Bob Dole who was characterised as an individual who was rooted in the past. By 2004, with the evolution of marketing strategies and an awareness that ordinariness was a feature of political campaigning it became clear that internally, within the Democratic party, there would be a uniform approach to campaigning. Two issues necessitated this approach. Firstly, there was a chance to portray Bush in a negative light and accentuate his wealth and elite standing. Secondly, the risk of seeming aloof from the problems of America by not playing an autobiographical card was too high to afford not to, and consequently the Democrats lined up to highlight their failings and problems while also asserting their merit for office.

Although the main bulk of this text considers individual leaders and those in office or who were in the process of challenging in a direct head-to-head race, the nature of the association and competition, in terms of positing a personal political identity and marketing it, among the Democrats in 2004 is instructive in an appreciation of how marketing impoverishment has evolved.

In the early days of Democratic candidate declarations of an intention to run against Bush the tone for individual marketing in the campaign was set down. Of all the candidates who advanced themselves on a platform of a populist identity perhaps the most effective was the man who was to become the Democratic candidate for the vice-presidency, Senator John Edwards. He advanced himself on a personal basis from the outset, highlighting, virtually at every opportunity afforded him, his personal attributes and how he could relate to the American people on a personal basis. In 2003 Edwards persistently advanced his cause, highlighting for example how his origins contrasted with those of President Bush. He stated, 'I hope you agree with me this is still a country where the son of a millworker can go toe-to-toe against the son of a president of the United States.' The *Washington Post* observed how Edwards advanced his personal case, 'As much as anyone in the nine-person Democratic field, Edwards is running on his autobiography – and not just because his political record is shorter and skimpier than almost all his opponents' records. The narrative of his life provides a theme of a great consistency and of potential force, a theme that would surely shape an Edwards presidency, should that ever occur.'[25] Edwards was a lawyer by trade, and a successful and wealthy one. His main contention however was that he protected individuals in the courts against corporations, and that he worked for ordinary people, with blue-collar individuals a consistent focus of his rhetoric and campaign. The *New Yorker* appeared appreciative of how Edwards intertwined his personal standing and a conveyance of populist and regular interests: 'this business of class in America is tricky. The Edwardses come from a middle-class, not a poor or working-class, background...his little-people consciousness, politically advantageous though it may be, seems real.'[26] Edwards lacked political experience in office and had not held any position as an executive. This was a potential Achilles heel; however by playing the personality card Edwards could accentuate particular strengths. In addressing connections with the American people he could also stress the personal and emotional experiences that he and his family had endured. He had lost a son in a car accident in the 1990s and argued that he could associate with those who had experienced loss, highlighting a personal warmth and association that was difficult for other candidates to replicate. At the start of his campaign he argued that he would be 'a champion for regular people in the Oval Office every day'.[27] *National Review* pinpointed the core theme of the Edwards bid at the outset, 'Just a regular guy, is Johnny Edwards. This image, of humble beginnings in the rural Carolinas and a young family man here in the capital city of Raleigh, has long been his trademark.'[28] Furthermore it emphasised Edwards' strength and gave advice for his Democratic opponents, 'Don't think you can beat him on personality or his trial-lawyer past. Your party has been fully Clintonized, and many of its activists and voters are now primed to value youth, energy, and charms above anything else. Don't try to contrast your hard-luck life with his.'[29] Edwards personally played the same card, emphasising his ordinariness as part of his campaign, while accentuating the social standing of his opponents. Having come second in the Iowa caucus, Edwards looked forward to the nominations race in the Southern states, while criticising the status of one of his opponents, Wesley Clark, 'I was elected in a tough Southern state and have spent my time in the Senate dealing every single day with the problems of a Southern state, with job loss, with the rural economy, all of the problems that affect people in Southern States. General Clark comes from a different place.'[30]

Edwards was supported by his wife during the campaign. She replicated many of her husband's arguments and tried to cast him as both an exceptional individual and, at the same time, as a person who was grounded and in touch with the American people. She stated, 'He's a regular guy who gets people's lives and who understands their issues. The guy's a winner. He knows how to win.'[31] Edwards advanced a populist Democratic ticket, trying to point out disparities of wealth within America, catering to a traditional Democrat constituency, but also trying hard to associate with a middle class that he argued had been neglected by Bush.

Of all the candidates who waged a marketing strategy designed to portray themselves as ordinary Howard Dean, an early front-runner, stands out. Dean characterised himself as an ordinary American who could associate with a broad swathe of society. In late 2003 he published a book designed to give him a profile in the run-up to the election and the pivotal primary races of early 2004. Throughout the book entitled *Winning Back America*, Dean emphasised his humble roots, commencing with claims to be a regular guy. He also accentuated and emphasised a number of areas which showed him to be impoverished, pointing out his 'agricultural minimum wage', and how he undertook menial jobs to make ends meet when young. Dean also tried to point out differences between himself and Bush. Both went to Yale, however Dean, looking to portray himself as more socially inclusive argued, 'Unlike George W. Bush, I had black roommates at Yale'.[32] This was not only an effort to discredit Bush, but also ensured that the minority communities within America could identify with him. When in power as a governor Dean still tried to maintain an ordinary presence, 'Our telephone number remained in the book'. Additional information was provided by Dean to give potential voters an insight into his life and character, including his favourite books, his weight and the car he owned. A large part of the information was superfluous to that needed to come to a sound political judgement about Dean, but tried to create an impression of a political figure extracted from mainstream society and one who had not forgotten his roots. Dean's strength lay not in reinventing his past or downplaying his wealth, but in selling his political and personal message. He used the Internet to good effect during the early stages of his campaign trying to reach out to a cross-section of voters.[33] This initially appeared to be revolutionary and a major step forward in political campaigning and marketing. Dick Morris, former political consultant to President Clinton, observed, 'It's part of a new era – back to basics. Howard Dean is using the Internet in an entirely guerrilla marketing approach. By this process, he's developed a massive grass roots list.'[34] This strategy however had its own pitfalls as the initial enthusiasm for peer to peer communication was mirrored by other candidates, and the actual affiliation of those who accessed and assisted with Dean's Internet campaign was uncertain. Although innovative and novel, the initial enthusiasm for Dean's approach, and its potential revolution for communication and national elections remained unfulfilled.

Although Dean tried to portray himself as the stock outsider in American politics, coming to turf out the political figures who had led the nation astray, 'those guys in Washington', some media sources were less sure of his credentials.[35] While he claimed to be of ordinary stock, and had displayed the resolve needed to come to be a challenger for the nomination for his party, the *Washington Post* had other perceptions of Dean as a candidate, 'Dean comes from money – his father, grandfather and great-grandfather were investment bankers; he summered in Sag Harbor, part of the Long Island playground that includes the Hamptons, and went to Yale. During the Vietnam War, he received a medical deferment from the draft for an unfused vertebrate in his back and moved to Vermont in 1978 for his medical residency. Entering politics there was relatively easy.'[36] In keeping with the stereotype of a tight-knit political elite Dean's grandmother invited President Bush's grandmother to be her bridesmaid. Dean's image was that of a working-class populist with rolled up sleeves and an aggressive manner. The reality was that he was of a similar background and standing to the other candidates contesting the presidency in 2004. Similarly, as Dean tried to invent himself to present a political identity that would embrace a broad cross-section of voters across America he appeared to be in danger of creating too many political identities, trying to cater to a number of groups, advocating policies that appeared inconsistent and out of tune with his previous declarations on policy in Vermont.[37] Nevertheless, as Dean progressed through an ultimately unsuccessful primary race he maintained his stance that there was a constituency, ill-defined yet pivotal, that was instrumental in shaping the destiny of the nation. In New Hampshire he railed against the corporate interests in the United States and argued that 'This government is run by a president who cares more about corporations than he does about ordinary Americans, and that is why I'm running'. Similarly, 'The ordinary people in this country are supposed to be running it.'[38]

A large part of the cause of Dean's undoing, following good poll statistics in mid to late 2003, was a televised speech where he was considered to have 'lost control' and to have lacked the poise necessary to lead the nation. Dean countered allegations of his appearance of being unpresidential by giving a confessional appearance on television. This evoked past memories of candidates who needed to bolster their image in the event of negative publicity, as the *New York Times* observed, 'From Richard M. Nixon's Checkers speech to Bill Clinton's "60 Minutes" interview about Gennifer Flowers, politicians have a history of going on television to quell accusations of misconduct'.[39] Dean presented himself as an individual who had made a one-off error, but insisted that getting enthusiastic about his cause was not a cause for concern. He did, as might be expected, allude to an impression that he was an ordinary man who had come to politics without necessarily bringing a fully fledged acumen with him. He confessed, on *ABC's Primetime* Thursday that he had made a 'zillion mistakes' during his campaign, and also to highlight his connection with the ordinary person, 'I wear cheap suits sometimes'.[40] For all the innovation of Dean's e-mail and electronic campaign, he faltered at an early stage and his impact petered away quite quickly following disappointing results. While he commanded a presence and attention in 2003 Dean was unable to portray himself as a credible contender when other candidates entered the race. His lasting mark on the 2004 race was his advocacy and use of electronic resources to advance his case.

John Kerry, as outlined at the start of this chapter, had considerable personal wealth. His challenge with respect to his individual standing was a complex one. He had to try to create a base of support among core Democratic voters and appear to associate with them, and this entailed an effort to appear to be largely aware of the plight of blue-collar America and be understanding of that community's needs. He also had to try to reach out to potential swing voters, address accusations concerning his personal wealth and fend off potential criticisms of his identity and personal position, namely that he was affected by his great wealth. Kerry's strategy and creation of a politically marketable identity is entirely in keeping with that of the other candidates and political figures mentioned previously. At an early stage of his campaign bid his personal life, social preferences and hobbies were advanced to the public. An objective was to make it easy to associate with Kerry, his interests and personal life being colourful and diverse. Kerry was said to enjoy shooting and eating doves, he rode a Harley Davidson motorbike, played ice hockey, snowboarded and wind-surfed, on top of being a husband and a senator.[41] In tune with the nature of the modern campaign, and in keeping with the assertions of this text, Kerry was encouraged to play upon his experiences as a person and to downplay policy, 'Kerry's advisers have urged him not to ramble, to speak less about issues and more about his life'.[42] Indeed Kerry did have an interesting life, spending time at a Swiss boarding school, assisting in campaigning for Edward M. Kennedy in 1962 and spending time serving his country in Vietnam. With regard to his social standing and wealth his early years do not appear to have been imbued with the financial acumen he would later possess. One of Kerry's friends observed that, 'John was from a prominent family, but he wasn't wealthy'.[43]

Running on an autobiographical ticket was one aspect of Kerry's campaign, yet in a similar vein to others discussed in this text he struggled to give the impression that he was derived from ordinary society and that he was a regular guy. Widespread information about the fortune largely derived from his wife's family legacy gave an impression that partly obscured Kerry's real origins. In an era of manufactured political autobiographies trying to get across a true and realistic picture of Kerry proved difficult. John Norris, who was Kerry's state director in Iowa, although unconcerned about its immediate effect upon the candidate's fortunes, observed, 'The East Coast press uses the word "aloof".[44] He was considered also to be 'too towering, too confident and too rich (His wife's fortune exceeds half a billion dollars) for people to walk away indifferently'.[45] Kerry's past, while it was portrayed as an asset by Kerry, became a target for the Bush campaign. Advertisements were designed to highlight aspects of the Senator's past, the accuracy of his Vietnam record, statements made by Kerry when he was young and to try to profile the flip-flop brand which would later cast a negative light upon Kerry's campaign strategy. Bush's director of polling and media, Matthew Dowd, argued that 'We have a job to do to correct the false impression given about us and the false impression about Kerry himself'.[46] Clearly the modern presidential campaign has become, in part, a contest about marketing the individual, a contest between camps to try to advance a personal image and identity that resonates with the public. Marketing this, by trying to manufacture a candidate's past so that they can be viewed subjectively by a large part of the populace as ordinary has become a meaningful campaign feature. It is now not only about what the candidate advocates, but also about who they are and where they have originated from, and increasingly this, as with policy, is open to vigorous debate and interpretation.

Kerry's campaign for both nominee and for President was carefully choreographed. Kerry met fire fighters during his campaign for the Democratic nomination. The *Washington Post* reported the event and raised the impression that it was artificial and strategic. 'This crowd has all the requisite types: a group of people, invited by the campaign, who are meant to appear as if they just happened to be there that day.... At these events candidates are judged for their authenticity, meaning less how much like a regular guy they are than how regular they can appear given the intrusive press entourage. This is a particularly important test for Kerry, given his rap for being aloof.'[47] The premeditated public relations opportunity produced its desired results, as reported: ' "I love him. He's awesome," says Beth Blake, one of the fire fighters. "He's very down to earth. He's a regular guy, just like everyone else. Look at this, he even got us our popcorn." '[48] This of course was hardly a challenging task for a multimillionaire, but gave the impression of a generous, considerate and earthy candidate.

Kerry however was not, it appears, as adept as Bush or his opponents in weaving together an integrated strategy of personal presentation. On the one hand he actively presented himself as an ordinary individual unaffected by wealth. On the other however there were occasions when Kerry appeared to let down his guard and his public identity became muddled and unclear. In his first campaign commercial on television in 2004 Kerry presented an outline of his life story, advancing a narrative profile of his character and experiences to the American people. While he mentioned his service to his country, he also discussed his educational background in the following terms: 'I thought it was important if you had a lot of privileges as I had had, to go to a great university like Yale, to give something back to your country.'[49] Westen considered this to be an issue which served to underscore, in an emotional context, divisions between Kerry and the voter. Westen argued that 'When Kerry added the reference to Yale, he fully activated the primary network that the conservative movement has worked for so many years to stamp into the American psyche to galvanize disdain and resentment towards Democrats: the liberal elite. Put together Massachusetts, liberal senator, and Yale and you have virtually the whole network activated.'[50] By contrast Bush rarely mentioned his education at Yale. In keeping with the spirit and practice of contemporary political marketing Westen believed that, 'The Bush campaign certainly understood what "average folks" think about intellectuals'.[51] While the candidates had similar backgrounds, were wealthy and shared social networks, what appeared to matter as an emotional bond between elector and the elected was how the presentation of the individual was accomplished. An elite education was an asset in many respects to become a figure of standing within politics; however it was a political liability when connecting to the voter.

Kerry was faced with challenges from within the Democrat camp, as well as from Bush and a cynical media corps. In the prelude to the pivotal New Hampshire primary a number of the hopeful candidates pushed themselves to the fore as being the most ordinary candidate, attuned socially and emotionally, while at the same time trying to assert credibility in the area of policy and display authority in leadership. While the political marketing of policy hinged upon several features related to party traditions, ideological convictions and the environmental context of the campaign, all candidates in the race adhered to a strategy designed to promote a political identity rooted in the mundane. As so few, if any of the candidates, actually had ordinary backgrounds the façade of ordinariness was important to convince voters that the candidates were in touch. In New Hampshire the infighting on these grounds was accentuated. A candidate, although not a very successful one, retired General Wesley K. Clark made a barbed comment about having to face other candidates from elite backgrounds. While Kerry, Dean and Joseph Lieberman, alongside President Bush all went to Yale, Clark argued, 'Unlike all the rest of the people in this race, I did grow up poor, I didn't go to Yale. My parents couldn't have afforded to send me there.'[52] In keeping with the central argument of this text that ordinariness, or its perception and portrayal, are central to contemporary politics Clark emphasised his target voter market. His campaign manager argued that in the aftermath of a disappointing New Hampshire showing Clark would concentrate on 'identifying with ordinary Americans'.[53] However, Clark's strategy was not particularly cohesive and his political marketing and public relations strategy was undermined when he referred to Kerry, a decorated Vietnam veteran, as a 'junior officer'. Dick Harpootlian, South Carolina Democratic Party Chairman was pessimistic about this interpretation. He believed that 'There are a lot more lieutenants out there than generals' and that the comment had taken away Clark's 'edge he had with the regular guy'.[54] Ultimately Clark was to make little headway either in New Hampshire or the primary contest in a meaningful way. Although he perhaps did have more genuine credentials with respect to casting himself as an ordinary individual, that all the other candidates in the race followed the same approach hindered his ability to cast himself as an exceptional figure in the Democratic primary race.

2008: A populist pitch

It is clear that perceptions remain that a populist persona can be exploited for electoral gain and that ordinariness and its associated political identity can be utilised to appeal to the contemporary voter. The presidential race of 2008 is a case in point. Barack Obama, frontrunner for much of the Democratic primary contest in 2008 and eventually America's president was eager to address issues of elitism and ordinariness on a frequent basis through his elongated campaign. This arose, in part, on account of perceptions that his family wealth created a social gulf between him and core demographic groups to whom he would have to appeal to both capture the Democratic nomination, and thereafter contest the presidential office. Obama defended himself against accusations of elitism stating, 'Michelle and I grew up in a pretty modest situation. I was raised by a single mum and my grandparents, Michelle's dad was a shift worker for the city in Chicago, her mother was a secretary. Neither of her parents went to college.' He also claimed that 'our parents saw struggle' and his wife's father had suffered from multiple sclerosis. On ABC's *Good Morning America* he argued, 'The irony is that I think it is fair to say that both Michelle and

I grew up in much less privileged circumstances that either of my two other potential opponents'.[55] In his autobiographical writings, released initially in 2007, Obama played to the conventional script of hardship, impoverishment and personal trial. He recalled, for example, his early career, 'And so, having sublet the cheapest apartment I could find, having bought my first three suits and a new pair of shoes that turned out to be a half-size too small and would cripple me for the next nine weeks, I arrived at the firm one drizzly morning in early June.'[56] In keeping with the other examples cited in this text Obama still retained the concept that the ideal candidate, as desired by the voter, was the person who could attest to impoverishment in their youthful and informative years, giving way to exceptional abilities in politics in the prelude to running for office. Across the duration of Obama's election campaign disclosures of his unconventional family life, relatives living in poverty and his linkage with Kenya characterised the interweaving of his public and private lives. How much these impacted upon voter choice or created an alluring mix of personal charisma alongside an attractive and substantive political platform is at present difficult to estimate, but nevertheless it is clear that Obama and his strategists were patently aware of the potential divisions that might be created concerning wealth and electoral credibility.

Significant concentration was given during the later stages of the 2008 race to the position entertained by Republican vice-presidential candidate Sarah Palin. Palin's emergence into the limelight of American politics was accompanied by criticism of her lack of experience on a national stage, alongside queries about her ability to understand America's foreign policy position, in particular the Bush doctrine. McCain's choice of Palin appeared to be both surprising and controversial and raised questions about his political judgement. Her candidacy evoked strong approval and strong criticism across a range of personal, political and ideological issues and raised pertinent questions about the extent to which ordinariness could be accentuated and marketed in the contemporary campaign. Despite extensive criticism there were thought to be redeeming qualities to her selection and her interweaving of her ordinary character with her political capabilities gave her a political appeal that temporarily, at least, bolstered the Republicans and threw the Democratic campaign off its intended course.

The selection of a woman as a vice-presidential candidate gave a superficial impression that Hillary Clinton supporters who were disaffected with the absence of a woman from the culmination of the election process might be drawn to Republican ranks. However, given the gulf between the ideological positions of Clinton and Palin it appeared unlikely that this gender-based component would act as a tool which might entice disillusioned Democrats. Palin's core appeal was unashamedly populist in nature. Following her first national speech which announced her to the American public CBS' Jeff Greenfield announced that it was a 'perfect populist pitch'.[57] Her candidacy created a number of questions about the nature of the modern leader and the use of populist criteria as a justification for election to office. One issue was the obvious dilemma that she was a heartbeat away from the presidency and her executive experience and political understanding were insufficient to sustain any real credibility in that office. Joe Hilley considered this to be a factor which was not pivotal in the election campaign of Palin: 'To win an election, Sarah was simply selling Sarah, travelling the state and telling voters she would listen to their issues and concerns. Her opponents had more time in public office, more business experience, and more money to spend on their campaigns. None of that mattered.'[58] A second dilemma was that she appeared popular among the right of the Republican party and exploited her social and emotional resonance with that ideological group. The extent of her appeal to other parts of the political spectrum, and swing voters in particular, remained unclear.

Several of Palin's media orchestrated events cast doubt on her political abilities, yet at the same time created the impression of a woman striving to be in touch with ordinary Americans. In particular, her Republican convention speech, a CBS interview with Katie Couric and her vice-presidential debate with Senator Biden were focal points which created discussion and controversy. Many of Palin's remarks about her ordinary background came in the form of self-reference and stressed areas tangential to politics. Her past, her husband and her family created a backdrop of note to her political campaign. Yet there were problems. In the CBS interview Palin had been unable to identify the magazines she read, could not cite a Supreme Court decision she opposed other than the abortion case of *Roe v. Wade* and struggled to address the meaning of the Bush doctrine in foreign affairs.[59] The interview raised questions over her command of the issues. In her vice-presidential debate with Senator Biden, Palin played a populist card. She referred to 'average, middle-class families like mine' and suggested that a perfect place to view popular opinion on the economy would be at a Saturday morning soccer match.[60] Similarly she argued that the ongoing emergence of financial concerns at the time, and the likelihood of a recession railed against the interests of the ordinary person, thereby associating herself with a classic populist stance. She declared 'Let's commit ourselves – just everyday American people, Joe Six-Pack, hockey moms across the nation – I think we need to band together and say "Never again." Never will we be exploited and taken advantage of again by those who are managing our money and loaning us these dollars.'[61] In essence the debate appeared to boil down to style versus substance, Palin being both criticised and complemented for her 'mom-next-door' image and her 'folksy colloquialisms'.[62] Although not a glowing success, the debate with Biden was, at the least, not as disastrous an appearance as the Couric episode, and gave some credence to claims that she was a plausible vice-presidential candidate.[63]

Critical evaluations of Palin as a populist candidate addressed not only her personal presentation skills, but also allegations of media bias which suggested that some outlets were duped by her folksy personality, while others simply saw politics as an issue devoid of character as a component which might condition voter choice. Republicans, and indeed Palin herself, perceived media coverage against her to be biased and disposed to present her in a negative manner, particularly the offerings of NBC. By way of contrast, Richard Cohen of the *Washington Post* thought the media coverage to be superficial, 'In effect, columnists, bloggers, talk-show hosts and digital lamplighters have adopted the ethic of the political consultant: what works, works. It did not matter what Palin said. It only mattered how she said it – all those doggones, references to her working class status (net worth in excess of $2 million), promiscuous use of the word "maverick," ... and, of course, the manic good cheer.'[64] In keeping with the other case studies addressed in this text, Palin presented herself as having working-class populist credentials, an ordinary background and commonplace interests, claims somewhat removed from the actuality of her personal situation. There were some extenuating circumstances. As a working mother she could in part advance these facets as credible and genuine. She was a mother of five and had grown up as part of small town America. Yet, in advancing populist credentials, her fashion choices – comprising in large part designer clothes, and her personal wealth were left open to scrutiny as they gave a contradictory message. Some, like conservative writer William Kristol perceived an elite media bias against Palin. In his interpretation she was the political manifestation of ordinary America. He commented, 'It's not just that many in the media don't like her politics and don't identify with her socially or culturally. ... McCain didn't just pick a politician who could appeal to Wal-Mart Moms. He picked a Wal-Mart Mom.'[65]

Accentuating her ordinariness, personal life and family background, Palin associated directly with 'Wal-Mart Moms' a phrase created by Democratic strategist Chris Lehane, referring to white working women with children who lived primarily in suburban and rural areas of key states.[66] Palin also identified herself with 'Hockey Moms' in an effort to cultivate an ordinary identity rooted in her home state and relate to a sport with working-class or blue-collar connections. At first sight it appeared that Palin's populist image was simply reflective of the historic traditions of political presentation in the modern era. In keeping with 'Soccer Moms' and 'Nascar Dads', target demographic constituencies, whether real or imagined, were courted in 2008 by candidates eager to seem to mirror the social and emotional attributes of these voting blocks. On this occasion 'Wal-Mart Moms' were identified as being important to the outcome of the election.[67] It was thought that they were initially torn between the two core candidates in the race, Obama and McCain, partly on account of the difficult economic conditions which provided the background for much of the pre-election discussion. The *Financial Times* observed, 'White women are crucial in every election because they vote in larger numbers than men and tend to be less partisan, and thus more open to persuasion. ... The Wal-Mart mom is less wealthy and education [sic] than her soccer mom sisters but could prove equally powerful this year.'[68] Palin was considered by those who welcomed her presence in the race to be either the embodiment of the spirit and sentiment of the ordinary American woman or a symbolic representation of American values, largely devoid of ideological baggage. Bob Moser defended Palin's cultural merits in *The Nation*: 'With this underrated grasp of the kind of substance free emotional symbolism that wins national elections, John McCain sniffed out in Palin a kind of Hollywood fairy tale: homegirl from a small town, reluctant beauty queen, plucky point guard, deadly shot and mother of five, suddenly – magically – plucked from obscurity and thrust into the national spotlight.'[69] Similar commentary made reference to the emergence of identity politics, including accusations that Palin represented a figure akin to a 'Caribou Barbie'. Gigi Georges, a Democratic strategist of the Glover Park group considered the core appeal of Palin on the Republican ticket. 'She represents an attitude of "I don't really care what anyone thinks. What the media thinks. What the elites think. I just don't give a damn." And plays not just to small-town America but to all women who feel they've faced something in their lives, that they've been put down, not recognized for their intelligence, not recognized for their character. And there she is – she's just like them.'[70] The concept of self-reference on the part of the voter was reminiscent of the marketing strategy and success of Ronald Reagan. Hilley considered this to be one of Palin's strengths, citing Reagan's own perception as an indicator of Palin's appeal, 'When asked what he thought voters saw in him, Reagan replied, "Would you laugh if I told you that I think, maybe, they see themselves, and that I'm one of them?" Alaska voters certainly seemed to find themselves in Palin, even as she found herself in them.'[71]

Ordinariness, or perceptions of ordinariness, clearly had an important role to play in shaping at least the overt and prevailing interpretation of one candidate in the 2008 presidential race. While McCain cast himself as a Maverick within the Republican organisation, and drew attention to his Vietnam war record and service to his country, Obama stressed his impoverished roots and his continuing awareness of the plight of those suffering under the threat of financial disrepair and possible recession. Both however had strong leadership credentials and engaged in robust debates on ideological and practical issues. Palin's appearance into the fray cast fresh light onto the difficult balance between marketing the image of being a regular person with the need to provide authoritative leadership and to have acquired a sophisticated understanding of policy issues. In large part her image was manufactured, laced with elements which lend credence to her claims of understanding ordinary people. When confronted with accusations of aloofness on account of the cost of her clothing during the campaign, she responded by contending that the clothes belonged to the Republican party, and promptly turned out to a rally wearing blue jeans. Her clothing costs amounted to $150,000 between August and October 2008. As debate raged about what this said about Palin's folksy image, the *Boston Globe* thought the issue to be problematic, at least on a superficial level: 'While the money comes from campaign donors, not from taxpayers, the clothing from high-end stores does seem to conflict with Palin's image as a Wal-Mart hockey mom.'[72] Nevertheless, Palin's successes in drawing attention to herself on account of her image and her family gave a short-term bounce for the Republicans in the polls, but queries about her ability to understand the demands of office and policy detail appeared to counteract the appeal of the ordinary image, and in the prelude to the national election in November she entertained poll figures which suggested that she was, albeit marginally, a liability for the Republican ticket.

Dick Polman observed the dilemma of populism, ordinariness and the contemporary appeal to the regular person on the grounds of character. 'Alexander Hamilton insisted in the 76th Federalist Paper that our leaders "would be both ashamed and afraid" to elevate people whose chief qualification appeared to be "insignificance and pliancy." But today Hamilton would probably be dismissed as an "elitist" who cannot related to the average Joe's apparent yearning for leaders who know just as little about the issues as they do.'[73] The race of 2008 continued the debate over political marketing, the portrayal of ordinariness as a political asset and its interplay with perceptions of effective political leadership.

Conclusion

The presidential elections of 2004 and 2008 brought together a number of key themes in political marketing and highlighted a core change in the presentation and identity of candidates. The identification of key voting segments in 2004 was not a new or particularly novel phenomenon. Nascar fans were thought by some to hold the key for the 2004 election, however although there was debate over their importance and whether they were a convenient tag to replace the soccer moms of past elections, the candidates did not, and perhaps could not, take the chance that they neglect the market and leave the door ajar for their opponents. As a consequence, in the narrow framework of trying to appear to be at one with the public Nascar received a prominence that had been previously been missing in past elections.

In understanding political marketing and how candidates might relate effectively to the voter it was clear that in 2004 the accommodation and use of voter profiles was the norm. Identifying the lifestyles, habits and preferences of the voter assisted those attempting to create a political identity for their candidates. Two themes were pronounced. Firstly candidates ran on their autobiographies. Where they had come from, socially and emotionally, were important factors in trying to create a relationship with the voting public. Secondly, wealth was evidently a political necessity for a candidate and a campaign but was, at the same time, a political theme to be minimised and kept largely out of mainstream public view. Instead impoverishment, or an appreciation of it, alongside pivotal moments in an individual's life which created social and emotional bonds was pushed forward so as to give legitimacy and authenticity to the candidates' claims of understanding the voter.

Although coverage of policy was key to voter choice alongside how pertinent political problems would be resolved by both the president and his opponents, the available evidence suggests that the attention given by candidates to who they were as people has had an increasingly prominent bearing upon the nature and outcome of the election process. It is not to suggest that candidate fortunes were dictated by simply who they were, after all, the two candidates who faced each other in the final presidential election contest were two of the wealthiest in the field. While arguments of impoverishment and populism held sway, it appears that as of yet the American public are accepting of the fact that the candidates, uniformly, come from a position of financial security. There is indeed no good reason to advocate that they should come from any other stock, or that an assembly of candidates from a different or a diverse range of social classes would be any better in politics. However, what was evident from 2004 was that those of an elite standing were eager to convey an impression that they had humble origins and could relate emotionally to individuals across the socio-economic spectrum.

For some candidates the task proved easier than others. Edwards' campaign rested strongly upon what appeared to be a genuine affiliation to blue-collar America, and an ability to attach himself to a number of emotional experiences, such as bereavement, which granted him sympathy and understanding. It suggested that there were issues which maintained a connection between elector and the elected and wealth, for all its impact in other realms of life, was not a pivotal factor in this particular circumstance. Wesley Clark too could claim to have background that put him in touch with ordinary people; however in reality errors of presentation afflicted his campaign, and also that of Dean, whose character came to be one of the attractions of the campaign in both a positive and negative capacity.

In keeping with the problems encountered in the United Kingdom by William Hague, leader of the Conservative party during the 2001 election, maintaining an impression of a genuine affiliation with other social classes proved difficult. On the one hand declarations of wearing cheap suits or having once endured social problems like alcohol abuse carried some weight in conveying awareness of common social issues. On the other they were superficial and tangential to meaningful policy issues and gave the impression of an elite social group utilising issues pragmatically simply to gain political and personal advantage.

The outcome of 2004 was a mixed one, with candidates advancing a uniform message of their being unaffected by wealth, but with a lack of comparative examples to see whether a candidate who genuinely was from a different social class would make any electoral headway.

Additionally, the number of attacks made by candidates on issues of wealth and populism, in both an intra or inter party capacity was limited, partly, one would assume because each candidate was open to the same criticism of being from a social position that removed them from ordinary society.

7
Cameron and Brown

The emergence of David Cameron as leader of the Conservative party, following his successful fight for the party leadership in 2005 presented a new and fresh development in British politics following the elongated tenure of Tony Blair. The marriage of the ordinary and exceptional components of politics were well entrenched in British politics by this time and political marketing was part and parcel of the spin oriented presentation of politics and political figures. Blair's ability to convey a sense of authoritative leadership in combination with populist rhetoric, and the presentation of him and his family as ordinary, appeared to suggest that a foundation for a successful leadership bid and an assault on power revoled around this type of political presentation. He was also able to position his party in the centre of the political spectrum and occupy a position where the Conservative party, and its leaders, appeared isolated and out-of-touch on the right. The move of the Conservatives to the centre, under the modernising strategies of Cameron put pressure on the voter to differentiate between the parties and thereafter to examine the role and identities of the leaders of the parties. In advance of Cameron's leadership Gerry Sussman observed, 'The catch-all British and American elections deflect attention from serious issues and elevate the importance of personality, "character", style, and the who's ahead elements of elections'.[1] In several respects Blair's success produced a consolidation of the strategies and techniques which were considered to have brought about his victory in the first instance.

Media coverage of the political establishment, and its leaders in particular, still earmarked ordinariness as a component which would endear political leaders with the populace. In the familiar realms of education, family background, home life and favoured pastimes media questions and scrutiny promoted personal life and the social attributes of candidates to the fore. Personal wealth was downplayed as an issue. Policy still mattered and was at the heart of party branding, but the convergence of the parties in the congested centre of the political market led to a lack of clear water and difficulty for the electorate in differentiating what each party stood for. The personification of politics assisted in allowing the voter to give additional meaning to the party identity through the perceived character of its leaders. In looking forward to the end of the Blair era, the Conservative party appreciated the problems that had afflicted its political fortunes in the period following 1997. The images of Cameron's predecessors William Hague, Iain Duncan Smith and Michael Howard were not thought to be in tune with the demands and expectations of the electorate. All were criticised for their appearance, their associations with the past legacy of the Conservative party and their lack of connection with the voting mass. They all pursued differing strategies in seeking to present themselves as socially and emotionally responsive, but all came unstuck at the hands of the Blair spin machine and a press hostile to political figures easily stereotyped and caricatured.

This chapter addresses primarily the strategies used by David Cameron, the Conservative leader from 2005 onwards in seeking to market himself and his party as an electable mix of the exceptional and the ordinary. While consideration is given to the strategies used by Gordon Brown, Labour leader and prime minister since 2007, the challenges posed to Cameron in presenting himself as electable are more intriguing. Coming from an elite background, entertaining the modern history of the Conservative party and engaging with the experienced spin machine of New Labour presented Cameron in particular with an array of challenges. His skill in presenting himself, against both Blair and Brown, as the leader who could best associate himself with the social and emotional needs of the voter would have a role to play in determining the nature and conduct of modern British politics.

The Conservatives: Still out of touch?

Cameron faced multiple challenges both during and after his leadership campaign to resurrect the fortunes of his party and to persuade the British voter that both he and the party had something tangible to offer in contemporary politics. The Conservative party were considered to be in some trouble following the 2005 election, and the range of candidates putting themselves forward to replace Michael Howard was not considered particularly encouraging for the party's future. Part of this outcome was related to the recent history of the Conservative party leaders. Hague was stereotyped as 'Tory boy', a political zealot out of touch with both his generation and with the British electorate as a whole. His efforts to appear to be in touch with the electorate and to be socially affiliated with popular culture floundered, as Chapter 5 outlined. His successors fared no better. Ian Duncan Smith advanced himself as a considered leader, one who mulled over the intricacies of policy and stood largely against the spin culture that pervaded the Blair era of politics. However, he failed to make any realistic indentations in the polls, and although considered both as a person who was a little more in touch with the electorate than his predecessors and as a caring individual, he failed to embrace fully the public relations machinery needed to elevate himself to the forefront of British politics. His self-reference as the 'Quiet Man' of politics, and as an individual who listened to the electorate rather than being a conviction politician condemned him to a position where his ongoing leadership proved untenable and he was replaced by veteran Conservative Michael Howard. Howard was an experienced politician by the time he assumed the leadership of the party. He had served on the front bench during the Thatcher government and had a strong public profile. He had been prominent at one point in time as Home Secretary (1993–97), advancing measures designed to convey an authoritarian approach to law and order. The main drawback for the Conservative party was that it was looking to its Thatcherite past in seeking to revitalise its future fortunes. This failed in both its intent and its outcomes, and made new demands of the party to be seen to be more inclusive and engaged with a wider cross-section of the voting public. While Margaret Thatcher had initially entertained voting groups who had defected from their Labour traditions, it was now the task of the Conservative party leadership to contest the centre-ground of politics, engage with a long served and largely popular leader in the shape of Tony Blair and reinvent the image of the party. All of these challenges would present Cameron with dilemmas on how to present himself to the British public and so change the face of contemporary British politics.

When compared to the previous leadership images of Thatcher and, to a lesser extent Major, the Conservative leaders in the twenty-first century, prior to the emergence of Cameron, do appear to have been somewhat more successful in conveying an impression that they cared about ordinary people and were in touch with the issues that affected their everyday lives. The party as a whole fared better in poll samples which addressed criteria of class, ordinary people and the popular interests. Naturally, part of the outcome may have been that the understanding of political marketing and the elevation of ordinariness was understood to be a feature of politics which necessitated some important consideration by the time Cameron led the party. However consideration of the position of the Conservative party as an institution suggests that through most of the first half of the decade figures made for relatively sorry reading. Under the stewardship of Hague 36 per cent thought the party out of touch with ordinary people. This rose to 42 per cent when Duncan Smith assumed the leadership, and then stabilised to some degree with figures in the early thirties during the remainder of Duncan Smith and Michael Howard's tenure. A notable change came when David Cameron was elected as leader of the party, the figure of those who considered the party out of touch falling to 23 per cent, a marked change and a distinctive one when long-term party trends are considered. This figure suggests, albeit superficially, that there is direct linkage between party image and the identity conferred on the party by its leader. The marked change in this particular area suggests that a change in the profile of the leader can initiate a change in how the party is perceived, and adds additional weight to the association between the character of the leader and the perceived political identity of the party as an institution.

In a similar vein there were changes in perceptions of Conservative leadership and its associations with those who defined themselves as ordinary in the post-Thatcher period. It is worth recalling that at the end of her tenure Mrs Thatcher was considered to be out of touch with ordinary people by in excess of 60 per cent of poll respondents. Although marginally more successful across time, John Major hovered around 50 per cent for most of his period in office. Following Major, however, the fortunes of the party, interwoven with a more subtle marketing of the characteristics of its leadership improved. The best result achieved by William Hague in this area was that recorded in April 2001; only 28 per cent thought him to be out of touch with ordinary people. This however was near the end of his time as leader and came in conjunction with the general election of that year. The figures gained thereafter made for more satisfactory reading with the statistics recorded for Cameron being among the best of the modern era. Duncan Smith was perceived to be out of touch by a mere 10 per cent in November 2001; however this rose to 24 per cent by September 2003. Michael Howard was considered to be out of touch with ordinary people by 30 per cent in 2005, and Cameron thereafter was thought out-of-touch by 14 per cent in September 2006.[2] The dynamic changes and improved fortunes of the party appear linked to the interpretations of the personality and authenticity of its leader, and Cameron displayed figures in the polls that were significantly better than those enjoyed by his predecessors. He was thought to be more down to earth, had more personality and was thought to be more in touch with ordinary people. Alongside interpretations of policy and ideological change within Conservative ranks it is evident that there were changes in terms of an understanding of leadership and political identity.

There are several conclusions that can be drawn from the available evidence. One is that the public perceived Cameron to be realistically more in touch with the electorate, and that he was genuinely a person derived from the mainstream and able to relate to ordinary people on the issues that concerned them most. The evidence however points to a contrary conclusion. Cameron's background was far from ordinary, and his life experiences, although possible to market as ordinary, were removed from those of mainstream British society. Thereafter the conclusion that is most likely, given the variables of policy change and ideological direction, which was not a primary product in the short term of Cameron's leadership, is that those polled considered the presentation of Cameron as a leader to bring about a marked change in the relationship between the party and the individual. Consequently, the evidence suggests that political marketing and its increasing sophistication with regards to the presentation of the identity of a leader can bring about a change in the way that a party, and its leader, is considered by the electorate. This is not to say that the modern Conservative party is simply the embodiment of its leader, but the evidence suggests that the social and emotional presentation of the leader of the party has a limited, but nevertheless important, role to play in shaping how the party is perceived.

In July 2005, in advance of the election of Cameron as leader political analyst Peter Riddell commented: 'The message is straightforward. The Tory party is out of touch with a large section of the electorate…the Tories suffer from being seen as not caring about ordinary people, being out of touch and opportunistic.'[3] The party's reputation as a whole seemed to reflect badly upon its candidates, Cameron in particular. The BBC commented in a similar vein: 'With his influential friends and blue-blooded heritage, Mr Cameron has been criticised for not being in touch with ordinary people.' Similarly, the *Times* listed what it considered to be Cameron's weaknesses in the midst of the Conservative leadership contest, 'His Eton and Oxford background set him apart from ordinary voters'.[4] It was not only the Conservatives who were charged with letting down the ordinary voter. In keeping with the poll evidence cited earlier which was detrimental to the Conservatives, New Labour was also accused of being increasingly out of touch and disconnected from its traditional constituents. As Patience Wheatcroft argued, 'If only the Opposition could sort itself out and line up a leader prepared to show some genuine respect for the "ordinary people", the arrogant Mr Blair and Mr Brown, and their cohorts could find out it is they who are given the kicking'.[5] Selective presentation was adopted to portray Cameron as a person at one with the British people. This was initially greeted critically by the media, keen to invoke stereotypes and labels on another Conservative leader who seemed neither innovative or new, but reflective of many Conservative leaders of the past. 'Cameron and his campaign team are so intent on downplaying the Eton-and-Oxford things, so worried about the Toff Problems, that it's hard to get them to talk about it at all.'[6] The challenge facing the party was clear. Not only did it have to try to offset stereotypes concerning the historical legacy of the party, but it had the very real challenge of portraying Cameron as a person who was connected to the populace both socially and emotionally. This was difficult given his social background. A positive result was sought through the replication of the strategies used in the past by political figures on both sides of the Atlantic, the portrayal of Cameron as a person connected strongly to his role as a father and husband, and efforts to minimise discussion of aspects of elitism that might prove detrimental to his own personal interests.

Cameron: Becoming an ordinary person

Cameron was largely unknown in advance of his leadership bid for the Conservative party, having been an MP for only four years. This gave him both advantages and disadvantages when presenting a marketable personal and political profile. His rapid emergence also had ramifications for his opponents. New Labour was forced to consider its options when confronting an opponent who could not easily be tagged as being part of the Thatcher generation, although limited attempts were made to link him to aspects of previous Conservative economic policy, most notably that undertaken by Norman Lamont, to whom David Cameron was an advisor. This became an emergent feature of the New Labour attacks on Cameron, but they had limited impact as time had elapsed since Lamont had been Chancellor, and Cameron's role was never outlined in such detail so as to hold him personally responsible for the economic woes that befell the nation during the mid-1990s.

Cameron enjoyed an outstanding education and possessed the traditional credentials to make him an engaging and effective politician. He was born in 1966 to a family in comfortable circumstances. His father was a stockbroker and he was educated at Eton and then studied at Brasenose College, Oxford. While there he was a member of the Bullingdon Club, a dining club reserved for those of wealth and status. He is related to several aristocratic families and is a distant relative of the Queen. The flourishing of his political career has been dramatic. He worked for the Conservative Research department, assisted in the preparation of briefings for Prime Minister's Question time, and was a Special Advisor at the Treasury and at the Home Office. He became a Conservative MP in 2001, was Shadow Minister for Local Government in 2004, and a member of the shadow cabinet in September 2004. In May 2005 he was made Shadow Secretary of State for Education and Skills, and announced his candidacy for leadership in September 2005. Outside of politics Cameron had business interests which underscored his elite social position. Between 1994 and 2001 he was Director of Corporate Affairs at Carlton Communications and until 2005 was a non-executive director of Urbium, operator of the Tiger Tiger bar chain.

Cameron's profile suggested initially that he had the education, contacts, experience and determination to lead his party. However, as already discussed in this text his elite credentials, while politically beneficial, threatened to create divisions between himself and the voter with respect to social and emotional associations – he was not ordinary enough and did not share the life experiences of the vast majority of the electorate. The electorate, and particularly swing voters, were instrumental to Cameron's political prospects, and his initial strategies were designed to demonstrate that he shared their concerns and way of life, and was not the product of a privileged elite. Balance was needed however. As demonstrated, many of the claims made previously in British politics about the activities of party leaders had been greeted with scepticism and mockery. Cameron had to be seen to be in touch with the ordinary voter without appearing fanciful, or overtly fabricating aspects of his past which simply would not endure scrutiny. The lessons derived from misplaced marketing ventures were still fresh in the memory.

Several core areas of Cameron's past and character were utilised to market him as a candidate who might appeal to the ordinary voter. These included salient areas such as his family and his age, alongside a carefully considered strategy to utilise Cameron's position as party leader in advance of Gordon Brown assuming the post for New Labour in the summer of 2007. Cameron had an 18-month period during which to anticipate the arrival of a new opponent, against whom he would likely contest a general election. As a consequence, when marketing his character and political identity he had one eye on establishing his authority and credibility as a party leader against Tony Blair, but also a keener eye for ensuring that he contrasted favourably against Gordon Brown. His approach to the marketing of his personality reflected this. He made his fondness for ordinary pursuits and pastimes clear and presented information that allowed the voter to relate to him as a person, as well as a political leader. He admitted to being a smoker in 2005, but intended to quit in 2006. He enjoyed real ale, music by The Smiths and The Killers, and exercised with a mountain bike. He played tennis and his wife played pool. While this sort of information, at first sight, has a marginal and superficial political role to play, it earmarked Cameron as an ordinary man, with an ordinary wife, and an ordinary background. It allowed the British public to assemble a character profile and to observe Cameron's personality across time. It was not a forlorn task as poll statistics, related later in this chapter, make clear.

Conservative leadership contest

In contending the leadership race for the Conservative party in the autumn of 2005 Cameron faced challengers who were well versed with both the party ideology, and the pitfalls faced by the party when seeking to give itself an identity and profile. The serious contenders were Cameron, David Davis and Kenneth Clarke, alongside party grandees such as Malcolm Rifkind. Clarke had a difficult position to defend as he had previously been prominent in the party and had expressed sympathies with a softer Conservative approach to the issue of Europe, which had previously proved to be a divisive issue within the Conservative party. He was also a former Chancellor and was Shadow Education Secretary at the time of the leadership election. For Cameron Clarke, his effort to elevate himself to the head of the party initially looked to be a challenging task. The *Times* reported in early October 2005, 'Mr Clarke, shown by polls to be the voters' favourite and neck-and-neck with Mr Davis among the membership ... (is) too head-on the European issue, the main obstacle to his winning the contest'.[7] The underlying message at the leadership election was one of unity with the populace as a whole and the need to be perceived to be more socially inclusive. This was largely in keeping with the way in which the individual leadership candidates pushed themselves to the fore and tried to portray themselves as embodiments of a party intent on fundamental change. Frances Maude, party chairman at the time of the leadership contest, argued that the issue at the heart of Conservative failure and party alienation since 1997 was about its values as much as its policies. He stated, 'So what's the problem? For me it's one simple word – values. Honesty, generosity, respect for all, compassion, fairness are all good values – that's how we try to live our own lives. But people don't see these values in our party. Only one in three thinks the Conservative party shares their own values. Half think we care about the well-off, not the have-nots.'[8] In part then, the leading contender for the party leadership would not only be the person who could advance policies which would touch a popular nerve with the voter, but the person who could, in terms of their identity and character, convey the impression that the Conservative party was a vehicle for change and social inclusion. Added to this the candidate needed to appear to transcend class identity and perceived class-based values.

Poll evidence on how the populace as a whole understood the candidates assists in an understanding of why Cameron was successful. Initial evidence suggested that he was by far the most impressive candidate in the eyes of the young. As modernisation looked to shape the future direction of the party this had an impact in reshaping the identity of the party, frequently portrayed in the media as being a bastion for the elderly vote in Britain. Cameron played to his age and to the youthful vigour he could bestow on his political party. Secondly, poll details presented material that was complex in its nature regarding the familiarity of the candidates to the public. This made a straightforward choice difficult. However, there were important areas where Cameron scored highly. To highlight the contradictory nature of the polls and the problem that faced the Conservative party, a panel polled by the *Guardian* newspaper were starkly divided with Kenneth Clarke ranked by some as the most charismatic candidate for the job, as well as the worst potential leader. There was no clear direction for the party to take and the leadership election, although enthusiastically contested, offered little immediate clarity about the best way forward for the party.[9] The *Guardian*/ICM poll is also instructive for the objective of this particular text. It was constructed to 'discover how voters react to candidates as individuals rather than to the political content of their message, with a panel shown silent film of the candidates in action'.[10] The poll demonstrated that 'Although some saw Mr Cameron as bland, shallow or too young for the job, he came across as presentable, confident and trustworthy. He was well ahead as the most likeable candidate and scored particularly heavily as likely to appeal to young voters, where Conservative support is weak. Only 18% of the panel thought

Mr Clarke and Mr Davis appealed to the young, while 54% thought Mr Cameron did so. He beat other candidates too as someone likely to change the image of the Conservative party.'[11] Image it appears counted when policy considerations were put to the side. As the party sought to modernise, with every leadership candidate repeatedly stressing a need for change, Cameron stood out as an individual who had the character, image and identity to appeal to demographic groups which had previously been out of the Conservative party fold.

To assist in the publicity and transparency of the leadership contest, Cameron and Davis met to debate with one another on the BBC politics show *Question Time*. In large part Davis was the contender who was more specific about his political beliefs, and outlined his policies in some detail for the future of the Conservative party. However, Cameron advanced himself as a candidate with the profile and political character to provide leadership, but he was far less forthcoming about policy. This was considered by Davis, as akin to a Conservative interpretation of the presentation of spin advanced by Tony Blair. He commented critically, 'The British public has seen three Blair parliaments. They are sick of spin. The era of spin is coming to an end. This is absolutely the worst time for the Conservative party [to engage with spin].'[12] Additionally, the emergence of Cameron's personality as a core feature in the leadership election irked his opponents, and they made clear that they considered a leadership change in favour of Cameron as one that might be considered superficial in its essence. David Davis's camp argued for example, in the aftermath of an unscripted speech that pushed Cameron to the fore of the leadership contest, 'The Conservative party is in danger of choosing a new leader on the basis of one speech. Politics is about substance as well as style.'[13] Nevertheless it was Cameron who was chosen by the party to lead it into a period where it would seek to modernise and change its identity to gain a broader appeal among voters. In the all-party ballot, taken in early December 2005 Cameron received 134, 446 votes and Davis 64, 398, a clear endorsement from the party membership.[14] The result was as much about the image and the portrayal of Cameron as an 'ordinary' person imbued with a dynamic character as it was about radical policy alternatives to those offered by the New Labour government. Sections of the media greeted this critically, 'Mr Cameron represents the victory not of Blairite ideology but of Mandelson–Campbell spin: the ultimate triumph of style over substance'.[15] Cameron was a modernising candidate, eager to change the image presented by his party, but he was also an individual conscious of the need for the transformation of the identity of the leader of the party, an area where it had suffered in a pronounced manner when compared to the Labour party alternatives.

Cameron set about the reformation of his party to change its political identity from the outset. He imposed a revision of how parliamentary candidates were selected, with an aim of getting the party to reflect society as a whole. He argued, 'We need people from diverse backgrounds to inform everything we do, to give us the benefit of their diverse experience, to ensure that we stay in touch with the reality of life in Britain. The conversation we have in the party must reflect the conversation in the country, and the sound of modern Britain is a complex harmony, not a male-voice choir.'[16] There was dissent within the party, and an impending threat that prominent members of the party might be ousted to allow them to be replaced by younger prospective parliamentary members. However, the intent, to get the party to appear to be more in touch with the electorate through the image of its membership was clear. This was not greeted enthusiastically in all quarters, as the absence of carefully crafted and designed policy was considered to paper over a void at the heart of the party and advance a political mandate based on copying Blair. Anatole Kaletsky observed that 'all these erroneous beliefs stem from one fundamental misconception: the idea that the Tories will be returned to government on the basis of what they look like, rather than what they stand for'.[17] The drive for a revised political identity, and the moulding of a leadership and party image that reflected the nature of modern Britain entailed allegations of superficiality, but given the success of Blair in pressing forth with politics based on this consideration, there appeared little to lose and much to gain in altering the course of the Conservative party to follow suit with a leader whom, it was assumed, could out-Blair Blair.[18]

In keeping with traditional political evaluations based on time periods, Cameron was evaluated as a political leader in the media following his first 100 days as Conservative leader. Bryan Appleyard observed that Cameron's class was a defining aspect of his personality and was central to the debate about what Cameron as a leader meant to the Conservative party, and thereafter to the nation. However, he also considered that the identification of class-based politics was also an element that was in need of further subtle differentiation and clarification. He argued that 'Cameron is New Eton, New Toff. He rides a bike, a toff thing to do but something that signals that he is not Old Toff and also reinforces the message that he can actually do it. Brown on a bike? No. Cameron seems to carry very little class baggage and yet he has that airy confidence, the sense that he always knows which fork to use.'[19] The converse view of Cameron was that he was indeed a toff, but one who was adept at shielding the public from that perception of him. One unnamed Conservative argued that it was an Eton cabal that came up with the ideas that aided in the reinvention of Cameron and the Conservative party, and 'the irony is that they are now desperate – to be more meritocratic, to bring on others outside their set, not least women'.[20]

The impact on potential national voting intentions aside, the leadership election left the Conservative party facing the prospect of having a political leader who appeared to face two directions at once in terms of his social profile and potential appeal. Writing in the *Guardian*, Oliver Burkeman evaluated the dilemma facing the party, alongside the skills displayed by Cameron in appearing to be a candidate who could fit many different leadership profiles at one and the same time. 'To his supporters...Cameron represents the holy grail. He's telegenic, approachable, sanely eurosceptic, socially liberal, unburdened by baggage: a Blair for the Tories... he stands a chance of addressing the party's central image problem...admitting to being a Tory has meant admitting not just to certain socioeconomic beliefs, but to being, somehow, a bit weird.' However there were potential limitations, 'His detractors see a wildly over-confident Old Etonian who has risen without trace....He would be unable to reach beyond the dinner-party circuit'.[21] Cameron, in the efforts to promote himself to party leader, played the same cards he would later deal when in the position itself. He accentuated his belief in a society rather than the state, and played heavily upon his domestic circumstances, particularly his engagement with the health services on the grounds of the disability of one of his children. He also identified himself with a central and flexible role within his family unit. He also stressed his youth, his awareness of social issues and the need to concentrate Conservative attention upon emergent demographic groups which had little connection, geographically and socio-economically with the party. While the message was not particularly populist in its nature it was Cameron as a person that was advanced as the primary asset and a vehicle for a perceived ideological change.

Social inclusion and autobiographical baggage

Cameron has remained guarded about certain aspects of his past. This has highlighted the limitations of using an autobiographical past as a tool through which to make connections with the electorate. Although able to use issues of family and health to make connections to voters, Cameron's personal past, particularly with respect to his education, threatened to create a social and moral divide with sections of the electorate. The underlying issue was one of trust, and Cameron's reluctance to openly discuss aspects of his past, however minor or detailed, left open questions as to his integrity and how selective aspects of his past had been omitted from discussion for the sake of political expediency.

A primary concern involved allegations of drug taking when at university. Discussion about the use of illegal drugs was a feature which plagued Bill Clinton's 1992 Democratic nomination campaign, and Cameron was aware that whatever his statement on the subject area there was no convenient excuse or safe haven that could be advanced to avoid media or popular criticism. Clinton, in 1992, explained and justified the allegations of drug use by claiming that although he had encountered marijuana he didn't inhale. This was greeted with scepticism and provided ample ammunition for American comedians. Cameron's strategy was altogether different. He simply refused to comment upon accusations that he had taken drugs, specifically cocaine. The stonewall response suggested that the candidate was being evasive and was offering selected parts of his past for popular consideration, aspects which would not alienate middle-class Britain and might attract other previously disillusioned voters. By way of contemporary contrast, several other figures in British politics have come to the fore to admit drug use prior to their entering politics. One individual who has advanced her case is that of Jacqui Smith, appointed Home Secretary by Gordon Brown. She admitted to smoking cannabis in the past and explained her actions as rooted in the naivety of her younger years and as a disclosure designed to highlight her openness and transparency with the British voting public.

Allegations of drug taking by Cameron were widespread and were presented in high-profile public forums, in particular in two major BBC presentations. For example, *Newsnight* anchorman and experienced political interviewer Jeremy Paxman alleged, 'From what you have said so far we take it you did take drugs as a young man but you have not done so since becoming an elected MP. Is that correct?' Cameron's response was terse and brief, 'I have been very clear that I think you are entitled to a private past'.[22] He was also questioned on Channel 4 news about past drug taking, and again addressed the issue on BBC's flagship *Question Time* program. He claimed, 'I'm allowed to have had a private life before politics, in which we make mistakes and we do things that we should not – and we are all human and we err and stray'.[23] This was a familiar and strategic defence very much in keeping with the defence advanced by President George Bush Jr with respect to his arrest for driving while under the influence of alcohol, decades before his assuming the presidential office. Bush too made the claim that everyone makes mistakes and that past transgressions need not tarnish contemporary impressions or perceptions of a candidate, particularly when the candidate has overcome the problem and reformed their actions.

Cameron's reluctance to discuss his past in detail appeared to fulfil his objective of not exposing himself to an expansive enquiry about all aspects of his character. It left him open to allegations of being selective about his past and of marketing a partial product, where only the parts that might not offend ordinary voters and embellish his character were presented.

An ordinary family man

Cameron used his family strategically to cultivate bonds between himself and the voter. At the time of writing David Cameron was married to Samantha, who grew up in comfortable surroundings on a 300-acre estate. She worked for a stationery firm in London, catering to a number of prestigious clients. Media commentary pointed to her 'blooming' appearance during the 2005 Conservative leadership election race, on account of her ongoing pregnancy at the time. Additionally, she was not marketed as the stereotypical Tory wife, as she had a tattoo on her ankle that suggested that she was engaged with contemporary culture in a fashion that had not previously been seen in Conservative ranks. Part of her political presentation was traditional and was in keeping with that advanced by Cherie Blair, and in part previously by Margaret Thatcher, although claims have been made that she was 'terrified' about comparisons with Cherie.[24] She conveyed an image of the busy working mother, pressed for time and constrained by both work and domestic responsibilities. In *Harper's Bazaar* in 2007 she argued, 'I'm a working mom. We have to pay for child care. I don't have huge amounts of cash to spend on designer clothing. I think all working moms are a bit like that. You feel poorer than you've ever been.'[25] She also claimed that 'Women in politics are almost always in suits. The fact that I don't tend to wear suits probably makes [what I wear] a bit fresher. I'm never in a navy Giorio Armani suit.'[26] This was in keeping with the marketing of the Camerons as a family that shared the experiences of the populace. On the one hand they were portrayed as part of an elite Notting Hill social circle, intertwined with the trappings of wealth and privilege. At the same time David Cameron and Samantha Cameron claimed that they avoided materials identified with the benefits that wealth brought, and presented themselves as individuals who had to take care with family finances.

At the time of the Conservative leadership election the Camerons had two children, Ivan and Nancy, and were expecting a third. Cameron's initial messages regarding the family were inclusive and designed to demonstrate his appreciation of modern family life, and to reach out to peripheral groups who were once sidelined by sections of the Conservative political movement in Britain. In a speech while Shadow Education secretary he claimed: 'Modern families come in all shapes and sizes – and they all need support.'[27] His appreciation of diversity reached out beyond the narrowly defined limitations of the nuclear family. Heavy play was made of Cameron as a family man. Having a severely disabled son allowed him to consider the difficulties posed in several areas of health care and a challenging domestic environment. He could relate directly to the issues of the National Health Service, the difficulties and emotional challenges posed to him and his family by disability, and convey to the public that, despite his wealth, education and background, he understood the pressures that faced numerous families in modern Britain. Cameron's openness with respect to his family was not merely an invitation to media intrusion and exploitation. He claimed 'People want to have a good look at their politicians. I am a young guy with a young family – that's a very important part of my life. ... What you did in the past has absolutely no bearing on what sort of politician you are. The fact that I am helping to bring up a severely disabled son has a huge impact on my politics today.'[28] In the same vein he advanced the hardship and concerns he faced in trying to get the care and attention required for his son: 'As parents of a severely disabled son Ivan, my wife and I were desperately concerned that we would never find a school where he could get the care attention, therapy and education he needs.'[29] This was a strong, realistic and persuasive argument. It deviated from many of the social and emotional issues advanced by contemporary politicians as Cameron could claim, legitimately, to have endured difficult experiences. When leader of the party Cameron built steadily upon the family oriented image. On Father's Day in 2006 Cameron announced that his family was far more important to him than becoming a future Prime Minister, 'And it goes without saying that my children couldn't care less whether I become prime minister or not'.[30] He has repeated this message on a frequent basis. As social experiences were accentuated, perceptions of family wealth and material benefits were duly downplayed. He claimed that he would not, or rather could not, buy his wife a fur coat arguing, 'It's just that I couldn't afford one'. This argument was a virtual mirror image of that presented by American presidential candidate Howard Dean, who alluded to an illusion of impoverishment by claiming that he wore 'cheap suits', which was, in turn, keeping with Nixon's 1952 Checkers speech about his wife and her respectable Republican cloth coat. Political marketing builds upon its own successes, with commentary and rhetoric that appears to gain credence with the public being reused and remoulded to suit contemporaneous concerns. Across the decades references to inexpensive clothing and moderate spending habits have earmarked the rhetoric of those who are both political figures of national note, but are also equipped with the finances to dress as they choose, and to avoid the financial decisions of many individuals within the nation who have to make clothing decisions based upon limited budgetary means.

In accordance with the overall marketing strategy that accompanied Cameron's rise to power all associations with wealth were minimised, all associations with ordinariness and associations with the mundane were accentuated and embellished. On its own this would of course be flimsy evidence upon which to suggest a surge of voting support and the reformation of the Conservative party image, but it served to suggest to voters that the Conservative leader and his party were divorced from stereotypes of a party narrowly serving the wealthy in modern British society.

Education and Eton

Perceptions of elite versus mass education have played an important role in shaping and defining political leadership. In this area there was relatively little to choose between Blair and Cameron, but Cameron's education still became an issue which threatened to create some division between himself and the marketing of his ordinariness as a component of his electability. Education, wealth and privilege had been used by the previous Conservative leader Michael Howard to attack Blair as elitist, as discussed in Chapter 5.[31] When against Blair, Cameron could make no such attacks. He and Blair shared similar educational backgrounds, with Blair educated at the Scottish public school Fettes, and Cameron having attended Eton. Both went to Oxford University. Cameron's problem was an association of terminology – Eton was well known in British political folklore, Fettes was not, and he experienced a disadvantage as a consequence.

Cameron's problems with respect to portraying himself as ordinary were initially more pronounced during the Conservative leadership race. Challenger David Davis's education at a comprehensive school stood squarely against appearances of elitism and compared favourably against Cameron's private education. This posed problems. Cameron simply minimised reference to his education, minimised discussion about his achievements, and explained his avoidance of student politics at University by claiming that he merely 'wanted to have a good time'.[32] Davis's class-based merits were largely nullified by Cameron's determination not to become embroiled in a class war debate he could not win in the nation at large. It might speculatively have held some strength within the ranks of the party faithful, but the prime consideration of the party was to place a person at the head of the organisation that could mix the exceptional with the ordinary, and Cameron therefore had to downplay the issue of his own education as both a weapon he could deploy and as an issue he could discuss throughout his time both as challenger and leader of the party.

Nevertheless, discussion of Cameron's Eton background resurfaced on a regular basis. In late 2005, soon after Cameron had become leader of the party, Labour Deputy Prime Minister John Prescott made light of the issue of class and education. He accused the Conservatives of being run by an 'Eton mafia'. Coming from an established working-class background Prescott could both make the accusation with the hope of wounding the image of the new Conservative party identity, and also consolidate the long-standing stereotype of Labour as being a party which had the interests of the working class at heart, and reflected its traditional roots. Prescott attempted to reopen a class war, largely on personal terms, as New Labour as an institution had moved strongly to the centre-ground and its political character was somewhat different to the identity that Prescott sought to cultivate. He claimed, 'It's the Eton mob isn't it? They used to fight their wars on the Eton playing fields. Now they win elections on the Eton playing fields.'[33] Class and education was however an uncomfortable battlefield for Labour to skirmish with the Conservatives. There were problems with Blair's background and social standing, and potential problems arose when evoking old stereotypes to wage future wars, 'a danger that by raising issues of class and privilege, Brown runs the risk of appearing a political dinosaur'.[34] There was in reality not a lot to choose between the parties in the realm of elite education, and that it was portrayed as an element that could be carried forth as an issue of importance between the parties was as much due to historical legacy as any other feature. In 2005, 13 MPs in the shadow cabinet had been educated privately, with 15 graduating from Oxford or Cambridge. Seven of the Labour cabinet graduated from Oxford or Cambridge. Only one person, Alan Johnson, Work and Pensions secretary, did not go to a university at all.[35] Gordon Brown made a simple accusation at the Labour Party conference when discussing Cameron in 2005, 'He's an old Etonian'. This simple comment was designed to convey images of an elite individual out-of-touch with ordinary Britain. Ben Macintyre commented in the *Times*, 'The Chancellor is partial to the class-based attack and he plainly intends to use Cameron's background against him. For people such as Brown, the very word Eton still sums up stiff collars, stiffer manners, noses of toffee and spoons of silver.'[36] Cameron's defence against accusations of elitism has remained consistent. He has defended his position by trying to look to the future rather than the past. 'It isn't the back story that matters. ... It's not where you come from, but where you are going.' Cameron was earmarked for attack by New Labour with an array of individuals assigned the task of probing weaknesses, among them a former Conservative MP who defected to Labour, Shaun Woodward. He was assigned the task of looking for weaknesses in Cameron's style and policies, while Lord Gould was assigned the task of evaluating the impact of Cameron in the polls. Alastair Campbell, former spin doctor to New Labour considered Cameron a 'good target'.[37] Kevin Maguire, a political columnist with the *Daily Mirror* and a supporter of Gordon Brown argued that he persevered in calling Cameron a toff because it irked Cameron and placed him on the defensive. He stated 'When we run stories in the Mirror his various spin-doctors lobby for me not to use the word "toff" because it upsets him so much. He spends enormous amounts of time spinning himself as an ordinary guy, but it just doesn't fit with his silver spoon life.'[38]

Education was marketed as a non-issue by Cameron, as an inevitable and unavoidable part of his past. Yet while he could not undo his personal history he could utilise the parts of his life which conveyed social and emotional issues and nullify the areas where separation from the electorate occurred. His Conservative party portrayed social class as a non-issue, where the past had no bearing upon how he should be perceived or of how he perceived others. In getting Cameron to a position where he could lead the Conservative party Eton probably meant a lot; however, in defining his leadership and shaping policies it was marketed so as to mean nothing.

Experience and age

Cameron has used his age and physical appearance as a means to market himself as fresh, new and young enough to breed new life into the

Conservative party and British politics as a whole. He made light of his age in his pivotal address to the 2005 Conservative party conference, 'We don't just need new policies or presentation or organization, or even having a young, passionate, energetic leader – though come to think of it, that might not be such a bad idea.'[39] His adoption of a discreet age-based strategy was important in trying to capture younger voters, and to portray Gordon Brown as the product of a bygone era. In 2005 Brown was 54, Cameron 39, and Cameron's appointed Shadow Chancellor George Osborne only 34. Cameron's strategy was reflective of Clinton's approach to the 1996 presidential election, and his aspiration to provide a 'bridge to the future' at the expense of his opponent Bob Dole, who was cast both as an elderly and, more importantly in the public mind, a distanced politician. Similarly, Cameron's new era strategy was designed to remove the legacy of Thatcherism from Conservative party rhetoric. The *Guardian*, a newspaper traditionally sympathetic to the British Left and to New Labour, romantically captured the appearance of Cameron following his election to leader of the Conservative party: 'Cameron's is a face unmarked by history, the ideal embodiment of a party that wants for a time to forget that it has a past, to strip away the burdensome memories of economic disaster and the end of society, the more persuasively to address itself to the future.'[40] Labour responded to this strategy with vigour, laced with some degree of concern over the potential ramification that age-based politics may bring. An unnamed cabinet minister stated, 'I do not buy the "old Gordon" line being a disadvantage. People will look at his experience and stature and compare it. …Of course if it turns into a Big Brother style choice about who people want and it turns into a whim decision, then we may have a problem. There is not a lot we can do about that, though.'[41] As previously discussed in this text, there is a contemporary correlation between the type of celebrity character those who watch reality game shows see as winners in a competitive forum and the selection of popular political leaders; it appeared to follow along similar lines and have the same character components viewed as desirable. This in itself suggests that the Big Brother popularity contest imprint cannot be wholly dismissed as trivial. It may pale in comparison to issues of taxation, public services and immigration, but it nevertheless has a role to play in shaping perspectives on the nature of political identity and the social connections that are open to individual candidates.

Anticipating the expected inheritance of the Labour party leadership by Gordon Brown, Cameron played heavily upon perceptions of both uniformity of intent between the Labour leadership and also the perceived differences that were anticipated once Brown assumed power. A Cameron aide outlined the strategy, 'We're not fighting Blair. We're fighting Brown. Everything we do is designed to make him look obstructive and reactionary.' Cameron's advantages here were clear but were not so much of his own making. They arose from Blair's decision to lead his party until an unspecified time during the 2005 parliamentary session. Although Brown was well known and aspects of his private life were in the public domain, he appeared relatively reserved about marketing himself as an individual when compared to Cameron and Blair, and based his political career upon a reputation for his financial management and prudence, rather than overt or flamboyant personal marketing. The *Telegraph* anticipated the problems, challenges and potential contrasts between Brown and Cameron: 'As Mr. Cameron forges a "new style of politics", a phrase Mr Blair of course used back in 1997, Mr Brown risks looking like a symbol of another era. His decision to eschew what he calls "all that touchy feely stuff" – while understandable – could make him seem inhuman to an electorate that sees his rival cycling to work and playing with his disabled son.'[42]

Cameron's efforts to minimise discussion of his class and wealth, and to portray himself as an ordinary person, at one with the issues and concerns of the British voting public were pronounced during his early leadership challenges. He utilised several marketing strategies and had clearly learned lessons from past candidates and from the strategic presentation of individuals, particularly party leaders in the United Kingdom and United States. Cameron's presentations, based on style, personality and association with ordinary voters, were greeted with scepticism by his opponents and with some guarded enthusiasm by elements in the media. Simon Jenkins, writing in the *Sunday Times* argued, 'The Blair project sought to make direct contact with voters through an accessible and likable personality. Since most politics is a turn-off, its practitioners must find a new conduit to the electorate. Blair seemed a friendly face at court. The power of celebrity is real, not synthetic or "spin". The Tories were right to start their climb back to power with Cameron.'[43] Alternate viewpoints pointed to Cameron as a practitioner of spin.[44] Nevertheless, poll statistics pointed to Cameron as the leader best placed to resurrect the fortunes of the Conservatives and challenge for power. He appealed to women, to the young and appeared, through the strategies outlined previously, to understand the issues affecting ordinary Britain and to personify its values.

The lessons of presenting the elite as ordinary are plentiful. Cameron assumed the short- and long-term risk that his image is considered

nothing more than a mask of convenience, and that his past, elite connections and downplaying of his wealth are exploited by opposition
forces. Cameron's strategy has however borrowed on the lessons learnt
from both his British political predecessors and leadership candidates
in the United States and the increasing sophistication of the practices
suggests that they are now well integrated into contemporary political
culture. His inherent strength and the reasons for his meteoric rise to
power lie not only in following routes to power, but in stressing the
mundane, pointing out the ordinary, and stressing the trials and predicaments that have characterised and continue to characterise his life.
While the objective of this text is not to chart the monthly fortunes
in the policy stakes or the ebbs and flows of short-term public support
Cameron did prompt a bounce in public opinion polls in the short term,
a bounce that, in the absence of radical policy innovation or presentation was largely based upon the issues of presentation and the remarket-
ing of the Conservative party as a new entity in British politics.

The demographic appeal

Cameron used strategies familiar from previous chapters of this text
when presenting himself and his party to the populace. Marketing was
a core element in the recreation of the party's image. Writing in the
Guardian James Harkin considered the approach to be one where alongside the marketing of the leader there also existed the effort to appeal
to specific demographic groups. While in the United States George
Bush had appealed to Nascar dad, and Bill Clinton had courted Soccer
Moms, Cameron was advised to appeal to a generation born between
the mid-1960s and mid-1970s, a 'Generation Gap' that appeared out of
touch with the ethos of the Conservative party and had voted in lesser
numbers for the party in modern general elections. Harkin argued,
'The last in-depth study of the British Conservative party, back in 1992,
found the average age of a Tory party member to be 62. Since then,
the party has ossified even further. But political parties only feel as
young as the leaders they elect. Many New Labour favourites, after all,
were elevated beyond their station in 1997 solely because they were
young enough not to seem tarnished with the trauma of Labour's past.
Cameron thinks he can work the same magic.'[45] Cameron's efforts to
court voting blocks also extended to a significant marketing campaign
directed at the youth vote. He went on Radio 1, a BBC radio station
directed at the young, to outline his music tastes and to emphasise his
socially liberal credentials. He also went to see the film about gay cow-
boys, *Brokeback Mountain*, on the day of its release. This prompted a gay

website to announce, 'Young gay professionals are the perfect group of people to support the Conservatives.' A MySpace entry also appeared with details of Cameron's personal tastes, although it was later proven not to be officially endorsed. At a later stage Cameron created his own website (essentially an offshoot of the main office Conservative party website) webcameron, which showed him undertaking mundane domestic chores and casting himself as an ordinary person. Through this type of activity Alan Finlayson thought that Cameron 'has demonstrated his understanding of political activity in the post-party political world'.[46] He was a modern politician, at ease with the Internet generation and marketing himself in a consistent manner across an array of media outlets. The Conservative party, when Cameron first became its leader, enjoyed increasing support from the young.[47] However there were potential problems. Paul Whitely, a professor from the University of Essex argued, 'It's a good idea only if he's not going to lose votes at the other end of the age range'.[48] Yet, there were potential benefits to an approach which alienated segments of the party. There was a risk that modernisation and youth might alienate the elderly and essentially right wing of the party, but one of Cameron's advisors, speaking in 2006 argued, 'The old fogey's are getting pissed off, but that is supposed to happen. Cameron needs pissed-off Tories to gain traction with the rest of the voters. It's all about being counter-intuitive.'[49]

In his early tenure as leader Cameron was also deemed to be a person who appealed specifically to women.[50] The issues behind the perceptions are complex, but the media suggested that Cameron was judged as much on his appearance as his policies. Moreover direct comparisons, particularly with then Chancellor Gordon Brown, ensured that he held sway with a particularly important voting block. Brown's policy measures such as tax credits, nursery reform and maternity benefits, should have at the least ingratiated him with the female voting block; however considerations appear to have been larger than simple policy measures. In the *Times* Alice Miles advanced suggestions that the ordinariness of the candidates, or at least the presentation of it, was a factor that needed serious consideration. She believed that women, 'are struck by images of the Tory leader with his children, a pose Mr Brown refuses to strike with his son, John. What is Mr Brown to do? He believes that the electorate admires the fact that he is a substantial character who refuses to do things – remove his tie, pose with his son – for image's sake. ... Mr Brown will have to do more. He may be right to scoff at manipulating his appearance, but in this instance being right doesn't matter. Being elected does, and for that, appearance counts.'[51] Cameron sought to avail himself of additional guidance from women, 'feminize' the Conservative party, create all-women shortlists, and cast himself as a modern man, at ease with the life balance of work and home life characteristic of the modern middle-class social idyll. He cooked, got his disabled son ready for school, took his daughter to swimming on Saturday mornings and provided support for his wife, who worked part-time. This was marketed in a prominent and consistent manner.[52] Added to that he was a supporter of Aston Villa and played his masculine credentials when needed.[53] Cameron was an identikit political figure, moulded to support the core themes of contemporary society and in touch with the day-to-day issues that underpinned it. By mid July 2006 in a *YouGov* Poll, a clear gender gap had appeared in voting intentions, with 43 per cent of women declaring their support for the Conservatives, against 28 per cent for Labour.[54] In essence the media considered there to be a stark divide between the two prospective prime ministers as Cameron took the reins of the Conservative party. He was appealing on a superficial image-based criteria, and Brown was appealing on the substance of policy, but Brown neglected the core issue of image presentation and the social and emotional traits that have come to characterise contemporary politics. In 2008, *Grazia* magazine, an award winning fashion magazine directed specifically at women, found that Samantha Cameron had the 'best First Lady style'. David Cameron was considered to be the politician most women wanted to marry and the political figure thought to be 'best in bed'. Conversely Gordon Brown was thought to be 'patronising', 'arrogant', and 62 per cent of those surveyed wanted to 'throw him off a cliff'. While *Grazia* might be considered the type of publication tangential to the formation or reflection of political understanding and identity, the Periodical Publishers Association believed it to be 'the sharpest reflection of what the modern female head currently holds'.[55] Its portrayal of politics largely ignored issues related to policy and ideology and concentrated on the political figure as a celebrity figure, over whom judgement was to be made on issues which were not necessarily political.

The downside of the marketing of the individual was the crossover into over-exposure of the character and the politics of celebrity culture. The birth of Cameron's son Arthur was described by *Times* columnist Tim Hames in the following manner: 'The whole saga of his birth has been politically stage managed in a manner so painfully reminiscent of the Prime Minister that it inspires uncharitable thoughts less of the christening font than the sick bucket.' Hames argued against the celebrity, Big Brother style of politics and the 'crass personalisation of politics'. The image marketing by Cameron appeared however to hold sway until Tony Blair left office, and Brown thereafter enjoyed a brief honeymoon period in the polls. The local elections of 2007 were a success for the Conservatives, with Cameron's popularity as a person having a positive impact upon impressions of a modernising and progressive party. A dip in the poll standing of Cameron in the summer of 2007, following impressions that he was detached from issues such as flooding in parts of England, prompted a reversal of fortunes. Cameron's standing, and that of his party, was sufficiently dented so as to encourage Brown to seriously consider calling a general election to exploit Conservative weakness. However, the Conservatives and Cameron responded. Dramatic policy announcements, particularly in the area of inheritance tax created a resurgent support for the Conservative party mandate. Similarly an inspired speech from Cameron resurrected the allure he entertained upon his assuming the leadership of the party. This brought about a retreat from Brown, the cancelling of the general election and a resurgence of the Cameron bandwagon. That Cameron has entertained the idea of personal marketing in a prominent way, and Brown has ultimately followed suit is testament to the fact that the change to an alternative and traditional presentation of politics is unlikely.[56]

Project Gordon: Marketing a prime minister

Brown's determination to resist the marketing campaign undertaken by Cameron has been clear, but the pressures to respond have ultimately pushed him to react in a manner similar to that of Cameron. He has mirrored many of Cameron's strategies, detailing aspects of his private life, his interests outside politics, giving attention to his appearance by having his teeth whitened, and making public his fashion preferences.[57] It appears on the surface that, irrespective of Brown's personal preferences, he has little choice in an era of political marketing but to confront Cameron on a personal as well as a political footing. In contrast to the initial interpretations that Brown would concentrate on exploiting his reputation as a politician of substance, and critique Cameron as a politician who was spinning a political web based upon the politics of personality, it was Brown who modified his image and adopted a political profile which stressed his ordinariness and his ability to socially and emotionally connect to the voter in the United Kingdom. Poll evidence from 2007 highlighted that there was not much to choose between Cameron and Brown in terms of being thought to be in touch with the electorate. While 17 per cent thought Cameron to be in touch with the electorate in July 2007, 20 per cent thought Brown to be in touch. By October the position had been reversed, with 23 per cent believing Cameron to be in touch and Brown remaining on 20 per cent. However, a fundamental difference between the two political leaders was in the area of charisma where Cameron had a clear advantage over Brown. Cameron entertained figures in the thirties, with 39 per cent considering him to be charismatic in June 2007. In stark contrast only 4 per cent thought Brown to be a charismatic individual, this figure falling to a mere 1 per cent in October 2007.[58]

Brown was a political figure of significant standing in the New Labour government, and had established a reputation as a chancellor who presided over a period of significant economic growth and economic stability. In 2006 it was clear that Brown would soon become Prime Minster, and although Blair paid a waiting game to announce his departure, much to the frustration of the media, Brown was in a position where he had to give serious and added consideration to his public image and whether he was a figure that the British people could identify with. The prior interpretations were not at all positive. Brown struggled to convey an image of ordinariness and advance any sense of personal warmth. Simon Jenkins, reflected that upon entering government Brown appeared to be 'a socially dysfunctional bachelor ... could not drive and could not handle money. He was personally shambolic.' Furthermore, he was 'charismatically challenged'.[59] The reflection of the strategies and tactics used by Blair and Cameron suggests that, although the results are subjective and often unquantifiable, Brown could not take the risk that he would be outflanked on the issue of being in touch with the electorate. As the political parties struggled for room in the congested centre-ground there was also a struggle to establish a clear political identity as both party leaders attempted to differentiate themselves from one another.

Gordon Brown's attempt to appeal to the electorate on the grounds of his personality and lifestyle was termed 'Project Gordon'. In 2006 the prospective Prime Minister started to discuss his private life, his personal history and his relationships. His image and appearance were to change, with his teeth being whitened and a new wardrobe selected to try to convey an improved and inclusive social image. One Labour MP was concerned about the potential problems resulting from an image makeover, 'Cosmetic dentistry – if it's bad, it makes your smile look false. Gordon recently had his teeth done, but the smile remains awkward. So that changed nothing really. But mess about with personality? I think that shows a lack of confidence, and one that will be jumped on by the Tories.'[60] Following the lead offered by Cameron and Blair, Brown identified the importance of his family to his personal well-being, and the changes in his life brought about by being a new dad. Moreover, like Cameron he had social life and interests that made him appear to be an ordinary member of society. He had an iPod, was a Raith Rovers football fan and at age 55 enjoyed watching Celebrity Big Brother. The *Times* observed how Brown's image had abruptly changed, 'This is the 2006 version of Gordon Brown, a startlingly different figure from the stern, introspective Scot who entered the Treasury in 1997 and whose passion and indeed life appeared to be geared around the public sector borrowing requirement'.[61] Brown had issues which also needed to be addressed in order that the interpretation that he was psychologically flawed did not get an established footing and create an unwelcome stereotype. There was also an awkward legacy to contend with. When Brown and his wife had no children of their own, Brown 'borrowed' a 3-year old child off one of their friends to make a more marketable photographic image. This publicity opportunity backfired and exposed the Chancellor as an individual who was desperately eager to look ordinary and part of mainstream society. In advance of his anticipated elevation to the position of prime minister elements of the media saw the problems posed for Brown if he did not address both the image of Cameron and his own political identity.

Looking to the future and the need to establish a cultivated political identity with the populace Brown engaged in a flurry of media appearances and discussed his private life and personal interests with previously unknown candour. He courted the pivotal British tabloids the *Sun* and the *Daily Mirror*, and discussed his personal life with the BBC, projecting his identity into the public domain. There were problems for Brown however. As Cameron had already marketed himself as a person, and had a relatively frank disclosure of his personal life, Brown appeared to be following rather than leading him in this area. The media did not miss the move to identikit politics, 'Samantha Cameron is pregnant, so is Sarah Brown. The Camerons gave their children the MMR jab, so did the Browns. The Camerons look lovely in a family snap at home, so do the Browns. Mr Cameron relaxes in a pair of Converse All Star trainers, Mr Brown wears Ralph Lauren at the weekend.'[62] There were a few areas which differentiated the leaders in terms of how much they were willing to address their social backgrounds. Brown was more reserved about posing for photographs with his family, and did not discuss detailed family issues, unless resolutely pressed to do so. Cameron was open about his son's disability, although frequently this was perceived to be a discussion which aided in demonstrating his awareness of issues of modern health care.

In his party conference address in autumn 2006 Brown advanced a new political identity designed to smooth over internal party relations and to suggest that he was not the 'control freak' that had been forwarded as part of his political make-up across a number of years. Philip Webster, political editor of the *Times*, observed the changes brought about on the Chancellor's image. 'It was a softer Brown, recognising that the public, according to the polls, is far from convinced by him, they find him dour, find him too serious. It was a real attempt by Brown today to show his human side, what drove him into politics, speaking at length about his parents, and comparing himself sharply by the man he is likely to take on at the next election, saying "I am not about image" – with the clear implication that David Cameron is just about image.'[63] The Conservative response to the image alterations undertaken by Brown was pronounced and unsurprisingly cutting. Shadow Chancellor George Osborne published his opinion in the London-based newspaper the *Evening Standard* in early 2006. Osborne observed that 'First we had the new Ralph Lauren shirt, then we had the trendy pink tie and last week we saw him in a helicopter helmet. I guess each outfit is meant to show a new human side to our Chancellor, Gordon at home, Gordon the urban sophisticate, Gordon the action man, anything in fact other than Gordon the dour old schemer whose been angling for the top job for so long.'[64] The attacks on Brown were predictable, but they were a risk. To attack the marketing of Brown as a strategy was to create further cynicism about the role of personal presentation in British politics. As Cameron was at the forefront of this type of approach, the Conservative party had to play on stereotypical personality attributes held about Brown and cast Cameron as genuine and authentic in the conveyance of his personality, and Brown as an unwilling and unpersuasive actor.

The use of the autobiography as a means through which to convey ordinariness has been a pronounced feature in the personal marketing of the modern politician as this text has demonstrated. While it was an area that was strategically downplayed in large part by Cameron it was an element that was accentuated by Brown. The lessons of Brown's past however were really only advanced as elements that could be utilised politically in the prelude to his elevation to the position of prime minister. In his 2006 Conference speech he made reference to the influence of his parents on the values he entertained and discussed his background. Advancing a spin on the conventional ideas of social hardship Brown argued that 'I don't romanticise my upbringing'. In a newspaper interview he did however advance his understanding that there was a need to be more open about himself and to consider how he might market himself. He stated, 'it was never my intention to draw my memories into the public arena. But people need to know what I stand for. You've got to explain your background and on that basis people may understand me better. I don't feel that talking and talking about yourself is...mmm.... People need to judge you on what you do, but they do want to know why you do what you do.'[65] By the time of the Labour party conference in 2007 Brown had fully come to embrace the contemporary strategy of marketing an autobiographical identity and presenting issues which would allow emotional linkages with the voter. He made continued reference to how his family and parents made him into a political figure who understood the needs of society. The backlash against this type of speech existed however, as its approach to politics reflected contemporary oratory strategy rather than ploughing untouched ground. Ann Treneman, writing in the *Times* observed, 'He told us about his family, the wonderful and wise Browns. They are like the Waltons, though more wholesome. I'm not sure the Waltons knew as many Bible verses as the Browns. They trade parables and talents over breakfast. Plus, the Browns all have moral compasses.'[66]

Efforts to market Brown proved, by the middle of 2008, to have been limited in their successes. Although the Prime Minister was criticised for not going to the polls in the autumn of 2007, few considered him at that time, as a political figure or as a person, to be a political liability for New Labour. However, following a number of policy problems involving banking, finance and tax restructuring the Labour organisation suffered a historic drubbing at the polls in the local government elections in the spring of 2008. The extent of the loss was sufficiently significant so as to raise questions about Brown's capacity to lead the party, and to accommodate the views of its members at both an elite and grassroots level. In part there were continued criticisms of Brown as dysfunctional and as a leader with Stalinist tendencies. However there were also criticisms of his policy leadership which interweaved the personal and the political into a particularly damaging episode for the Prime Minister. This was underscored by harmful revelations from John Prescott and Cherie Blair in memoirs published in 2008 which cast Brown in an unfavourable light. Immediately following the electoral disaster, which affected local government rather than seats in Westminster, the Prime Minister took to the media circuit to discuss how he intended to address issues of tax policy and re-engage with the policy debate. Of note for this text however was Brown's appearance on the *This Morning* talk show, which had a daytime audience and was classified as a light entertainment programme. This type of move was partly inspired by a Labour backbencher, Chris Mole, who contended that Brown should look to the light political interview opportunities because people did not know who, as a person, he really was.[67] *This Morning*'s host Fern Britton introduced the slot with Brown with the somewhat caustic remark that 'It's an opportunity for you to be human'. In keeping with the issues raised in this text Brown was asked about his family and proceeded to discuss how one of his children has cystic fibrosis. He was able to paint a portrait of a home life that was far removed from the trappings of elite office, and to suggest that he faced personal challenges and responsibilities that might also be understood by the voter. It was suggested on blogs that it had been arranged prior to the interview that Brown would not discuss personal issues, however he appeared content to answer the questions put to him and to use an opportunity to present social and emotional issues at a time when the public policy realm was in some disarray.[68]

Ultimately Brown struggled to convey impressions of him as a person with whom the public could relate and to convince the watching public that he was derived from an ordinary background or understood the issues which affected the populace. Looking ahead to a future general election in the immediate aftermath of the May 2008 problems encountered by Brown, veteran political commentator Max Hastings observed the social and emotional trappings of high office, and the issue of authenticity that had come to play a key role in contemporary British politics, 'So much in politics, as in all human affairs, is about feeling sufficiently comfortable with oneself to make others feel likewise. Tony Blair's triumphs as a politician derived in part from his brilliant impersonation of a real person. Try as he will, Brown cannot match this, and Cameron can.'[69]

Conclusion

The modern experiences of Cameron and Brown indicate that both leaders are acutely aware of the need to advance, into the public realm, a cohesive understanding of them as individuals who have lives and interests that are in common with the general populace. Political marketing was employed by engaging with media strategies that advanced social and emotional meaning in both formal political occasions and in media appearances designed specifically to advance social settings as integral to the identity and character of the individual. In advancing these characteristics the tone of British politics, for the two main parties, has become remarkably similar. As both have sought to occupy the centre-ground in terms of policy and an ideology of modernisation, both have also become similar in their efforts to demonstrate that they remain unaffected by their positions of influence and power.

It is clear that in British politics there are still social locators which are perceived to be political liabilities. Cameron's education gave him the confidence and elite standing to appeal to the Conservative party as a credible leader with the appropriate social associations and intellectual credibility for that position. His study at Oxford also lent credence to his political ambition. However, as a package, although politically beneficial, they were publicly downplayed. Brown too had an educational record that made for political credibility but also gave the impression that he was not of ordinary stock and was, largely on account of his intelligence, divorced from mainstream society. The minimal marketing of education and concentration on issues which offered themselves as socially and emotionally appealing leaves a gulf between the educational expectations and requirements of the modern political leader, and the willingness of the populace to accept and embrace that exceptionalism. Elitism and ordinariness are not comfortable partners yet are bedfellows in modern British politics.

The use of the family to advance a positive and warm personal image is not a new development in British politics, but its emergence as a core feature of a permanent campaign now earmarks it as a form of marketing that can be used to exploit new media and expand the appeal of the political leader into realms beyond conventional political broadcasting. Both Samantha Cameron and Sarah Brown are considered to be political news, and both have social roles to play in earmarking the identities of the parties their husbands lead. Their children are news, the domestic habits of their husbands are news, the lifestyle balances they choose to engage with are news, and the consequence of the aggregate media coverage is to provide a multilevel discourse on the social habits of the party leaders that offers access into a broad range of media outlets. The benefits of the strategy are clear, with political transparency enhanced through an ability to see the characteristics of the individual, and to evaluate how these are reflected in policy projections and political identity. The drawbacks of contemporary political marketing is also evident however, with increasing cynicism about what is being marketed. Whether the real social background, or one that is thought appealing to the voter, is displayed is open to question, and the evolution of identikit candidate experiences is apparent.

The extent of political marketing has outcomes that are significant for the political process and the nature and role of political leadership. The clear objective of political marketing in the areas of social and emotional association are to show that candidates are of ordinary stock and share both the life and lifestyle of the voting populace. However, it becomes increasingly clear that to become a political leader requires facets and experiences that are not ordinary or normal and the marketing of the leaders paints a false impression. The exercise, as highlighted in Chapter 5 with William Hague, requires of the candidate a reinvention to suit political mores, and the creation of a candidate who has to present a past and an image which conforms to the best marketing strategy. This, rather than opening politics out to a wider spectrum of society and broadening the opportunity for ordinary people, or indeed those of elite stock to engage with politics, simply means that there is a position which is thought to be the most marketable that has to be aspired to for electoral gain. The evolution of this image has taken time to mature but it is clearly an important part of modern British politics, and has been in place in America for some time. The American model of log cabin to White House political development has become transposed to British politics. There is pressure for political figures to have common origins, to display exceptional talents in politics, and thereafter to retain social and emotional attributes which create affinity with the voter. Past circumstances are important and added to this it has become clear that political leaders have to be seen to remember that these are instrumental in creating a political understanding and identity. That all the major political players return to this same stock message has created a political environment where origins and their impact on character have become important facets in the competitive marketing of political leadership.

Conclusion

Political marketing has a central role to play in contemporary politics. The methods and means of accumulating information about voter preferences have developed significantly in the modern era with databases which outline demographic information, socio-economic status and personal lifestyle preferences being amassed by major political parties. These aid political party organisations in understanding how voters think, act and behave during election cycles in particular, and serve to cater for voter needs and demands as identified by focus groups and market research.

While the breakdown of the voting block has been researched quite comprehensively with respect to party affiliation and election activity, aspects of emotional affiliation with respect to political leaders appear to be more complex and are based on issues and information which are not necessarily derived from rational voting behaviour. In the main voters evidently process political information on matters related to economic behaviour and class-based politics, and appeals to voting coalitions on grounds of demographic sensibilities is commonplace in democratic nations. In part, leaders of political parties play to these pre-assembled coalitions and entertain ideas related to class-based partisan issues. However, as this text has demonstrated there are, in the contemporary period, other issues which suggest that political understanding is now also founded upon perceptions of who a candidate is, how they are perceived socially, and how their emotional understanding impacts upon the electorate. Several features underpin the emergence of social and emotional considerations as important in creating the association between elector and elected. Of prime consideration is the presentation of the candidate as a person who is similar to, and shares the experience of, the electorate. This presentation has both breadth and depth, how to achieve it being the subject of extensive research directed at campaign and leadership presentation. However, there is also a superficial aspect to the presentation as there exists a crossover into celebrity culture that threatens to reduce politics, and the practice of democracy in particular, to a personality contest where policy discussion and understanding are secondary features for elements within the voting block.

In large part the emergence of associations beyond the immediacy of substantive policy is based on the presentation of the political candidate as being derived from an ill-defined 'ordinary' or 'regular' realm of society. The core essence of ordinariness is that it is self-conferred by the voters, who ascribe to them a social position which is often unrelated to their contextual socio-economic standing. It is therefore appropriate and opportune for political leaders, as representations of the values of the party they lead, to seek to aspire to a similar realm of ordinariness. Understanding the social and economic pressures faced by the populace and the lifestyle choices of sections of the voting block, or seeking to act them out for the cameras, can portray an image of a political figure who is still, despite their social position of prominence and responsibility, largely unaffected by the trappings of political office. Because of safety and security fears, an ordinary existence for party leaders is not possible. Additionally, the historical evidence suggests that to become prominent in politics normally requires significant personal wealth. What is conveyed thereafter is political theatre which gives the impression that leaders have come from mundane or ordinary backgrounds, still understand the issues which affect mainstream society and present, as an ongoing political campaign, their lives as being interwoven with mainstream society.

In parallel with the presentation of policy or the branding of political parties, the presentation of the regular or ordinary individual clearly hinges on a number of features which are easier to realise for some candidates over others, it being based largely on how easy the candidate finds it to portray themself as authentic in their communications to the public. There appears to be an aversion within voting blocks to elitism, and this appears on both sides of the Atlantic in the contemporary era. Perceptions that political leaders come from a social position of wealth and esteemed social connections appears to be perceived as suggesting aloofness and the inability of the leader to form an emotional bond with the electorate. Additionally, the possession of wealth suggests an inability to understand commonplace issues. The outcome of this impression is that political leaders present and market themselves as either unaffected by the trappings of wealth, as undertaken by

John Kerry, not discussing their wealth as with David Cameron, or stressing the aspects of association with the impoverished and those facing economic challenges as advanced by Bill Clinton when he felt the voters' 'pain' during the 1992 presidential election campaign. With the advent of the permanent campaign there is now a pressing need to continually convey an impression to voters that gives a longer-term aggregate picture of how candidates live their lives, and are thereafter able to convey this existence into the public sphere. The use of the media is essential to this communication, with the utilisation of a number of different forums and means through which to present an ongoing life narrative, concentrating on the mundane, to the public. While Nixon used a prime time and pivotal speech to convince the voter of his political standing and to express the limitations about his wealth in 1952, other political leaders across time realised that a more elongated release of information concerning social standing and autobiographical background could be used to persuade the voter that bonds could be formed with leaders of political institutions. Elements of populism and an appreciation for the ordinary person were laced into Reagan's political rhetoric, and Thatcher and Major used the media to give generalised impressions of ordinary upbringings, culminating in the political branding of the Grocer's Daughter and the Boy from Brixton. The use of the media allowed the presentation of messages across several forums which targeted social groups from an array of socio-demographic backgrounds. Cameron's use of the Internet to advance a regular personal message is testament to this. In the contemporary era daytime chat shows are used to appeal to voters, largely addressing ideas not related to political policy. Clinton and Blair both exploited this forum. The objective was to advance a persona that could be used to socially market the political leader to the populace.

In other areas, such as in social pastimes, sport, and music similar activities prevail, with political leaders trying to gain favour by appearing to be at one with sections of the voting block in sharing popular passions. In the United Kingdom this has witnessed political leaders enthusiastic to declare their support for football teams, Blair with Newcastle, Howard with Liverpool, Brown with Raith Rovers and to be in touch with the traditions of cities and sporting clubs. In the United States a burst of enthusiasm for Nascar racing was testament to a perceived need to socially associate with a voting block identified as having social values, alongside a strategic voting location, which could be exploited politically. Although Bush's love of baseball was well known, the arrival of Nascar on the lawn of the White House was more of a political than a personal gesture to that sport. Traditional political policy themes and economic policy issues were factors which remained instrumental to voter association, but the added components of social and emotional connection could be enhanced through the exploitation of values interests central to the lifestyles and interests of many voters. The social conservatism of Bush and the appeal to working-class and blue-collar America on grounds slightly divergent from traditional appeals to an economic rationale were important to an appreciation of how and why Bush was able to both win the 2000 election, and thereafter consolidate his position in 2004.

The ongoing nature of the elite–ordinary partnership shows no signs of abating. In both British and American politics the issue of class and its interplay with political credibility and authenticity is manifest in prominent campaigns. Following the death of veteran member of parliament Gwyneth Dunwoody the Labour party faced a by-election in May 2008 in Crewe and Nantwich. Following the pronounced losses in the local elections earlier in the month the seat was pivotal in shoring up the battered credibility of the party. The Labour campaign effort sought to minimise the impact of Prime Minister Gordon Brown who was suffering in the opinion polls, and instead focussed its attention on the background of the Conservative candidate Edward Timpson. It argued that he was from elite stock and highlighted his 'excessively privileged background'. Part of its political attack was to have individuals dressed in top hat and tails on the streets of Crewe to try to convey a negative impression of Timpson, who was a barrister and the son of a multimillionaire. Class, wealth and social position was still, at least in the eyes of Labour strategists, an issue that could be raised to convey the impression that a candidate was out of touch with the issues that faced the electorate. Wealth was perceived as a political liability. Conservative party leader Cameron dismissed the attacks commenting, 'This class warfare stuff is ridiculous, out of date and makes the Labour Party look stupid'[1] The class-based attacks largely backfired on Labour during the campaign, with the loss of the seat and an improvement in the fortunes of the Conservative party. Significant criticism was levelled at Labour for its actions in utilising class as an issue through which to create social and political division. Tamsin Dunwoody, the New Labour candidate argued her case on familiar grounds, 'I don't have a £53m pound fortune supporting me. I don't have a one-and-a-half-million-pound mansion. I am just a single, unemployed mother of five fighting hard for a job.'[2] In the midst of pressing concerns over fuel prices, dissatisfaction with Labour tax reform and concern over the potential depths of a recession, the blunt class-based presentation failed to hold sway with voters who were dissatisfied with government.

The appeal to the voter on social grounds and on considerations of wealth and its impact on character has followed largely familiar paths across the modern political era. In large part the changes in this area are grounded on the increasing sophistication of market research and an appreciation on the part of candidates and parties that ongoing presentation of social origins and character attributes has to be achieved if the candidates are to look authentic in their presentation of themselves both as an ordinary yet exceptional member of society. The manifestation of ordinariness has hinged upon the continued presentation and portrayal of issues that are universally enjoyed or endured by the nation the candidate seeks to represent. The area of economic hardship has clearly been one that has been exploited by candidates and marketed as a form of both social and emotional association. Interestingly, in the modern era the use of the autobiography has become a means through which to interweave perceptions of grounded ordinariness, which can then be played alongside contemporaneous exceptional political ability. This allows an impoverished and trying past to sit comfortably alongside talent which sets the political leader apart from mainstream society. In virtually every case related in this text the candidates who wished to compete for party leadership or national office advanced personal recollections of family or personal hardship when growing up, and of how these hardships shaped their character and political understanding. In several cases, most notably those of John Major and Tony Blair, the past was used to try to gain credence with the voter in a direct form through a political party broadcast. In the United States John Edwards has proven particularly adept at sharing the impoverishment of his family background, and he tried to use it to compare himself favourably with other opponents in recent election races. The marketing of candidates therefore in the modern era hinges not only upon policy or a pragmatic use of environmental conditions to win public favour. Rather, in social and emotional terms it also rests upon the entire life story of the candidate under question and how that life might be spun to elicit a positive voter response either in a sympathetic or empathetic way. An additional advantage is that in many cases the recollections of family discussions, personal illnesses and their social ramifications are unique to the candidate, and allow an authoritative and largely unchallenged source to form the bedrock for this type of appeal. On occasion, as experienced by British Conservative party leader William Hague, this can backfire, but it nevertheless allows leaders to advance images and impressions which have flexibility inherently built in. The leader can tailor their past to accommodate prevailing contemporary opinion.

The personal recollections of leaders generally have the mundane at their core, with issues and themes that can be experienced by mainstream society presented as essential facets in public presentation. This has built upon itself across time and is transferable across political parties and national boundaries. Nixon's reference to a respectable Republican cloth coat in 1952 was built upon by Howard Dean's cheap suit remark in 2004 and thereafter Conservative party leader Cameron declared that he was unable to afford to buy a fur coat for his wife. These mundane and seemingly meaningless remarks all had the same desired effect, to bond the candidate with the mainstream of society and to convey, somewhat artificially, that the realm of the political leader, socially and economically, mirrored that of the ordinary person. Wealth was not an issue which would be raised as an asset to leadership. Rather it was considered a social handicap. This text has also shown that the areas of health, childhood, social habits and particularly in the modern era the nature and role of the party leader within the family unit are important. All of the major party leaders in the modern era have made play of their understanding of the family as a key social unit and have exploited and utilised their own social positions as marketing tools to form associations with voters, going so far, as was the case with British Prime Minister Gordon Brown, as to borrowing a child to embellish a photo of him in advance of him having his own family.

The marketing of the candidate in the modern era as an individual largely devoid of elite socio-economic standing is not without its problems, as other areas of political understanding evidently serve to obscure and make difficult an unadulterated portrayal of the individual candidate. Party profiles, stereotypes and investigation and reporting by the media have played a major role, particularly in the United Kingdom, in shaping popular perceptions of candidates' personal profiles and origins. Tony Blair undoubtedly benefited from the general stereotype that prevailed within the United Kingdom, that the Labour party he was chosen to represent was the party of the left and was representative of working-class interests. The background of Blair, as a person who had enjoyed an elite education and possessed an esteemed social standing, was minimised as it conflicted with his representation of the interests of poorer sections of society, while the marketing of Blair as a person who was in touch with these interests was enhanced by the party profile he occupied. In contrast the leaders of the British Conservative party had experienced problems in disassociating themselves from party stereotypes. John Major, in many ways the ideal embodiment of an ordinary person made good in the world of politics, struggled to cast aside the perception that the Conservative party was elitist and privileged in nature. In this respect political marketing had to accommodate, embrace and at times offset the wider perceptions of parties as vehicles for entrenched class interests. In the United States party affiliation appears to have a lesser impact. Part of this is on account of divergences between economic and social conservatism and the appeal of the Republican party to social conservatives on ground of morality, placed alongside sophisticated Republican appeals to the emotional understandings of the electorate.

An important facet of political marketing and the presentation of leadership is that it appears difficult for party leaders to sustain perceptions of ordinariness across time. In virtually every case where sufficient evidence exists, there was a deterioration in the perception of ordinariness across time and interpretations that the political leader had lost touch with the issues that faced the electorate. In part this might be expected as a consequence of the presentation of the political figure as being imbued with the trappings of office. This was enhanced through the ability of political leaders to gain access to media coverage and to control aspects of presentation that can further the dissemination of their desired image. Blair, for example, made a continued effort to convey an image of him as being a normal family member unaffected by his office, giving impressions that he was a family man who aspired for a commonplace domestic life as much as he desired political life. Nonetheless across time Blair was considered to be increasingly out of touch with ordinary people. In America efforts to capture social positions which could be offset against the grandeur of the presidency have also been pursued, with the objective being to be seen to be in touch with middle America and to accentuate the symbolism of the president being derived from the populace.

A large part of the debate on ordinariness, elitism and the perception that wealth corrodes the credibility for public office hinges on a popular understanding of how wealth is thought to create a barrier between the political elite and the ordinary person. As indicated by President Bush in the 1992 presidential debates, it serves to suggest that in order to address a social or economic problem, or understand an issue, a political leader must have experienced it personally to fully accommodate it and appreciate its magnitude. There appears to be little logic to underpin the idea that leaders should share the experiences of the populace. However in a practical sense, and in an era when political convergence in the centre-ground of politics is considered an issue and popular interest in politics appears to be on the wane, associations based on interpretations of social understanding may have resonance with the voter. Certainly the studies involving the type of character considered appealing to reality TV viewers, where ordinariness was considered an appealing attribute, appears persuasive when transferred into the political realm. It allows the voter to make associations on grounds that require little in the way of political knowledge, and to base evaluations on attributes to which they can relate. Because it involves self-identification it transcends class boundaries. While it makes for little sophistication in the realm of serious politics, it allows a level of political involvement and appreciation that lends itself to political marketing. The more a candidate can portray themself as in touch with the voter the better the chance to appeal to sections of the community who do not entwine themselves with political detail. While this, as argued by Hames in Chapter 7, may reduce political discussion to that of a superficial celebrity contest it nevertheless has become a mainstay of political presentation and of political marketing. As a consequence while the 'towering intellect' of Prime Minister Brown might be celebrated in the corridors of Westminster, Cameron's efforts to appeal to the social and emotional whims of the voter appear to have held as much, if not more, sway.

There are dilemmas facing political leaders with respect to the extent to which the marketing of the individual should proceed and be exploited as a resource for political gain. Blair encountered problems with the use of his family in political presentations strategically designed to show he was a family man. However this conflicted with a desire to maintain a level of privacy about the education, health and financial position of his family members. Similarly, his wife experienced problems, both in terms of her visual appearance and her reputation as a working woman, when details of her private life were exposed in an uncontrolled manner in the media. The portrayal of candidates and their families as authentic, and therefore appealing to the voter, runs substantial risk. A core theme of political marketing in this realm is that the candidate and their family need only be perceived to be authentic and ordinary. Conventional spin, manipulation and selective media images naturally serve to grant candidate's leeway in this area. However, ongoing cynicism about the authenticity of the classless position of the political elite makes a genuine presentation of material difficult to accomplish. Contemporary politics also highlights other realms where the marketing of the individual has limitations. The experience of Sarah Palin, who advanced a prominent populist campaign in 2008 also suggests that many voters seek a balance between folksy presentation and an understanding of the detail and substance of policy. Palin suffered from being thought to have little command of policy, even if some considered her to be the manifestation of the 'Wal-Mart mom'. There were also problems with her image and the budget used to furnish her clothing for the campaign. By the end of the campaign it was not essentially clear what the image of Palin was. As a consequence, the opportunities to differentiate between those who are from genuinely ordinary backgrounds and those who are strategically presented as being ordinary is often difficult for the voter to discern.

The future of marketing with respect to the presentation of the individual candidate remains unclear. In both British and American politics the ongoing presentation of individuals who appear unaffected by the trappings of office is obvious, particularly at times of election but also in a broader form as an ongoing concern which allows the presentation of individual characteristics to resonate when policy considerations do not dominate political debate. There remain problems for political figures in being seen to provide leadership and exceptional ability while at the same time being perceived to follow social trends or conform to social norms which appear prevalent in society. That the background of political candidates appears to have changed little in the modern era, specifically that they are moneyed with elite educations and esteemed social networks, suggests that the selling of candidates as ordinary is now commonplace in modern politics. Additionally, that the same trends appear in both the United States and the United Kingdom suggests that there is an appreciation that interpretations of personal character, ordinariness and authenticity are considered to be important to the voter across democratic systems.

Notes

1 Leadership and ordinariness

1. Thomas Frank argued, 'it is the Democrats that are the party of workers, of the poor, of the weak and the victimized.' *What's the Matter with America?: The Resistible Rise of the American Right* (London: Vintage Books, 2006) p. 1.
2. Ibid., p. 6.
3. Darren G. Lilleker and Jennifer Lees-Marshment, *Political Marketing: A Comparative Perspective* (Manchester: Manchester University Press, 2005) p. 3.
4. Cited in Richard W. Waterman, Robert Wright and Gilbert St. Clair, *The Image-Is-Everything Presidency* (Boulder, Colorado: Westview Press, 1999) p. 74.
5. Gareth Smith and John Saunders, 'The Application of Marketing to British Politics' *Journal of Marketing Management* 1990, Vol. 5, No. 3, p. 299.
6. Michael Billig, 'Political Rhetoric' in David O. Sears, Leonie Huddy and Robert Jervis, *Oxford Handbook of Political Psychology* (Oxford: Oxford University Press, 2003) p. 226.
7. Nicholas Jones, *Soundbites and Spin Doctors: How Politicians Manipulate the Media – and Vice Versa* (Guernsey: Guernsey Press, 1996) p. 27.
8. S. Mark Pancer, Steven D. Brown and Cathy Widdis Barr, 'Forming Impressions of Political Leaders: A Cross-National Comparison' *Political Psychology* Vol. 20, No. 2, 1999, p. 346.
9. Lilleker and Lees-Marshment, *Political Marketing* (2005) p. 6.
10. See Terence Blacker, 'The Voice of the People? Just Ask a Hairdresser' *The Independent* 9 January 2007.
11. See James David Barber, *The Presidential Character: Predicting Performance in the White House* 4th Ed. (New Jersey: Prentice Hall, 1992).
12. Peter Wilby and Cahal Milmo 'Private Moments and Public Motives: Leisure "Interests" of Public Figures' *The Independent* 17 August 2005 [http://news.independent.co.uk/media/article306409.ece].
13. Bruce I. Newman, *The Marketing of the President: Political Marketing as Campaign Strategy* (New York: Sage, 1994) p. 6.
14. Leo McKinstry, *Fit to Govern?* (London: Bantam Press, 1996) p. 19.
15. Anne Perkins, 'Never Underestimate the Force of Political Personality' *The Guardian* 6 December 2005.
16. The advert is available on any one of a number of video websites and can be accessed for free. For example, http://www.youtube.com/watch?v=bRKhTQHrtdk
17. Samuel Kernell, *Going Public: New Strategies of Presidential Leadership* 3rd ed. (Washington DC: CQ Press, 1997) p. 106.
18. Leonie Huddy, 'Group Identity and Political Cohesion' in David O. Sears, Leonie Huddy and Robert Jervis, *Oxford Handbook of Political Psychology* (Oxford: Oxford University Press, 2003) p. 542.

19. Dan B. Thomas, Lee Sigelman and Larry R. Baas, 'Public Evaluations of the President: Policy, Partisan and "Personal" Determinants' *Political Psychology* Vol. 5, No. 4, (Dec 1984), p. 533.
20. Newman, *The Marketing of the President* (1994) p. 73.
21. Drew Westen, *The Political Brain: the Role of Emotion in Deciding the Fate of the Nation* (New York: Public Affairs, 2007) p. 194.
22. Ibid., p. 15.
23. Huddy, 'Group Identity and Political Cohesion' in Sears, Huddy and Jervis, *Oxford Handbook of Political Psychology* (2003) p. 512.
24. Cited in Ibid., p. 514.
25. Erik D. Aker, 'The American Character' *Policy Today* Vol. 5, No. 4, April 2008 [http://www.policytoday.com].
26. Raymond Kuhn, '"Vive La Difference"'? The Mediation of Politicians' Public Images and Private Lives in France' *Parliamentary Affairs* Vol. 57, No. 1, p. 31.
27. Philippe J. Maarek, *Political Marketing and Communication* (Paris: John Libbey, 1995) p. 44.
28. Per-Anders Forstorp, 'Participation in the State of the Ordinary: Being "Yourself" as a Representative' *The Public* Vol. 4, No. 3, 1997, p. 72.
29. Ibid., p. 73.
30. Frank Rich, 'When You Got It, Flaunt It' *The New York Times* 23 November 2003.
31. Cited in Kevin Phillips, *Boiling Point: Democrats, Republicans and the Decline of Middle-Class Prosperity* (New York: Harper Perennial, 1993) p. 58.
32. Ibid., p. 74.
33. Jon Gertner, 'The Very, Very Personal Is the Political' *The New York Times* 15 February 2004.
34. Bruce Miroff, 'The Presidency and the Public: Leadership as Spectacle' in James P. Pfiffner, *The Modern Presidency* (New York: St. Martin's Press, 1994) p. 305.
35. Mary E. Stuckey, *The President as Interpreter in Chief* (Chatham, New Jersey: Chatham House, 1991) p. 96.
36. Peter Wilby, 'Private Moments and Public Motives: Leisure Interests of Public Figures' *The Independent* 17 August 2005 [http://news.independent. co.uk/media/article306409.ece].
37. *The Independent* 9 January 2007.
38. *The New York Times* 23 November 2003.
39. See Scott Keeter, 'The Illusion of Intimacy: Television and the Role of Candidate Personal Qualities in Voter Choice' *Public Opinion Quarterly* Vol. 51, No. 3, 1987.
40. Ibid., p. 345–6.
41. Dieter Ohr and Henrik Oscarsson, 'Leader Traits, Leader Image and Vote Choice' Paper delivered at European Consortium for Political Research (2003), Marburg [http://www.essex.ac.uk/ecpr/events/generalconference/ Marburg/papers/14/7/Ohr.pdf].
42. Ibid.
43. Ibid.
44. Christina Holtz-Bacha, 'The Private Life of Politicians: New Image Making Strategies and How They Have Changed Relations between Politicians and

the Press in Germany' *Political Communication Report* Vol. 13, No. 2, Spring 2003 [http://www.ou.edu/policom/1302_2003_spring/commentary.htm].

45. See for example, J. Curtice, 'Was It the Sun Wot Won It Again? The Influence of Newspapers in the 1997 Election Campaign' Crest (Centre for Research into Elections and social trends) Working paper No. 75, September 1999 [http://64.233.183.104/search?q=cache:L0cGeNR8pvYJ:www.crest.ox.ac.uk/papers/p75.pdf+its+the+sun+wot+won+it&hl=en&ct=clnk&cd=2].

46. 'Third of Mps Privately Schooled' *BBC News* 12 December 2005 [http://news.bbc.co.uk/go/pr/fr/-/hi/education/4514156.stm].

47. Kenneth J. Cooper, 'Quayle Opens Fanfare to the Common Man: First Re-Election Campaign Swing Stresses Plight of "Ordinary People"' *Washington Post* 10 January 1992.

2   Cloth coats and Camelot

1. 'Today's Political Ads Use Yesterday's Tactics' *ABCNews.go.com* 10 October 2004 [http://abcnews.go.com/GMA/story?id=149990&page=1].

2. Theodore H. White, *The Making of the President 1960* (New York: Atheneum Publishers, 1961) pp. 70–1.

3. Richard M. Nixon, *RN: The Memoirs of Richard Nixon* (London: Arrow Books, 1978) pp. 6–7.

4. Lewis Chester, Godfrey Hodgson and Bruce Page, *An American Melodrama: the presidential campaign of 1968* (London: The Literary Guild, 1969) p. 237.

5. Cited in Ibid., p. 93.

6. Ibid., p. 99.

7. Richard Nixon, 'Checkers Speech' [www.historyplace.com/speeches].

8. Ibid.

9. Rae Lindsay, *The Presidents' First Ladies* Revised ed. (Englewood Cliffs, New Jersey: R & R Writers, 2001) p. 29.

10. Hal W. Bochin, *Richard Nixon: Rhetorical Strategist* (Westport, Connecticut: Greenwood Press: 1990) p. 42.

11. Stella Bruzzi, *New Documentary: a Critical Introduction* (London: Routledge, 2000) p. 136.

12. Chester et al., *An American Melodrama* (1969) p. 229.

13. Nixon, *Memoirs* (1978) p. 214.

14. Ibid., p. 221.

15. Ibid., p. 304.

16. Joe McGuiness, *The Selling of the President 1968* (New York: Pocket Books, 1970) p. 20.

17. Ibid., p. 21.

18. Ibid., p. 24.

19. Ibid., p. 120.

20. Ibid., p. 131.

21. Chester et al., *An American Melodrama* (1969) p. 619.

22. Ibid., p. 618.

23. Ibid., p. 141.

24. Louis W. Liebovich, *The Press and the Modern Presidency: Myths and Mindsets from Kennedy to Election 2000* 2nd ed. (Westport, Connecticut: Praeger, 2001) p. 32.

25. Thomas W. Benson, *Writing JFK: Presidential Rhetoric and the Press in the Bay of Pigs Crisis* (College Station: Texas A&M University Press, 2004) p. 9.
26. Liebovich, *The Press and the Modern Presidency* (2001) p. 25.
27. James N. Giglio, *The Presidency of John F. Kennedy* (Lawrence, Kansas: University Press of Kansas, 1991) p. 255.
28. Ibid., p. 282.; Melvin Small, *The Presidency of Richard Nixon* (Lawrence, Kansas: University Press of Kansas, 2003) p. 11.
29. 'Presidents and History' *Pollingreport.com* [www.pollingreport.com/wh-hstry.html].
30. Cited in Robert Dallek, *John F. Kennedy: An Unfinished Life 1917–1963* (London: Penguin, 2003) pp. 30–1.
31. Cited in 'The Catholic Issue' *Time* 18 April 1960 [http://www.time.com/time/magazine/article/0,9171,874023,00.html].
32. Cited in Nicholas J. O'Shaughnessy, *The Phenomenon of Political Marketing* (Basingstoke: Macmillan, 1990) p. 55.
33. 'Transcript: JFK's Speech on His Religion' *National Public Radio* 5 December 2007 [http://www.npr.org/templates/story/story.php?storyId=16920600].
34. Bruce I. Newman, *The Mass Marketing of Politics: Democracy in an Age of Manufactured Images* (New York: Sage, 1999) p.14.
35. Waterman, Wright and St.Clair, *The Image-Is-Everything Presidency* (1990) p. 50.
36. White, *The Making of the President 1960* (1961) p. 96.
37. Ibid., p. 101.
38. Ibid.
39. 'The Richest President, How Much He Has, How Much He Gets' *U.S. News & World Report* 18 January 1962, p. 82.
40. Lord Longford, *Kennedy* (London: W.H. Allen and Co., 1976) p. 29.
41. O'Shaughnessy, *The Phenomenon of Political Marketing* (1990) p. 159.
42. Theodore C. Sorensen, *Kennedy* (London: Hodder and Stoughton, 1965) p. 107.
43. Ibid., p. 11.
44. Ibid., p. 107.
45. Ibid., p. 18.
46. Ibid., p. 141.
47. Dallek, *John F. Kennedy: An Unfinished Life* (2003) pp. 232, 246–7.
48. Thomas Reeves, *A Question of Character: A life of John F. Kennedy* (Roseville, California: Prima Publishing, 1997) p. 114.; Giglio, *The Presidency of John F. Kennedy* (1991) p. 10.
49. George E. Reedy, *The Twilight of the Presidency* (New York: New American Library, 1970) p. 152.
50. Dennis Kavanagh, *Election Campaigning: The New Marketing of Politics* (Oxford: Blackwell, 1995) p. 218.
51. Longford, *Kennedy* (1976) p. 29.
52. O'Shaughnessy, *The Phenomenon of Political Marketing* (1990) p. 41.

3   Thatcher and Major: Marketing a Conservative identity

1. See Dominic Wring, 'Political Marketing and party development in Britain: a "secret" history' *European Journal of Marketing* Vol. 30, No. 10/11, 1996, pp. 92–103; Margaret Thatcher, *The Path to Power* (London: HarperCollins, 1995) pp. 410–11.

2. E. H. H. Green, *Thatcher* (London: Hodder Arnold, 2006) p. 127.
3. Ipsos MORI polls [www.ipsos-mori.com].
4. Margaret Thatcher, 'Speech at Conservative Party Conference' *Margaret Thatcher Foundation* 16 October 1981 [Margaretthatcher.org].
5. 'The Truth About Thatcher, Thatcher, Milk Snatcher' *BBCnews.com* 1 January 2001[http://news.bbc.co.uk/1/hi/in_depth/uk/2000/uk_confidential/1095121. stm].
6. Ian Aitken, 'First Lady Will Put the Tories Right' *The Guardian* 12 February 1975 [http://www.guardian.co.uk/politics/1975/feb/12/past.ianaitken].
7. See, James Thomas, ' "Bound in by History": The Winter of Discontent in British Politics, 1979–2004' *Media, Culture & Society* Vol. 29, No. 2, pp. 273–7.
8. Thatcher, *The Path to Power* (1995) p. 12.
9. Wendy Webster, *Not a Man to Match Her: The Marketing of a Prime Minister* (London: The Women's Press, 1990) p. 29.
10. John Campbell, *The Grocer's Daughter* (London: Pimlico, 2001) p. 2.
11. Cited in Ibid., p. 23.
12. Margaret Thatcher, 'Speech at Conservative Party Conference' *Margaret Thatcher Foundation* 16 October 1981 [Margaretthatcher.org].
13. Margaret Thatcher, 'TV Interview for Channel 4 A plus 4' *Margaret Thatcher Foundation* 15 October 1984 [Margaretthatcher.org].
14. Margaret Thatcher, 'Radio Interview for IRN (Conservative Leadership Election)' *Margaret Thatcher Foundation* 31 January 1975 [Margaretthatcher. org].
15. E. H. H. Green, *Thatcher* (2006) p. 127.
16. Webster, *Not a Man to Match Her* (1990) pp. 30, 38.
17. Cited in Ibid., p. 44.
18. Margaret Thatcher, 'Ruthlessly Ambitious? When People Say This They Are Wholly Wrong: Interview for the Times' *Margaret Thatcher Foundation* 19 May 1975 [Margaretthatcher.org].
19. Margaret Thatcher, 'Radio Interview for IRN (Conservative Leadership Election)' *Margaret Thatcher Foundation* 31 January 1975 [Margaretthatcher. org].
20. Cited in Webster, *Not a Man to Match Her* (1990) p. 54.
21. 'Labour's Trouble with Women' *The Observer* 20 February 2005.
22. Webster, *Not a Man to Match Her* (1990) p. 35.
23. Ibid., pp. 45–6.
24. Margaret Thatcher, 'TV Interview for Channel 4 A plus 4' *Margaret Thatcher Foundation* 15 October 1984 [Margaretthatcher.org].
25. Margaret Thatcher, 'A Lot More to Life Than Slickness: Interview for the Times' *Margaret Thatcher Foundation* 11 June 1987 [Margaretthatcher.org].
26. Webster, *Not a Man to Match Her* (1990) pp. 49–50.
27. Ivor Crewe, 'The Thatcher Legacy' in Anthony King et al., *Britain at the Polls 1992* (Chatham, New Jersey: Chatham House Publishers, 1993) p. 25.
28. Craig R. Whitney, 'Gray Flannels or Not, John Major Is Riding the Crest of Popularity in Britain' *New York Times* 28 February 1991.
29. Gary Taylor, 'Media Review: Tile Major Government' *Contemporary Review* January 2001.
30. Alan Watkins, 'A Victory for the Repressive Society Looms, Leaving Mr Clarke Defeated Again' *The Independent* 16 October 2005.

31. Philip Norton, 'The Conservative Party from Thatcher to Major' in King et al., *Britain at the Polls 1992* (1993) p. 59.
32. Ibid., p. 134.
33. Cited in, Michael Leapman, ' "Rush of Blood" Was Kinnock's Downfall' *The Independent* 26 November 1995.
34. Ipsos MORI polls [www.ipsos-mori.com].
35. Sarah Hogg and Jonathan Hill, *Too Close to Call: Power and Politics – John Major in No. 10* (London: Warner Books, 1995) p. 221.
36. Laurence Rees, *Selling Politics* (London: BBC Books, 1992) p. 78.
37. Cited in Ibid., p. 91.
38. Philip Norton, 'The Conservative Party from Thatcher to Major' in King et al., *Britain at the Polls 1992* (1993) p. 156.
39. Rees, *Selling Politics* (1992) p. 91.
40. Hogg and Hill, *Too Close to Call* (1995) p. 222.
41. '1992: Tories Win Again against Odds' *BBC News* 5 April 2005 [http://news.bbc.co.uk/1/hi/uk_politics/vote_2005/basics/4393317.stm].
42. Nicholas Jones, *Soundbites and Spin Doctors* (1996) p. 38.
43. John Major, *John Major: The Autobiography* (London: Harper Collins, 1999) p. 290.
44. Ibid., p. 291.
45. Cited in Nicholas Jones, *Soundbites and Spin Doctors* (1996) p. 39.
46. Major, *Major* (1999) p. 387.
47. Ibid., p. 388.
48. 'Basildon man has long been seen as representative of the average Briton. The new town's voters backed the Tories throughout the Thatcher and Major years and then swung to Labour in the 1997 landslide, with a 13,000 majority, reduced to 7,738 at the last election.' Sarah Hall, 'Basildon Man Bonds With the Chancellor' *The Guardian* 18 March 2004.

4 Confronting an elite identity

1. Robert Lindsey, 'Creating the Role' in Hedrick Smith et al., *Reagan: the Man, the President* (New York: Pergamon Press, 1980) p. 21.
2. Cited in 'Land of Reagan' *Chicago Tribune* 18 September 2003 [http://www.law.northwestern.edu/inthenews/article_full.cfm?eventid=994].
3. Lou Cannon, *President Reagan: The Role of a Lifetime* (London: Simon and Schuster, 1991) p. 207.
4. Ronald Reagan, *Ronald Reagan: An American Life* (London: Hutchison, 1990) p. 55.
5. Jeffrey M. Jones, 'Historical Favorability Ratings of Presidents' *Gallup.com* 29 July 2003 [http://www.gallup.com/poll/8938/Historical-Favorability-Ratings-Presidents.aspx].
6. Media Advisory, 'Reagan: Media Myth and Reality' *Fairness in Accuracy and Reporting* 9 June 2004 [www.fair.org].
7. Robert Dallek, 'The American Experience: Reagan' *PBS online 1999–2000* [www.pbs.org].
8. Cannon, *President Reagan* (1991) pp. 32–3.
9. Edmund Morris, *Dutch: A Memoir of Ronald Reagan* (London: Harper Collins, 1999) p. 411.

10. Terri Bimes, 'Reagan's Rhetoric Targeted His Populist Appeals' *Institute of Governmental Studies: Public Affairs Report* Vol. 43, No. 2, Summer 2002 [http://www.igs.berkeley.edu].

11. Robert J. Bresler, 'The Roots of Conservative Populism' *USA Today* May 1996.

12. Ibid.

13. Cited in Ibid.

14. Cited in Terry Bimes, 'Ronald Reagan and The New Conservative Populism', *Institute of Governmental Studies* Working Paper 2002–1, 2002 [http://repositories.cdlib.org/igs/WP2002-1].

15. Ibid.

16. Harold Meyerson, 'Populism Without Heavies' *Washington Post* 28 July 2004.

17. Adapted from, 'Appendix D: the Republicans and the Rich: Popular Perceptions in the Opinion Polls, 1981–1988' in Kevin Phillips, *The Politics of Rich and Poor: Wealth and the American Electorate in the Reagan Aftermath* (New York: Harper Perennial, 1990) p. 243. (Figures as sourced)

18. John Kenneth White, 'A Presidency on Life Support' *The Polling Report* 10 October 2005 [http://www.pollingreport.com/whitejk.htm].

19. Nanette Asimov et al., 'As Governor, He Led State through Turbulent Times' *San Francisco Chronicle* 6 June 2004 [http://www.sfgate.com/cgi-bin/article.cgi?f=/c/a/2004/06/06/LOCAL.TMP].

20. Maureen Dowd, 'A Regular Guy Goes to the White House' *New York Times* 15 January 1989 [http://query.nytimes.com/gst/fullpage.html?res=950DE3D7133DF936A25752C0A96F948260].

21. Linda Feldmann, 'Bush Tour to Tap "Regular Guy" Appeal' *The Christian Science Monitor* 3 May 2004 [www.csmonitor.com].

22. Bill Clinton, *My Life* (London: Hutchinson, 2004) p. 422; Clinton also argued, 'It took us, and the national media, to places in the American heartland too often overlooked. America saw us reaching out to the people we had promised to represent in Washington'. Ibid., p. 423.

23. Cited in O'Shaughnessy, *The Phenomenon of Political Marketing* (1990) p. 225.

24. Ibid.

25. Kevin Phillips, *The Politics of Rich and Poor* (1990) p. 30.

26. Richard Stengel, 'The Likability Sweepstakes' *Time* 25 October 1988.

27. Cited in O'Shaughnessy, *The Phenomenon of Political Marketing* (1990) pp. 236–7.

28. Peter Goldman et al., *Quest for the Presidency 1992* (College Station: Texas A&M University Press, 1994) p. 599.

29. 'George H. W. Bush Interview, 2 June 1995' *Academy of Achievement* [http://www.achievement.org/autodoc/page/bus0int-1].

30. See Mitchell S. McKinney, 'Let the People Speak: The Public's Agenda and Presidential Town Hall Debates' *American Behavioral Scientist* Vol. 49, No. 2, October 2005, p. 202.

31. '1992 Debate Transcript' *Commission on Presidential Debates* [http://www.debates.org/pages/trans92b2.html#q-debt].

32. Anne Wortham, 'Making Sense of the White Male Stigma of not "getting it" ' *The World and I.com* Vol. 9, No. 3, August 1994 [http://www.worldandi.com/specialreport/1994/March/Sa12156.html].

33. J. Maggs, 'The Format That Saved Clinton' *National Journal* 2 October 2004, p. 2996.

34. Lance Morrow, 'William Jefferson Clinton' *Time* 3 January 1993.

35. McKinney, 'Let the People Speak: The Public's Agenda and Presidential Town Hall Debates' *American Behavioral Scientist* (2005) p. 202.

36. '1992 Debate Transcript' *Commission on Presidential Debates* [http://www.debates.org/pages/trans92b2.html#q-debt].

37. Ibid.

38. Wortham, 'Making Sense of the White Male Stigma of not "getting it" ' *The World and I.com* (1994) [http://www.worldandi.com/specialreport/1994/March/Sa12156.htm].

39. Martin Walker, *Clinton: The President They Deserve* (London: Vintage, 1997) pp. 48–9.

40. Clinton, *My Life* (2004) pp. 384–5.

41. Gwen Ifill, 'The 1992 Campaign: Media; Clinton Defends His Privacy and Says the Press Intruded' *The New York Times* 27 January 1992.

42. Cited in Kavanagh, *Election Campaigning: The New Marketing of Politics* (1995) p. 135.

43. Cited in, Walker, *Clinton* (1997) pp. 137–8.

44. Kavanagh, *Election Campaigning: The New Marketing of Politics* (1995) pp. 218–19.

5   New Labour and Tony Blair

1. Gerry Sussman, 'The Rise of Election Spin' *Spinwatch* 20 April 2005 [http://www.spinwatch.org].

2. Peter Wilby and Cahal Milmo 'Private Moments and Public Motives: Leisure "Interests" of Public Figures' *The Independent* 17 August 2005 [http://news.independent.co.uk/media/article306409.ece].

3. Rachel Oldroyd, 'Labour, the Party of the Rich' *The Mail on Sunday Review* 28 September 2003, p. 47.

4. Stephen Coleman, 'How the Other Half Votes: Big Brother Viewers and the 2005 General Election' *International Journal of Cultural Studies* Vol. 9, No. 4, 2006, p. 465 [online version: http://ics.sagepub.com].

5. Ibid., p. 466.

6. Ibid., p. 468.

7. Ibid., p. 470.

8. Jennifer Lees-Marshment, 'Political Marketing as Party Management – Thatcher in 1979 and Blair in 1997 *National Europe Centre Paper* No. 110 [http://www.anu.edu.au/NEC/Archive/Political%20Marketing.pdf].

9. Brian Wheeler, 'The Tony Blair Story' *BBC.co.uk* 10 May 2007 [http://news.bbc.co.uk/1/hi/uk_politics/6506365.stm].

10. Lees-Marshment, 'Political Marketing as Party Management' *National Europe Centre Paper* No. 110 [http://www.anu.edu.au/NEC/Archive/Political%20Marketing.pdf].

11. David Butler and Dennis Kavanagh, *The British General Election of 1997* (Basingstoke: Macmillan, 1997) p. 54.

12. Anthony King, ed., *New Labour Triumphs: Britain at the Polls, 1979 – a Study of the General Election* (Chatham, New Jersey: Chatham House, 1998) p. 201.

13. Lees-Marshment, 'Political Marketing as Party Management' *National Europe Centre Paper* No. 110 [http://www.anu.edu.au/NEC/Archive/Political%20 Marketing.pdf].
14. David Denver, *Elections and Voters in Britain* (Basingstoke: Palgrave, 2003) p. 121.
15. Cited in Andy McSmith, *Faces of Labour: The Inside Story* (London: Verso, 1996) p. 296.
16. Ibid., p. 297.
17. Ibid., p. 297.
18. Ibid., p. 308.
19. Ibid., pp. 308–9.
20. Michael Pearce, '"Getting behind the Image": Personality Politics in a Labour Party Election Broadcast' *Language and Literature* Vol. 10, No. 3, 2001, p. 212.
21. Ibid., p. 213.
22. Ibid., p. 214.
23. Harold D. Clare, David Sanders, Marianne C Stewart and Paul Whiteley, *Political Choice in Britain* (Oxford: Oxford University Press, 2004) p. 50.
24. Jenny Lloyd, 'The 2005 General Election and the Emergence of the "Negative Brand"' in Darren G. Lilleker, Nigel A. Jackson and Richard Scullion, *The Marketing of Political Parties: Political Marketing at the 2005 British General Election* (Manchester: Manchester University Press, 2006) p. 67.
25. Cahal Milmo, 'Private Moments and Public Motives: Leisure "Interests" of Public Figures' *The Independent* 17 August 2005 [http://news.independent. co.uk/media/article306409.ece].
26. Ibid.
27. Sue Evison, 'Tony Blair Opens His Heart to the Sun' *The Sun* 27 February 1997.
28. Alastair Campbell and Richard Stott, eds, *The Blair Years: Extracts from the Alastair Campbell Diaries* (London: Hutchinson, 2007) p. 89.
29. Vincent Hanna, 'Shadow Play with Tony and Kevin' *The Guardian* 5 October 1995.
30. Barney Ronay, 'Party Poopers' *When Saturday Comes* 220, June 2005.
31. Ibid.
32. Cited in 'A Great Feat of Ballot-Rigging' *The Guardian* 23 February 2000 [http://www.guardian.co.uk/politics/2000/feb/23/londonmayor.uk].
33. Ipsos MORI polls [www.ipsos-mori.com].
34. Ibid.
35. Ibid.
36. Cited in Greg Hurst, 'Blair Taunted over Public School' *The Times* 4 December 2003.
37. Rosemary Bennett, 'Selection is Good for Us, Not for You' *The Times* 24 May 2006.
38. Madeleine Bunting, 'Be a Man of the People Tony' *The Guardian* 7 June 2000.
39. Michael White, 'Fourteen Pints of Trouble: Poor Old William Hague – He Just Can't Get the Personal Stuff Right' *The Guardian* 10 August 2000.
40. 'Hague: I drank 14 pints a day' *BBC News Online* 8 August 2000 [http:// news.bbc.co.uk/1/hi/uk_politics/871543.stm].

41. Ibid.
42. Ibid.
43. 'Hague Challenged to Drink 14 Pints' *BBC News Online* 9 August 2000 [http://news.bbc.co.uk/1/hi/uk_politics/872280.stm].
44. *The Guardian* 10 August 2000.
45. *BBC News Online* 9 August 2000 [http://news.bbc.co.uk/1/hi/uk_politics/872280.stm].
46. Kevin Toolis, 'A Party That Is over – and Out' *The Observer* 10 June 2001.
47. Julia Langdon, 'William Hague: Never Had It So Good' *The Independent* 28 September 2007.
48. Ibid.
49. Irwin M. Stelzer, 'The Bill Clinton of the Sceptered Isle' *American Enterprise Institute for Public Policy Research* (AEI Online) 14 October 1996 [http://www.aei.org/publications/pubID.6995,filter.all/pub_detail.asp].
50. Piers Morgan, 'Tony Blair: His First Interview as Prime Minister' *Daily Mirror* 29 July 1997.
51. Helen Wilkinson, 'Time to Deliver on the Family' *The Independent* 21 November 1999.
52. Carole Malone, 'Arrogance with a Cherie on Top' *The Sunday Mirror* 15 December 2002.
53. Ibid.
54. Ibid.
55. 'Blair's Son "Drunk and Incapable"' *BBC News Online* 6 July 2000 [http://news.bbc.co.uk/1/hi/uk/822238.stm].
56. 'Blair Denies "Using" His Children' *The Telegraph* 22 March 2002 [http://www.telegraph.co.uk/news/1388509/Blair-denies-'using'-his-children.html]; 'Blair Denies "Exploiting" Family' *BBC News Online* 22 March 2002 [http://news.bbc.co.uk/1/hi/uk_politics/1886754.stm].
57. Lilleker and Lees-Marshment, *Political Marketing: A Comparative Perspective* (2005) p. 26.
58. Cited in Simon Jenkins, *Thatcher & Sons: A Revolution in Three Acts* (London: Allen Lane, 2006) p. 232.
59. Ibid., pp. 242–3.

6 Bush, Nascar dads and Wal-Mart moms

1. Nicholas Lemann, 'The Newcomer: Senator John Edwards Is This Season's Democratic Rising Star' *The New Yorker* 6 May 2002.
2. Howard Kurtz, 'The Big Mo' *Washington Post* 5 February 2004.
3. Ibid.
4. Alex Knott, 'It's a Millionaires' Race: New Financial Disclosure Database Details Assets of 2004 Presidential Candidates' The Buying of the President 2004, *The Center for Public Integrity* 27 January 2003 [http://www.publicintegrity.org].
5. Ibid.
6. Ibid.
7. See Charles Lewis, The Buying of the President 2004: Who's Really Bankrolling Bush and His Democratic Challengers – and What They

Expect in Return' *The Center for Public Integrity* [http://www.publicintegrity.org/bop2004/].

8. Joshua Green, 'In Search of the Elusive Swing Voter' *The Atlantic Monthly* January/February 2004.

9. Ibid.

10. Jeff MacGregor, 'The New Electoral Sex Symbol: Nascar Dad' *The New York Times* 18 January 2004.

11. Ibid.

12. Gary Langer, 'Driving the Election: Speculation that "NASCAR Dads" Will Decide the 2004 Vote May be Off Track' *ABCNews.com* 15 February 2004 [ABCNews.com].

13. Patrik Jonsson, 'Dems Target "NASCAR Dads"' *The Christian Science Monitor* 12 September 2003 [http://www.csmonitor.com/2003/0912/p03s01-uspo.html].

14. Ibid.

15. Ibid.

16. Mike Allen and Liz Clarke, 'Gentlemen, Start Your Campaigns: President Takes the Race for "NASCAR Dads" to the Daytona 500' *Washington Post* 16 February 2004.

17. Ibid.

18. Paul Krugman, 'Succeeding in Business' *The New York Times* 7 July 2002.

19. Ibid.

20. 'Bush Acknowledges 1976 DUI Charge' *CNN.com* 2 November 2000 [http://archives.cnn.com/2000/ALLPOLITICS/stories/11/02/bush.dui].

21. 'George W. Bush on Drugs: Identifies with Former Addicts Based on Former Alcoholism' *Issues 2000* [http://www.issues2000.org/George_W_Bush_Drugs.htm].

22. *New York Times* 23 November 2003.

23. Jonathan Alter, '"Let Them East Cake" Economics' *Newsweek* 28 July 2004.

24. 'Text: President Bush on NBC's "Meet the Press"' *Washington Post* 8 February 2004.

25. David S. Broder, 'Running on the Story of His Life' *Washington Post* 8 June 2003.

26. Lemann, 'The Newcomer' *New Yorker*, 6 May 2002.

27. John Hood, 'Just a Regular Guy' *National Review Online*, 2 January 2003 [http://www.nationalreview.com/comment/comment-hood010203.asp].

28. Ibid.

29. Ibid.

30. Randal C. Archibold, 'In Iowa Edwards Counts the Reasons to Be Upbeat' *The New York Times* 20 January 2004.

31. Andrew Marshall, 'Presidential Candidate John Edwards' Wife Visits Ames' *Iowa State Daily* 13 October 2003 [http://media.www.iowastatedaily.com/media/storage/paper818/news/2003/10/13/News/Presidential.Candidate.John.Edwards.Wife.Visits.Ames-1097080.shtml].

32. Cited in Chris Suellentrop, 'A Browser's Guide to Campaign 2004' *MSN Slate* 17 November 2003 [http://www.slate.com/id/2093412/].

33. Alan M. Webber, 'Super Web Site Helps Dean Surge Ahead' *USA Today* 7 December 2003.

34. Lois Romano, 'Dean, Driven by the Grass Roots' *Washington Post* 22 September 2003.
35. Tony Allen-Mills, 'Dean Takes Tip from the Terminator with Power Lunge' *Sunday Times* 19 October 2003.
36. Evelyn Nieves, 'Short-Fused Populist, Breathing Fire at Bush' *Washington Post* 6 July 2003.
37. Roland Watson, 'Vote for Me, Says Howard Dean. Which One, Asks America' *The Times (T2)* 16 January 2004.
38. Howard Kurtz, 'Tripping Over His Message' *Washington Post* 30 January 2004.
39. Alessandra Stanley, 'A Smiling Dean Turns to Television to Undo the Damage From Television' *New York Times* 23 January 2004.
40. Ibid.; Jim Vandehei, 'Dean Tries a Self-Deprecation Strategy' *Washington Post* 23 January 2004.
41. Laura Blumenfeld, 'John Kerry: Hunter, Dreamer, Realist' *Washington Post* 1 June 2003.
42. Ibid.
43. Ibid.
44. Ibid.
45. Ibid.
46. Howard Kurtz, 'Kerry's Past to Star in Bush's Ads' *Washington Post* 20 February 2004.
47. Hanna Rosin, 'In the Woods With John Kerry' *Washington Post* 16 November 2003.
48. Ibid.
49. Cited in Westen, *The Political Brain* (2007) p. 8.
50. Ibid., p. 9.
51. Ibid., p. 10.
52. John F. Harris, 'In New Hampshire, A Testy Primary Eve' *Washington Post* 27 January 2004.
53. Paul Schwartzman, 'The General Says He'll Keep Soldiering On' *Washington Post* 28 January 2004.
54. Ibid.
55. Alex Spillius, 'Barack Obama Turns to Wife to Win Back Voters' *The Telegraph* 2 May 2008.
56. Cited in Barack Obama, 'Barack Obama: My Long-Lost Father Was a Drunken Down-and-Out' *Daily Mail Online* 9 June 2008 [http://www.dailymail.co.uk/news/article-1025301/Barack-Obama-My-long-lost-father-drunken-out.html].
57. David Bauder, 'Palin Provides a "Perfect Populist Pitch" ' *Associated Press/USA Today* 4 September 2008 [http://www.usatoday.com/news/politics/2008–09-03–2226980962_x.html].
58. Joe Hilley, *Sarah Palin: A New Kind of Leader* (Michigan: Zondervan, 2008) p. 166.
59. 'One-On-One With Sarah Palin' *CBS News* 24 September 2008 [http://www.cbsnews.com/stories/2008/09/24/eveningnews/main4476173.shtml].
60. Robert Barnes and Juliet Eilperin, 'Courting Middle-Class Voters' *Washington Post* 3 October 2008.
61. Ibid.

62. Tom Shales, 'Palin Takes on A New Foe: Her Image' *Washington Post* 3 October 2008.
63. Dana Milbank, 'Joe, and Sarah Six-Pack' *Washington Post* 3 October 2008.
64. Richard Cohen, 'This Debate's Biggest Loser' *Washington Post* 7 October 2008.
65. William Kristol, 'A Heartbeat Away' *New York Times* 8 September 2008.
66. William Kristol, 'The Wal-Mart Mom and the Media' *San Diego Tribune* 9 September 2008 [http://www.signonsandiego.com/uniontrib/20080909/news_lz1e9kristol.html].
67. Jane Sasseen, 'The Wal-Mart Sisterhood' *Business Week* 17 April 2008.
68. Andrew Ward, 'Obama Winning over Wal-Mart Moms' *Financial Times* [Ft. com] 29 September 2008.
69. Bob Moser, 'The Sarah Palin Show' *The Nation* 4 October 2008.
70. John Heilemann, 'The Wal-Mart Frontier' *New York Magazine* 14 September 2008 [http://nymag.com/news/politics/powergrid/50277/].
71. Hilley, *Sarah Palin* (2008) p. 162.
72. Foon Rhee, 'Palin Clothing Bill up, Poll Standing Down' *The Boston Globe* 22 October 2008 [www.boston.com].
73. Dick Polman, 'The American Debate: Populism Gone Wild: Palin Latest Example of Push to Mediocrity' *Philadelphia Enquirer* 21 September 2008 [http://www.philly.com/inquirer/columnists/dick_polman/20080921_The_American_Debate__Populism_gone_wild__Palin_latest_example_of_push_to_mediocrity.html].

7   Cameron and Brown

1. Gerry Sussman, 'The Rise of Election Spin' *Spinwatch* 20 April 2005 [http://www.spinwatch.org/content/view/139/8/].
2. Ipsos MORI polls [www.ipsos-mori.com].
3. Peter Riddell, 'Moaning Tories Will Never Win Back the Middle Class Voters They Have Lost' *The Times* 21 July 2005.
4. 'The Rivals' *The Times* 4 September 2005.
5. Patience Wheatcroft, 'Gordon Waves Two Fingers: the Chancellor's Latest Action Typifies This Government's Concept for the Ordinary Voter' *The Times* 22 July 2005.
6. Oliver Burkeman, 'To His Fans He Is the Tories' Answer to Blair – Clever, Telegenic and Bent on Modernising His Party. To His Critics He Is a Ludicrously Inexperienced, Metropolitan Toff.' *The Guardian* 29 September 2005.
7. 'Tory Rivals Square up in Fight for Leadership' *The Times* 4 October 2005.
8. Cited in 'Get Real, or Get Out: Blunt Message from Modernisers' *The Times* 4 October 2005.
9. 'Cameron Rated Best Candidate to Lead Tories to Power' *The Guardian* 3 October 2005.
10. Ibid.
11. Ibid.
12. 'Davis Revives Bid with Win on Points in Tight TV Duel' *The Times* 4 November 2005.

13. 'Cameron Goes Green as Fight for Leadership Gets Heated' *The Times* 31 October 2005.
14. Andrew Denham and Kieron O'Hara, 'Cameron's "Mandate": Democracy, Legitimacy and Conservative Leadership' *Parliamentary Affairs* Vol. 60, No. 3, 2007, p. 419.
15. Anatole Kaletsky, 'The Tories Have Chosen the Right Man – and What a Disaster That Will Be' *The Times* 9 December 2005.
16. 'Mps Can No Longer Be Male-Voice Choir Says Cameron' *The Times* 12 December 2005.
17. *The Times* 9 December 2005.
18. See Peter Kerr, 'Cameron Chameleon and the Current State of Britain's "Consensus"' *Parliamentary Affairs* Vol. 60, No. 1, 2007, p. 48; also, Francis Elliott and James Hanning, *Cameron: the Rise of the New Conservative* (London: Fourth Estate, 2007) p. 308.
19. Bryan Appleyard, 'What's He Got To Look Forward To?' *The Sunday Times Magazine* 5 March 2006.
20. Quoted in 'Reservoir Toffs' *The Sunday Times* 8 October 2006.
21. Oliver Burkeman, 'To His Fans He Is the Tories' Answer to Blair – Clever, Telegenic and Bent on Modernising His Parry. to His Critics He Is a Ludicrously Inexperienced, Metropolitan Toff' *The Guardian* 29 September 2005.
22. Fraser Nelson, 'Cameron in TV Spat over Drugs Claim' *The Scotsman* 18 November 2005 [www.news.scotsman.com].
23. Helen Rumbelow, 'I Strayed – but Cameron Dodges Drugs Questions' *The Times* 14 October 2005.
24. See, Sophie Goodchild, 'Samantha Cameron Turned David into a Modernising Liberal' *The Independent* 11 March 2007.
25. 'A Fashionable Life: Samantha Cameron' *Harper's Bazaar* September 2007.
26. Ibid.
27. 'Cameron Speech on Quality of Life', *Conservative party website* 12 June 2005 [www.conservatives.com].
28. Alice Thompson and Rachel Sylvester, 'What Precisely Are Your Politics, Mr Cameron?' *The Telegraph* 22 October 2005 [www.telegraph.co.uk].
29. David Cameron, 'What My Son Has Shown Me about Caring' *Conservative party website* 12 June 2005 [www.conservatives.com].
30. 'Cameron: My Family Means More Than No. 10' *The Sunday Times* 18 June 2006.
31. 'Question Time Briefing' *The Times* 4 December 2003.
32. Brian Wheeler, 'The David Cameron Story' *BBCNews* online 9 January 2006 [www.bbc.co.uk].
33. 'How Desire for Reform Became a Class Struggle for the Cabinet' *The Times* 19 December 2005.
34. 'As Labour Sharpens the Knives for Cameron, Which Blade Will It Use?' *The Times* 6 January 2006.
35. *The Times* 19 December 2005.
36. Ben Macintyre, 'Who Cares about the E-Word?' *The Times* 9 December 2005.
37. *The Times* 10 December 2005.
38. James Silver, 'Who's Responsible For "Toff Nonsense?"' *Sky News* 29 May 2008 [http://news.sky.com/skynews/article/0,,91211–1317513,00.html].

39. 'Full Text : David Cameron's Speech to the Conservative Conference 2005' *The Guardian* 4 October 2005 [www.politics.guardian.co.uk].
40. Anne Perkins, 'Never Underestimate the Force of Political Personality' *The Guardian* 6 December 2005.
41. David Cracknell and Andrew Porter, 'Coming Soon: Toff Gun v King Con' *The Sunday Times* 11 December 2005.
42. Rachel Sylvester, ' Brown Doesn't Do "Consensus Politics" – Which Is His Loss' *The Telegraph* 12 December 2005 [www.telegraph.co.uk].
43. Simon Jenkins, 'Cameron's Face Fits – but He Can't Look Both Ways at Once' *The Times* 11 December 2005.
44. *The Times* 9 December 2005.
45. James Harkin, 'Generation Gap' *The Guardian* 7 January 2006.
46. Alan Finlayson, 'Making Sense of David Cameron' *Public Policy Research* March–May 2007 p. 6.
47. See 'Young, Tory and Proud: The Conservative Revival on Campus' *The Independent* (supplement) 23 February 2006.
48. Cited in Andy Beckett, 'Hi Kids, I'm Dave Cameron. Keep It Real' *The Guardian* 12 January 2006.
49. David Cracknell, 'The Changing Face of Tory Boy' *The Sunday Times* 26 November 2006.
50. 'Is It Time for Dave's Babes?' *The Times* 21 November 2005.
51. Alice Miles, 'All Right Then, Girls: What Is It Exactly about Young Dave That Ticks Your Box?' *The Times* 14 December 2005.
52. For example see, 'David Cameron: up Close and Personal, One Year On' *The Times* (Magazine) 2 December 2006.
53. Sam Macrory, 'Football and Politics' *larevueparlementaire.fr* 1 December 2005.
54. 'Blue Swoon' *The Sunday Times Magazine* 30 July 2006.
55. 'A Wife Less Ordinary: Samantha Cameron Trumps Sarah Brown in Style Stakes' *The Guardian* (blogs) 23 May 2008 [http://blogs.guardian.co.uk/politics/2008/05/what_women_want_david_cameron.html].
56. 'Now We've All Met Arthur, His Dad Should Say Goodbye to Hell! Politics' *The Times* 20 February 2006.
57. David Cracknell and David Smith, 'Can They Rebuild Him?' *The Sunday Times* 12 February 2005.
58. *YouGov/Sunday Times* polling 2007.
59. Simon Jenkins, 'Tory Boy' *The Sunday Times* (News Review) 17 September 2006.
60. James Cusik, 'Project Gordon : How Do You Turn an Analytic and Distant Chancellor Into an Amiable, Expressive PM in – waiting?' *Sunday Herald* 17 September 2006.
61. 'How Project Gordon Failed to Put a More Human Face on the Iron Chancellor' *The Times* 11 February 2006.
62. Ibid.
63. Philip Webster, 'Analysis: New Softer Brown Lays Out His Stall' *The Times* 25 September 2006.
64. George Osborne, 'Project Gordon Is Doomed' *Evening Standard* 20 February 2006.

65. Bel Mooney, 'The Odyssey of Gordon Brown' *The Times* [Times 2] 8 November 2006.

66. Ann Treneman, 'So, Gordon, How Wonderful, Wise and Talented Am I?" *The Times* 25 September 2007.

67. Andrew Sparrow, 'Brown Faces ITV's Fern to Reveal His Human Side' *The Guardian* 8 May 2008 [http://www.guardian.co.uk/politics/2008/may/08/gordonbrown.labour?gusrc=rss&feed=media].

68. See Nick Robinson, 'Opening Up' *Nick Robinson's Newsblog* 8 May 2008 [http://www.bbc.co.uk/blogs/nickrobinson/].

69. Max Hastings, 'The Tories Only Need Fly a Straight Course as Brown Force-Lands Labour' *The Guardian* 12 May 2008 [http://www.guardian.co.uk/commentisfree/2008/may/12/conservatives.gordonbrown].

Conclusion

1. Russell Jenkins, 'Cameron Cries Foul as Campaign Turns into Class War' *The Times* 13 May 2008.

2. '"Tory Toff" Campaigning Defended' *BBCnews.co.uk* 19 May 2008 [http://news.bbc.co.uk/go/pr/fr/-/1/hi/uk_politics/7408464.stm].

Index